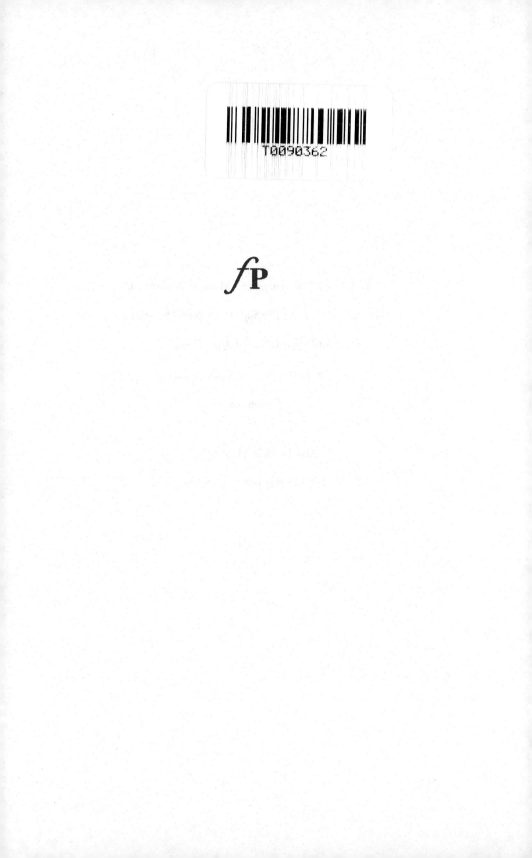

*f*P

Also by Dale Maharidge and Michael Williamson

*Journey to Nowhere: The Saga of the New Underclass
And Their Children After Them*

The Last Great American Hobo

Homeland

Also by Dale Maharidge

The Coming White Minority

DENISON, IOWA

Searching for the Soul of America
Through the Secrets of a Midwest Town

Dale Maharidge

Photographs by Michael Williamson

Free Press

New York London Toronto Sydney

*f*P

FREE PRESS
A Division of Simon & Schuster, Inc.
1230 Avenue of the Americas
New York, NY 10020

FREE PRESS and colophon are trademarks of Simon & Schuster, Inc.

For information about special discounts for bulk purchases,
please contact Simon & Schuster Special Sales: 1-800-456-6798
or business@simonandschuster.com

Designed by Jeanette Olender

Manufactured in the United States of America

1 3 5 7 9 10 8 6 4 2

Library of Congress Cataloging-in-Publication Data

Maharidge, Dale.
Denison, Iowa: searching for the soul of America through the secrets of a Midwest town / Dale
Maharidge; photographs by Michael Williamson.
p. cm.
1. Social change—Iowa—Denison. 2. Denison (Iowa)—Social conditions.
3. Denison (Iowa)—Economic conditions. 4. Denison (Iowa)—History.
I. Williamson, Michael. II. Title.
HN80.D34 M35 2005
977.7'45034—dc22 2005050730

ISBN 13: 978-0-743-25566-0
ISBN 10: 0-743-25566-6

To my mother, Joan, my first reader

CONTENTS

DENISON, IOWA

THE WHITE BUFFALO

WESTHOPE, N.D.—Between August 17 and September 2, 2002, four non-albino white buffalo calves were born on the ranch of Dwaine and Debbie Kirk. There were now some ten white buffalo in the American bison population of 350,000, according to Bob Pickering of the Buffalo Bill Historical Center in Cody, Wyoming. Pickering estimates the odds of a single non-albino calf being born at sixteen in one million; an albino, eight in one million. The National Bison Association puts the odds higher for an albino: one in ten million.

The Great Plains Indians told a legend about two warrior hunters who were observing a buffalo herd. One animal was snow white. They marveled over the creature. The white buffalo suddenly raced toward them and was transformed into a beautiful woman. One warrior grew aroused. The spirit woman told him she knew what he was thinking and asked him to step forward. He did, and they were engulfed in a cloud. When the woman stepped out as the cloud dissipated, all that remained of the warrior was a pile of bones swarming with maggots.

The other warrior fell to his knees. The spirit woman told him to return to his encampment and in four days she would visit. On the fourth day, a cloud descended at the camp. From it emerged a white buffalo calf, which materialized into the woman. She held a sacred bundle and taught the people sacred ceremonies: sweat lodge purification, healing, marriage, the Sun Dance.

Some of this legend is recorded in the 1932 book *Black Elk Speaks: The*

Life Story of a Holy Man of the Ogalala Sioux, by John G. Neihardt. Black Elk fought against the invaders with Crazy Horse and survived the massacre at Wounded Knee on December 29, 1890. Now blind and very old, Black Elk recounted stories passed down over generations, including the White Buffalo Calf Woman story. When she arrived on the fourth day, said Black Elk, she sang this song:

> With visible breath I am walking
> A voice I am sending as I walk
> In a sacred manner I am walking
> With visible tracks I am walking
> In a sacred manner I walk

"Then she gave something to the chief, and it was a pipe with a bison calf carved on one side to mean the earth that bears and feeds us, and with twelve eagle feathers hanging from the stem to mean the sky and the twelve moons, and these were tied with a grass that never breaks," Black Elk said.

In other accounts, the White Buffalo Calf Woman said that when a white buffalo was born, it would prophesy her return, and harmony would visit the world. Other accounts interpret the birth of a white buffalo as heralding a return to the old ways.

" 'Behold!' she said," according to Black Elk, speaking of the sacred pipe. " 'With this you shall multiply and be a good nation' . . . she sang again . . . and as the people watched her going suddenly it was a white bison galloping away and snorting, and soon it was gone."

Hundreds of years later, Europeans crossed the Alleghenies and came to the Midwest flatlands. By 1869 the white population of Iowa surpassed 1 million. The Sioux, who had occupied the northern and western parts of Iowa, were pushed onto a 35,000-square-mile reservation in the Dakotas, which stretched from the Missouri River west to the 104th Meridian. After 1876 the government changed the boundary to the 103rd Meridian, carving off a 50-mile strip that included the gold-rich Black Hills. Still, with more settlers arriving, the whites wanted even more acreage. So the Indians were cheated or attacked, and the great Dakota reservation was broken up by 1889.

The Sioux were defeated in battle, but hope emerged in the Drying

Grass Moon on October 9, 1890, when word came to the Sioux about a Paiute messiah named Wovoka in Nevada, who had founded a new religion, a Christian-pagan fusion called the Ghost Dance.

"All Indians must dance, everywhere, keep on dancing," Wovoka commanded.

Wovoka did not invoke the white buffalo—his was more of a Christlike vision—but his message was essentially the same as the old Sioux legend. If they danced enough, it would bring back the buffalo. Their ancestors would rise from the dead, the whites would vanish, and the Indian people would again rule the Plains. There would be harmony. The Sioux and other tribes embraced the Ghost Dance that November of 1890. They danced for hours at a time.

"This was the Moon of Falling Leaves, and across the West on almost every Indian reservation, the Ghost Dance was spreading like a prairie fire under a high wind," Dee Brown wrote in *Bury My Heart at Wounded Knee*. "Agitated Indian Bureau inspectors and Army officers from Dakota to Arizona, from Indian Territory to Nevada, were trying to fathom the meaning of it. . . . Official word was: stop the Ghost Dancing. [It] was so prevalent on the Sioux reservations that almost all other activities came to a halt. . . . At Pine Ridge the frightened agent telegraphed Washington: 'Indians are dancing in the snow and are wild and crazy. . . . We need protection and we need it now.'"

This led to the roundup of Indians in December and the massacre at Wounded Knee Creek at Pine Ridge. U.S. soldiers followed fleeing women and children into the brush, executing an estimated 300 unarmed Sioux.

Wounded Knee marked the end for the Great Plains Indians.

* * *

Over a century later, on June 15, 2002, a freight train stopped in Harlingen, Texas. Seven men and four women climbed into an empty blue Union Pacific railroad grain car. Two were sisters from Honduras, traveling with their teenage cousin: Lely Elizabeth Ferrufino, age thirty-five; Rosibel Ferrufino, age twenty-nine; and Lesly Esmeralda Ferrufino, age eighteen. Among the rest were Mexican Omar Esparza Contreras, age twenty-three; Salvadoran Domingo Ardon Sibrian, age thirty-six; and Guatemalan Byron Adner Acevedo Perez, age eighteen.

A man sealed the hatch. The eleven were engulfed in darkness.

The train moved toward Kingsville, near Corpus Christi, where someone was supposed to unseal the hatch. The object was to avoid U.S. agents at the Sarita Border Patrol checkpoint. The agents wouldn't suspect a sealed car, and thus the eleven would make it to a safe house. From there they'd continue on their journey to *El Norte*, for which they had each paid their smugglers up to $1,000. The smugglers had slipped $550 to a rail worker to assist with the operation.

When the train stopped in Kingsville, no one opened the hatch.

The grain car went into storage in Oklahoma. Summer passed. The car was dispatched to Iowa, to a grain elevator in the town of Denison, fifty miles from the Nebraska border. In mid-October, harvest time, the cars were readied to be filled with grain. A worker walked atop the train, breaking open hatches; he smelled an odor. He peered in the car and saw eleven mummified bodies.

The first law officer on the scene was Crawford County Sheriff Tom Hogan. He noted that the bodies were evenly spaced around the circumference of the sloping pitch of the compartment, with all feet pointed into the well in the center.

It's like they're flower petals, he thought.

Hogan saw that the rubber seal around the hatch had been picked at. They'd tried to escape. And when that failed, it was clear to Hogan, the last to die had cared for the others.

From the valley floor of the Boyer River where the grain car sat, one could see a distant blue-and-white water tower peeking above the trees atop a hill to the east. Upon it was written,

DENISON

"IT'S A WONDERFUL LIFE"

The town's slogan comes from the 1946 Frank Capra Christmas movie classic starring Jimmy Stewart and Donna Reed. Denison laid claim to the appellation because Donna was born on a farm south of town and went to high school here.

This Great Plains town formed what viewers saw in Donna on both the large and small screen. A brochure published by a Denison museum

4

noted that at her family's farm, she spent time "helping her mother bake great fluffy loaves of bread and wonderful pies. . . . Donna also helped feeding and watering the chickens, gathering eggs, milking cows." Donna, active in 4-H, "specialized in cooking, needle craft and sewing." She relished going to movies at the old opera house and sitting at the soda fountain in the adjoining Candy Kitchen. During the Great Depression, Denison was similar to the fictional Bedford Falls in the Capra movie— all white, with humble and churchgoing folks.

On September 1, 1938, Donna, seventeen, boarded "The Challenger" for California with $60 in her handbag. She lived with an aunt while attending Los Angeles City College. In 1940 she was crowned campus queen. Her picture appeared in the newspapers, agents called, and by February 1941, she had a lead role in a B-movie. After *Wonderful Life,* Donna was cast in the 1953 film *From Here to Eternity,* a role for which she won an Oscar. She then starred in *The Donna Reed Show* on television from 1958 to 1966, which presented an idealized family. For a generation of Americans "Donna Reed" was synonymous with wholesomeness.

When Donna died of pancreatic cancer in 1986, the demographics of her hometown were unchanged from her youth. But when the grain car was opened sixteen years later, Denison had become multicultural. The U.S. Census had counted 98 Latinos in all of Crawford County in 1990, but in 2000, Denison had 1,364 Latinos out of 7,339 residents. This likely was an undercount, because many Latinos are undocumented and fear cooperating. And still more came. Many whites believe that Denison is half Latino; this is likely not accurate, though to them it seems that way. A conservative estimate is that by 2004, there were 2,000 Latinos in town, though one official insists the number was 3,500.

Luis Navar was among these newcomers. Luis had left Mexico as a teenager in the 1980s, entering the United States by sneaking across the border. Luis did day labor in Los Angeles and was often homeless. He worked hard, married, had four children, and ended up in a cramped apartment in the MacArthur Park area of Los Angeles at the end of the 1990s. There was violence. Luis worried for his children's safety. He was drawn to make an exploratory trip, to visit Denison.

"I came, and I saw the green stuff [corn and soybeans] all over, no matter which direction you looked out of town," Luis recalled. "I said,

'This must be a good place.' I saw this as a place full of life. In L.A. the view out of our window was of a big alley wall full of graffiti."

Luis convinced his reluctant wife that it was time to move, and the family drove to Denison. It was a new beginning, their chance at a wonderful life in *El Bedford Falls*.

* * *

A few months after the eleven bodies were discovered inside the grain car in Denison, novelist Rob "Levi" Levandoski was walking in the woods of his family farm in northern Ohio. Levi had moved back to a trailer on the farm, on which his brother commercially raised pumpkins, after his wife left him and he needed to retreat from the world and write, and to see things. The pumpkin farm was in the town of Hinckley, at the base of the westernmost ridge of the Allegheny Plateau. It's here that the Midwest flatlands begin on the glaciated plains. From this final hill, it's virtually level west to the Rocky Mountains.

After the defeat of the indigenous Ohio peoples, there was a massive hunt in Hinckley in 1818 to kill off animals that were in the way of farmers. Great piles of elk, fox, bear, and woods buffalo were stacked and left to rot. Buzzards came to feast on the carrion, and today locals honor their return from southern migration with Buzzard Day, an annual festival on March 15, the day of the Great Hinckley Hunt.

Levi grew up watching the buzzards, a reminder of the violence of the past and with the spirits of his ancestors who had settled the land stolen from the Indians. He'd find arrowheads and upon picking them up would have the tingling sensation that he was the first to touch the points since the person who'd made them. He felt the power of transference. As his beard whitened, he increasingly had shamanlike visions of the great arc of history that really was not all that much time; the past compressed and was connected with the present.

One day when Levi was out by the creek on the farm, he discovered a snapping turtle of a kind that he'd not seen since he was a boy. They had vanished, along with the whitetail deer in the decline of all native flora and fauna in the twentieth century. Then Levi found another turtle. They were back, as if by magic, as were the deer, which were now so numerous as to constitute a problem. He had a vision.

Levi reasoned that the North American continent was being repopulated by all manner of once-native species. In New England, moose have come down from Canada, as have wolves and grizzly in the West and wolverines, seemingly, in Michigan. Around him in Ohio, black bears and beavers were reappearing, as were smaller creatures such as the turtle. It was logical, he reasoned, that the coming of Latinos to the Great Plains in doubling numbers over the previous decade was part of this process.

After all, Levi felt, many Mexicans and Central Americans who migrate are mostly indigenous, unlike the lighter-skinned Mexicans who hold positions of power in their native land. These Latinos are the largest pool (more vast than any remaining North American tribes) of native peoples proximate to the United States. Was their migration out of the South a century after the Ghost Dance predicted by the vision of Wovoka, to correct an imbalance caused by the injustice of the past? There were now 3 million Latinos in the Midwest, double the 1990 number, according to the 2000 Census. Most were in cities such as Chicago. There were concentrations in rural Kansas, Nebraska, Minnesota. Iowa was still overwhelmingly white, but Latinos were the largest minority in 2002, at 89,000, comprising 3.1 percent of the state's population. They were located in a handful of small cities in addition to Des Moines and Davenport—among them Denison, Marshalltown, Perry, Postville, and Storm Lake.

"It's the repopulation," Levi announced as he stood on the bank of the creek where he'd discovered the turtles. "It's the white buffalo."

PART ONE

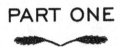

SUMMER

THE GROTESQUES

Evening. I was lying in bed, sweating from the midsummer heat. A slow-moving fan in the ten-foot ceiling did little to cool the chamber. A Mexican polka boomed from a car passing the evangelical *iglesia* across the street, rattling the panes. Earlier I'd taken a meal at La Estrella. Miguel, the restaurant's manager, had cooked me *birria*, goat. In my half-sleep state with memory of the goat dish that was as good as any I'd ever eaten in Mexico, I had the vaguest of notions where I was. Then I remembered: Denison, Iowa.

I was here because of Jim, the editor from the first book Michael Williamson and I had published, now our agent. I'd been teaching at Columbia University in New York City when Jim had an idea about a book set in the middle of the country at this curious time in history. I term it curious because the nation had been so unsure and unsettled after 9/11. People sought inner peace while at the same time there was great societal angst. We were now The Homeland, a term that conjured an image of tranquility, the middle, isolation. A lot of people in my circle were leaving cities, heading to rural areas. Yet a desire for an idyllic country existence predated 9/11. Why had Thomas Kinkade's paintings, after all, been selling well for so long?

In addition, cultural change was no longer limited to the coasts. Now nonwhite immigrants were pouring into the center of the nation, on a different kind of search. Perhaps the big city was not only passé but dead to both whites and nonwhites, due to suburban sprawl and hideous commutes. For immigrants, country life was also an escape from urban violence. But was the small town they were coming to also dead because of Wal-Mart and global economic forces? Or was it America's future? What could be learned about the soul of the nation in a rural place that in so many ways might be a microcosm of the country?

Jim is a New Yorker who understands the middle, doesn't consider it flyover country—he often takes a train or a car inland to spend time listening to people in small towns. When Jim and I talked, it became rapidly clear that this book had to take place in Iowa. One reason was that the state is geographically in the center of the nation. Another reason was its neutrality. Many Americans have built-in prejudices against certain regions and states. "Alabama" said to a northerner conjures stereotypes, just as "New York" uttered to a southerner evokes another type. And to southerners and easterners, "California" has, well, its own baggage. Iowa's neutrality is why so many fictional stories from popular culture are set in the state: *The Music Man, The Bridges of Madison County, Field of Dreams.*

Jim convinced the publisher of the necessity of this book, and with insane speed, Michael and I went on the Internet and hacked around. When the Denison web site came up on the screen, I stared at an image of the water tower and the slogan, "It's a Wonderful Life." Aside from being in Iowa, Denison appealed to us because it has a large immigrant population. But it was much more than this. There was an instant connection, as if Denison were calling out to us, "Come." No other town would do. I later came to firmly believe that we didn't find Denison. Rather, it found us. We fibbed slightly to our publisher by saying that we'd been here— we'd driven through a few times but hardly lingered—and now weeks later, I was living in this town where I would dwell for most of the ensuing year. The process was only marginally more precise than having thrown a dart at a wall map. I didn't want to tell the publisher that I actually wanted to know as little as possible about the town in advance. The discovery of whatever truth I was seeking would be best if it were to happen spontaneously.

Before I made my drive to set up house in Iowa, Jim had suggested that I visit the cemetery immediately upon my arrival.

"See who has the biggest monument. That should tell you something."

I'd long placed great trust in Jim's editorial guidance. So while checking in at the historic Park Motel on the fabled Lincoln Highway (the first transnational automobile road), I asked the deskwoman how to reach the cemetery. After dumping a few bags in the room, I headed out.

This part of Iowa is not the Midwest of monotonous flatness. It has minor hills that roll to the Missouri River to the west, where the land does indeed give away to the ceaseless level of Nebraska's Platte River watershed. Oakland Cemetery was located atop the tallest of the hills south of town, with a forever view. The sun was about to vanish in the mist when I spotted a massive granite mausoleum, more impressive than any other stone amid the oaks and cedars. It was far larger than the monument for J. W. Denison, the huckster who had been the town's founder.

I breezed past Denison's grave and went to the six-crypt mausoleum in the orange twilight as the cries of cicadas wound from the treetops. Large letters announced,

SHAW

Several plaques read:

LESLIE M. SHAW
1848–1932
GOVERNOR OF IOWA
1897–1901
SECRETARY OF TREASURY
DURING THE ADMINISTRATION
OF PRESIDENT THEODORE ROOSEVELT
1901–1907

ALICE CRAWSHAW SHAW
1848–1935

EARL BOARDMAN SHAW
1883–1937

ERMA LOVISA SHAW.
BORN OCTOBER 9, 1885. DIED OCTOBER 9, 1918.
SHE DIED ON SHIPBOARD EN ROUTE TO FRANCE
TO SERVE, AT HER OWN EXPENSE, IN THE WORLD WAR,
UNDER THE AUSPICES OF THE AMERICAN RED CROSS.

I peered through a glass window in the brass door. A plate on the middle white marble left crypt said "Father"; on the middle right, "Mother." Erma was below her father. Earl was below his mother. The top two crypts were empty.

* * * *

A few nights later, I was writing and sleeping in the Shaws' master bedroom. After my visit to the cemetery, I'd rented a piece of their decaying mansion that had been completed in 1892.

The family had lived here until early 1902 (the inscription was in error), when Leslie Shaw and his wife went to Washington. The Shaw children—including the oldest daughter, Enid, who is not in the crypt—remained while finishing school and then moved east. Yet the Shaws did not sell the house until 1910, when it became clear that the former governor and his wife were never coming back home from life on the eastern seaboard. It was purchased by an opera star and his wife, who lived in it until they grew senile; their son disposed of the house in 1956.

The buyer broke the mansion into seven apartments. The 1956 sale began a decline for the stately home, as not much work was done to keep it in good repair. The buyer also built an apartment building a few steps out the back door, crowding the house and ruining any immediate hope that someone would use it again as a single-family residence.

Now it was just me and an ancient woman downstairs. The other five units were empty. The last occupants besides the woman were some methamphetamine cookers who trashed the third-floor ballroom that had been Apartment Number 7 and took fire from some Mexicans they'd ripped off; a bullet-shattered window remained broken. The screaming and crazy crankheads were evicted after they climbed out the windows and scaled down the paint-scabbed side of the vine-covered house.

The house was owned by a seventy-five-year-old guy who had little interest in it. It had been his late wife's real estate investment. I heard from townspeople two theories about why he didn't sell. One was that she wished the Shaw Mansion not be sold without their kids' okay and that the kids kept resisting. The other theory was that for reasons of nostalgia or lethargy, he simply ignored the properties. When I asked him about this, he just shrugged and muttered, "I've got to get that upstairs cleaned up and get an appraiser in." But he never came to clean.

Whatever the reason, he'd allowed the place to go to hell. The cranksters' ballroom was ravaged and fetid, knee-deep in soiled clothes and detritus. In addition, there was a crack den down the hall in what had been Apartment Number 3. Number 3's carpet was cigarette scorched, and the bathroom mirror had been ripped from the wall and placed on a coffee table to cut drugs.

Now all but the part occupied by the woman was virtually unlivable. The house was nearly a ruins, rooms waterstained from the leaking roof, rot having taken a toll. There was another factor beyond all this that made the house difficult to rent—one that I'd discover a few weeks after I'd moved in.

My apartment in Number 4 on the second floor was funky but habitable by my minimalist standards. I'd been tipped to the house by Nathan Mahrt, a de facto town historian, who turned me on to the owner. The old man was surprised when I wanted to rent a spot in the home. Number 4 had last been occupied in September 2001; a calendar turned to that month remained on the kitchen wall. The picture was of Union Square in New York City. I stared at the image and the 11th for a long time that July afternoon that I set up residence. My life was still frozen on that September day. I had just finished *Homeland,* a book on post-9/11 America that began the morning I watched from my Manhattan rooftop as the second tower fell. I had been immersed for over two years in the lives of those most affected by the events of that morning. It was as if I were stuck in my own version of the movie *Groundhog Day,* living the same dreadful twenty-four hours over and over. For this and other personal reasons, it had been a rough few years.

I left the old calendar on the wall.

Teddy Roosevelt may have slept in the room adjacent to my quarters. TR was friends with Leslie Shaw and others here in town before he became president. Though not officially recorded, stories circulated among old residents of his staying in the home. Roosevelt gave Shaw a gift: a fireplace facade with bear heads on it that remained downstairs.

Teddy might have slept soundly, but I kept waking through the night to the blare of diesel horns echoing up the Boyer (pronounced Boo-yer) River valley on average every twelve minutes, from the Union Pacific trains barreling through, many carrying strip-mined Wyoming coal to the power plants that fuel Chicago and other Midwest cities. There was a frantic quality to the horns. They kept a schizophrenic tempo as they faded and the units moved east or west, and there was the clatter of metal thundering from the valley bottom.

I was living a sudden inversion of Dorothy from the Wizard of Oz—dude, you're no longer in New York or San Francisco, my urban centers for the previous dozen years. From just about any street in Denison, due to the hilly topography, one can see corn growing beyond the town's boundaries. For reasons that defy easy explanation, I was drawn to those fields. I spent afternoons walking corn rows for hours at a time, lost in a green dream. I was looking to connect with the Sioux by finding arrowheads, and for something else as I tried to figure my life out and move on from the calendar date on the wall of the Shaw Mansion. The closest manner to describe the emotions of this quest comes from two cinematic depictions of corn: picture the desolation of Cary Grant in *North by Northwest* after the bus left him alone at the prairie crossroads; then the mystical whispering emerging from the corn in *Field of Dreams*. My psyche was somewhere in the middle, at times veering to that of the extreme when Grant was running for his life down the corn rows when the crop duster was trying to kill him. *What the hell am I doing here?*

I didn't find arrowheads. I did discover patches of marijuana growing wild, as it has from old times when it was planted for hemp to make rope. The female plants were ripe with buds that had not yet seeded; it was a drought year, and the buds had a strong odor.

I came home those days to the Shaw Mansion and other odors. When the wind blew straight from the west, it carried the scents of curing hams, boiling hides, the making of pet food from cooked blood. Denison has two major meatpacking plants—one for beef, the other for pork—plus additional processing facilities. These plants were responsible for the town's existence. They were also the reason the town had a large Latino population.

For years, packing plants all over the Midwest had a white-dominated workforce, but when unions were busted in the early 1980s, wages fell. In days of old, workers say, the plants rotated jobs, and production lines were run more slowly, which meant fewer injuries; now, workers on sped-up lines were suffering severe carpal tunnel syndrome, a common affliction. There were also cuts, pulled muscles, and other physical problems. The packing industry is by far the most injurious category of job in Iowa, according to the U.S. Department of Labor: 24.3 recordable cases per 100 full-time workers in 2002, compared with an average of 7.4 cases per 100 workers for all industries.

Constant turnover is required due to injuries or because workers don't last at the hard labor.

White kids who had automatically gone into the plants from the 1960s until the early 1980s now sought other options—85 percent of the 140 or so annual Denison High School graduates were now going on to postsecondary schools, and some of the remaining white kids "couldn't pass the drug test," as one politician said. There was a dearth of workers. Latinos were eager to do the hard labor, and they passed the drug tests. They now worked grueling hours slashing at pork and beef in 34-degree rooms.

At Farmland Foods, as many as 9,400 hogs met their demise each day—a "perfect kill day" when the eight-hour production line did not break down, fewer if there were malfunctions. This plant employed 1,445 people. In one recent year, 2.3 million hogs, about 15 percent of all those raised in Iowa, were made into over 360 million pounds of pork products.

At shift change there were mini–rush hours. A lot of people were working. This masked a different reality. Things were on edge, economically and otherwise. Crank was a growing problem. The downtown was not as dead as many other midwestern cities, for sure. There were just a few vacant storefronts. Most businesses, however, clearly were not thriving. For now, the plants were keeping Denison's lights glowing.

The odor often changed on summer days. At times it smelled like cooking paper, other times like frying bacon. It was the smell of cold hard cash.

* * *

Nathan, who got me into the Shaw Mansion, was among the first people Michael and I had encountered. We'd immediately driven to town after selling the idea for this book and met him in a group of men. Nathan sat quietly, but his demeanor belied an intensity.

Nathan, thirty-two, is a balding and serious man whose life is devoted to the past. From his earliest age, he loved all things old. He preferred the past to anything new and quite possibly just about any living creature, except for his wife, Amber; his two-year-old daughter, Sophie; and a 110-pound St. Bernard–German shepherd mix, Schotze, "sweetheart" in German.

Nathan was born a hundred years too late. One day he showed me a 1949 aerial photograph of Denison. He pointed out all that was torn down after the photo was taken—the most prominent edifice being a Victorian-era hotel that had been replaced with a concrete pillbox surely inspired by Stalin's Moscow architecture, now the Topko Drug store. There was the J. B. Romans house, a Victorian mansion crafted by a German artisan, replaced by a Safeway, which itself was leveled to make way for the current Hy-Vee Supermarket.

It was a sunny and crisp winter day when the photograph was taken. Nathan stared at the eight-by-ten black-and-white glossy for a long time, not wanting to put it down. He wanted me to see what he saw, and I too stared. Then I noticed the picture was well-thumbed at certain corners. I realized that it had been made this way over a long period of time by Nathan's hands.

"Boy, wouldn't you like to go back in time and be in that picture for a day, walking around?" I asked.

"I think about that all the time," Nathan said dreamily, as he continued staring at the town scene. To Nathan, each old building was a friend. He could take you around and tell you who had lived where, what they had done, as if he were a Methuselah who'd known all the early residents.

He couldn't do anything about what was gone before his birth in 1971, but at an early stage in his life, he began a quest to save what remained. It started at age twelve when he grew curious about his mother's nearly century-old house. He tracked down the daughter of the original owner, an ancient woman, and talked her into giving him pictures of the house from its heyday.

Each year he curated, moving on to larger objects. At age sixteen, he bought a wrecked 1969 Roadster and pieced it back together. At seventeen, he was in a local pawnshop, and the owner told him about a Wurlitzer Model 1015 jukebox—the chromed variety one sees in vintage 1950s diners—that he was going to buy from a businessman to sell to a distant man. Nathan felt the jukebox belonged in town. He went to the businessman.

" 'He's offered me $4,000 for it,' " Nathan recalled the owner saying about the pawnshop owner. "He asked me, 'What will you pay for it?' "

Nathan's face fell. He had $950 in his bank account. He said he couldn't top the pawnbroker. The owner insisted on Nathan's telling him how much he could spend.

"Nine hundred dollars," Nathan said, sheepishly.

"Sold," the man said. Shocked, Nathan asked why.

"That guy only wants to make money on it. Thirty-one hundred dollars doesn't mean that much to me."

These bits of fortune continued as the stakes grew. A famed institution closed in 1985—the Candy Kitchen, a soda fountain and café next to the Ritz Theater. It was filled with objects dating to before 1920, the most revered being the long counter that Donna Reed leaned on when she drank "phosphates"—what we now call Italian sodas.

The kitchen was shuttered for years, gathering dust. Then one day it was empty of the fountain, the candy counter (inlaid terra cotta with a varying ground-stone pattern, weighing 2,100 pounds), mahogany benches, mirrors. A local man had bought everything for $10,000; later he auctioned items on eBay, the Internet trading company. A New Jersey man had purchased the counter, and the only reason it wasn't whisked away was that it would cost $14,000 to transport it. Nathan intervened, convinced the seller to let it go for $1,000. It was money he didn't have, but he couldn't bear to see the counter leave town.

This pursuit continued. He located a 1920s gas pump and restored it. While looking for parts for the pump, he discovered an Indian motorcycle. He restored it. He was at an auction house and spied a 1915 icebox. It was one of the first electric refrigerators, but it still used the same metal-covered wooden chamber that the "ice man" would fill with ice cut from winter lakes and stored in insulated barns. It was a wreck, missing handles. Nathan asked about it.

"No one wants to buy it. I'm going to take it to the dump. They're going to charge me fifteen dollars because of the Freon," he recalled the auctioneer telling him. "Tell you what. If you take it, I'll pay you eight dollars."

Nathan loaded it on his truck. He located handles, made parts by hand, had the metalware re-nickeled. The compressor was shot. He learned that General Electric had never changed the motor: a brand-new one meant for a modern refrigerator fit exactly. It was a process that took many months. When done, he had a showroom-perfect 1915 refrigerator worth a small fortune.

Did he wish he were rich enough so he could save more endangered items? I asked this question absent-mindedly one afternoon.

"I thought about what you said, about being rich," he said a few days later. "I don't think so. Like my refrigerator. If I were rich, I would have bought a new one. Or I would have bought one that was restored. I had to work for it. I think I would have missed out. I guess it's the struggle that I enjoy."

When Nathan married, he didn't purchase a tract home. Denison is filled with the mansions of merchants and lawyers and bankers from before the turn of the century. Some had long been torn down, and others were in terrible shape. He could have gotten any for a relative pittance, but he chose the most ruined—one slated to be bulldozed in 1997. It had been built by Charles Bullock, who was remembered as a hero for shooting three circus showmen who tried to rob and burn down his drugstore in 1875. The Queen Anne–style home, with a round turret and a cone-shaped roof, had been in long decline, last used as apartments. When looking at it, Nathan leaned against a wall and heard crunching. He peeled back the wallpaper to find dozens of cockroaches. Undeterred, Nathan stripped the interior walls to bare studs and entirely rebuilt the house.

"Some people go home to their ranch-style house and put their feet up, and don't think about anything like this. They're missing something. My brother isn't like me. I feel sorry for him. He'll never feel the soil in his fingers, the *need* to do something. So that's why I don't want to be rich. There are other ways."

Nathan rescued many other things—so many that he stored items from his burgeoning collection in spare corners of the homes of family and friends. He was compelled to curate not for the vice of possession but to save things from loss. If he didn't do it, no one else would.

But there were numerous defeats.

When Donna Reed died, her estate left the town her papers, still pictures, and other career-related items—10,000 objects in all. The Ritz

Theater was run down. One plan was to demolish it to create a parking lot, but locals rallied and created the Donna Reed Foundation. (The foundation would later hold the Donna Reed Festival for the Performing Arts, a weeklong June event that brought Hollywood to Denison, teaching aspiring young actors from all over the country.) Grant monies were found, and it was decided to restore the building to its 1914 state when it had opened as an opera house, and that meant taking off the 1940s movie marquee and replacing it with one designed like the original.

Nathan drew the plans for the 1914 replica, but he figured the town should keep the 1940s marquee, for it was part of the history and would be valuable someday to be used elsewhere. So he went to one of the managers at the construction company and asked if he could take the marquee as it was being removed with a crane.

"'No, you can't have it,'" he recalled him saying.

Nathan thought this was ridiculous, so he waited until a truck took the marquee to the dump. A short time later, he went to the dump and saw the marquee waiting to be pushed into the hole. Nathan asked the dump operator if he could have it.

"Sure."

A voice came from behind. It was the manager.

" 'Crush it,'" he said, Nathan recalled.

Nathan argued. What was the problem? The manager grew more agitated.

" 'Crush it!'"

The dump operator moved the bulldozer forward, and Nathan watched in horror as the marquee was smashed to pieces.

* * *

In that first meeting in which Nathan had sat quietly, we were on the high school campus adjacent to the water tower that announced "It's a Wonderful Life" in the office of Denison Schools' superintendent, Bill Wright. Bill was a big reason we were in town. After the eleven Latinos were found dead, he'd told the *Los Angeles Times,* "Immigration is what's keeping us alive."

That comment had caused me to telephone. Bill invited us out, and Michael and I drove from the East Coast on the Lincoln Highway—U.S. Route 30—to Denison. We didn't know Bill had planned a larger meeting. When we walked in, in addition to Nathan, we met Mayor Ken Livingston, a retired sales manager for Equifax Services, an insurance underwriting and financial services company; and Joel Franken, a retired high school art teacher and former city councilman.

"There are two kinds of people in this town," Joel announced not long after we sat down. "The negatives. And the positives. You're looking at some of the positives."

By *positives*, he was talking about those who wanted to move business forward in Denison and saw good in the cultural change. Both Ken and Joel said it was vital to be positive and welcome Latinos. As Joel saw it, the *negatives* were resistant to spending tax monies to encourage economic activity and wished Latinos were gone. Ken cut in and said he wanted to see Latinos included in the city, running for office, thriving economically. The negatives expressed their displeasure, Joel said, each morning at roundtable coffees at Cronk's Cafe on the Lincoln Highway or the Hy-Vee Supermarket's dining area. The negatives disliked things such as the Donna Reed Festival, which they dubbed "Dead Donna Days."

A definition of *positives* and *negatives* seemed to be a bit black and white. I'd learn Joel's branding was a lot more complicated and had nothing at all to do with being a Republican or a Democrat, a liberal or a conservative, or any other simple label.

Joel's language harkened to that of Sherwood Anderson in his 1919 novel, *Winesburg, Ohio*, which revealed the secrets of a small fictional Ohio town. I'd read *Winesburg* in college. Anderson had been influential as a mentor and a literary stylist to writers such as William Faulkner and John Steinbeck and Ernest Hemingway. Anderson called his characters "grotesques." As he termed it, "The grotesques were not all horrible. Some were amusing, some almost beautiful." To become a grotesque, as Anderson described it, one had to attempt to embrace a truth. There were many forms of truth—"the truth of virginity and the truth of passion, the truth of wealth and of poverty, of thrift and profligacy, of carelessness and abandon. Hundreds and hundreds were the truths." But by embracing truths, they inevitably became falsehoods, he wrote, because a truth cannot be embraced.

Denison, I would come to understand, is a place of the grotesques. I made this discovery as I became immersed in the life of the town and attempted to learn its truths. It was a process in which I too became a grotesque. What I mean will become clear as the story of Denison unfolds. The truth of Denison is found in an amalgam of its voices. Not all voices will be attached to their real names. It is, after all, a small town. Among those whose identities I'll keep secret is someone I shall call Kate Swift, who had read *Winesburg* when a student at Denison High School; for a time, the book was required reading.

"I'm going to call you Willard," Kate Swift announced not long after I had arrived.

George Willard was the young reporter to whom the characters in *Winesburg* revealed their stories. In turn, I am calling her Ms. Swift, the teacher in *Winesburg* who strives unsuccessfully to seduce Willard. Denison's Kate Swift and others sought me out after my presence became known. As with Anderson's Willard, they came to me to present truths. Thus, in many cases, in addition to using pseudonyms, I've also fudged some identifying characteristics. Otherwise everything is accurate as told to, or witnessed by, me. In the chapters called "Willard's Diary" I present myself in the third person because, as these citizens' confidant, I became their Willard. In other cases, material comes from spylike observations.

A few words on what this book is—and is not.

This is a town book. It's not about farming. Denison is a blue-collar factory city. The packinghouse work was once done in Omaha or Chicago, and the workers here are about as removed from farming as are people in those cities. Agriculture is out there beyond the town's lines, but there's little to remind you of that unless you listen to local radio, which gives constant reports on the price of corn or soybeans, or kill numbers: today 132,000 cattle, 382,000 hogs, 12,000 sheep. One imagines farmers listening with a sense of comparison with last week, last month, or last year, but the townies find no meaning in the figures.

It's also not an exposé on the meatpacking industry. Others have done this, from Upton Sinclair in *The Jungle* to Barbara Kopple in her Oscar-winning *American Dream*, a documentary film about a 1985 strike at a Hormel plant in Minnesota. In Denison the plant operators avoided me and did not return phone calls. I sent a letter to Farmland Foods, the largest of the plants owned by Smithfield Foods, kindly requesting an interview. The response, from Jerry Hostetter, vice president–investor relations and corporate communications, said in part,

> As much as we would like to, we cannot possibly grant all the interview requests that we receive. Therefore, we examine each request based on its merits, and then we make a determination whether the request is compatible with our company's overall communications priorities.... In that regard, we regret that we cannot honor your request for an interview at this time. However, we wish you much success with your current project.

When I occasionally ran into one plant official who nightly frequented Denison's watering holes, he eyed me as if I were packing a nine and waiting for the right evening to pull it and shoot him.

What this book is: it's about an American town, from Latino packing plant workers to the white overclass. The struggle of Denison mirrors that of hundreds of other towns—how to endure in the twenty-first century in economic, cultural, and personal terms.

In contemporary America, a small town's economy is affected by Wal-Mart. But this is not a book on Wal-Mart either, as others have told that story in great detail. Yet I do touch on the company. Before moving to Denison, I'd been in a Wal-Mart just three times: once in Oklahoma in the 1970s to purchase a hat and on two subsequent occasions as research for a story. For a variety of reasons, I chose not to patronize the chain. In Denison, however, I had no choice. For a wide range of vital goods, there are no other options without driving to Omaha, seventy miles away. If you live in Denison, you will shop at Wal-Mart.

So as I set up my life in the Shaw Mansion, I made repeated Wal-Mart visits to purchase a cheap desk, a swivel chair, and a CD/radio—all made by de facto slaves in distant lands. The radio was an immediate failure: it picked up few FM stations, and the CD player was temperamental. The chair functioned for two weeks; then the backrest snapped off. I discovered that I could balance the backrest on the metal post, and if I were careful, the chair continued to be usable, more or less. If I stood up rapidly, however, the backrest flopped to the floor. Thus began a nightly ritual of constantly resetting the seat back.

Why not simply return these items? If I were to do so, my only choice was to have them replaced by the very same inferior goods because there were no other brands in the store. Or I'd have to waste a day going to Omaha to shop. So I lived with the junk. Yet the desk wonderfully performed its job. My Wal-Mart success ratio stood at one out of three. Despite my negative outlook, many locals embraced Wal-Mart with near-worship; others were like Nathan, who referred to it as "Satan's Hollow."

* * *

I was surprised by how fast change was happening in Denison. A bank had just torn down its century-old quarters on the town square to replace it with a larger building. An adjacent old brick building not in the way was suddenly marked for demolition. Nathan worked feverishly to save the building—he thought it could be moved—but because of the construction schedule, he had only days to act. He met with the bank president, but there wasn't enough time. The building was demolished.

Then came word of a new threat.

Nathan had learned that my landlord was talking about finally selling the Shaw Mansion. A man wanted to buy it. His plan was to gut the interior woodwork and transport it to Des Moines to put in a house that he was building. The home was a Victorian time capsule. There were hand-carved posts and banisters, and fancy fretwork over the doors. This buyer would then modernize the Shaw Mansion and make it into apartments.

The potential buyer had heard about Nathan and had telephoned him.

"He told me to butt out," Nathan said.

I was aghast. I'd moved in just as someone wanted to ruin the home after it had stood for 111 years. Nathan was frantic, on a mission to try and preserve the mansion. Could he save the most historic home in town?

I knew about dispassionate reportage from my years of newspapering, but to hell with all that. I was already involved, so I decided to help Nathan. I began spreading the word to the town's elite. Many were alarmed. One banker said, "That's the most famous house in Denison!

We can't lose that!" The reaction was a common response. As Nathan noted, however, it was extremely difficult to get people to act in Denison.

Nathan worked on two fronts: trying to line up a buyer who would restore the house and trying to locate the descendants of Shaw in the event that they had enough money to make it into a museum. But my landlord was not returning Nathan's telephone calls.

*　*　*

Not long after I moved into the Shaw Mansion, I awakened with a start. It was near dawn, and I was sleeping with a T-shirt over my eyes to blot the light. I had a feeling I was being watched by someone standing over my bed, but when I pulled away the shirt, no one was there.

When I returned after a short trip to California, this same thing happened at the same hour.

Then, a few nights later, I awakened with the feeling that someone was lying on top of me, smashing my chest. I was in a sleep of the kind one has to struggle to escape, and I was not able to breathe. I gasped for air.

There was another watching incident.

Then came a night when I was asleep on my side; something behind me was pushing, not just against my back, but moving *into* my insides. It was like a shimmering sheet of electricity traveled evenly through my organs. I flung out of bed as if being ejected. I stood, befuddled. My heart would not settle. Predawn light colored the eastern sky.

About a week after this incident, I was interviewing a woman in town. She asked where I was living.

"Oh, you're in the haunted house," she commented.

I dismissed the comment until a few days later when I was talking to Nathan about the latest turn of his trying to get in touch with my landlord and his desire to bring a few potential buyers through on a tour.

"Don't tell anyone it's haunted."

"What do you mean?"

"Oh, you don't know about the ghosts?"

I replied that he'd neglected to inform me of them.

"Over the years people have had things happen who rented in the attic. The woman who worked at Topko who rented it kept waking up, feeling a weight on her. She couldn't breathe."

Then the woman began seeing things out of the corner of her eyes,

26

movement in the shadows, Nathan said. Other tenants had reported seeing ghosts: a tall man and a short, overweight woman.

One day the woman who worked at Topko was in the kitchen. She
turned around and was facing a tall man who had walked through the
wall. She fled from the house in terror—and moved out not long after.

The same week Nathan informed me of the house's spirit residents, the
ancient woman who lived downstairs moved out and went into a nursing
home. I realized she was gone when the house seemed extra quiet and
then noticed her drapes were open for the first time. I peered in the window and found her quarters vacant. I went up the stairs to Number 4.
There was a door that separated my area from hers; it was at the top of
the grand staircase and had been sealed to everyday use since 1956. I
pulled away a chair that leaned against it, unlatched the bolt. I expected it
to be latched from the other side. But someone had loosened the bolt,
and the door swung open.

I stepped to the railing at the head of the stairs. The only light was that
of dusk weakly filtering through a stained glass window across from the
banister. An early winter prairie storm was blowing in, and the stained
glass rattled; a loose downspout banged against the side of the mansion.

I was now alone in the house. I didn't go down the stairs.

It was just at freezing. Icy rain hammered the windows. Thousands of
starlings had taken roost in the silverleaf maples outside my window, and
they were chirping at 3:00 A.M. in what I imagined to be bird screams of
discomfort. Trains wailed in the valley bottom. Sleep was impossible.

LA MAESTRA I

Forty-three Latino men and women filled the classroom at Denison High School, seated at six tables. Eyes darted to the clock on the back wall. It was three minutes to seven o'clock in the evening. In front was *La Maestra,* the teacher. Georgia Hollrah stood at an overhead projector readying the lesson she would give in the coming hour and a half. A two-sided typing-paper-sized sign was affixed to the projector with a string. During the day it announced to the white kids,

ESPAÑOL

This sign was now flipped and declared,

ENGLISH

At the back center table was Jesús from El Salvador, who works on the killing line. He examined a device he'd just purchased for $145—a hand-held computer that translates Spanish to English. At a front table to the right of Georgia was Antonio, who works farther down the line. Antonio slashes a blade at the same spot on ribs all day long in a 34-degree room wearing metal gloves. Antonio's knuckles were fantastically swollen from repetitive stress injury, and he rubbed his hands trying to work out the pain. After class Antonio would do the same as always: go home, take vitamins so he could be strong, and fall into bed. He needed to be ready for work the next morning.

At my table were five women and one man. Mina, only twenty or so, had just arrived from Mexico and didn't have a job; she'd also been attending an English-language class in the morning at the Lutheran church. There were Virgen and two Marias, who work in another meat plant. The younger Maria is in her twenties and wore a red "New York" sweatshirt. The older Maria had a silver-lined front tooth and a seven-year-old daughter, who sat quietly by her side.

To my right was Jesús from the state of Michoacán in Mexico, and a third Maria at this table—his wife. This was their first-ever English class. The couple had been in the United States for twenty-seven years, mostly in Merced, California, where Jesús had driven a tractor and Maria picked peaches. Jesús had a stiffness to his walk, the movement of a farmhand who had spent a lifetime in the fields. He'd moved with Maria as if in formation with her when they'd entered the classroom. It was a proud walk. One does not see native-born American men walking like this with their women. Jesús had a full, thick mustache that was finely trimmed, and he wore a baseball cap, as did half of the men in the room.

These caps are worn in a curious manner. The bills are especially curved, the arch made more exaggerated by the hands of the men to be much like a duck's bill missing the bottom beak, worn low over the brows even indoors—the habit of people who have worked in the sun and instinctively understand its power and the need to shield their eyes.

Nearly everyone had put in a long day. Most had spent it killing, cutting, or chopping at pork or beef. Georgia had already taught five Spanish-language classes to 160 English-speaking students, and her day had begun twelve hours earlier. Eyes were heavy, but all faces were eager, Georgia's being the most enthusiastic. She was fifty-two but appeared younger, not only because of her long blond hair, but by the manner in which she moved and used her hands to speak as she taught.

The clock struck seven. Georgia looked up, smiled.

"Good evening!"

"Good evening!" the room said in unison. There was a distinct "b" sound in place of the "v" in the reply.

"What is today?"

"Monday!" said a man to Georgia's left.

"That's right. And what is today's date?"

"October six," someone said.

Georgia wrote, "Monday, October 6" on the blackboard. Below she wrote "sixth."

She pointed to the "6" and then the "th" in "sixth," underlining it.

"It is a six. But we say 'sixTTTHHHH. SixTTTHHHH.' What is today?"

"Monday, October sixth," some of the class replied in unison. Others used "six."

Georgia had cocked an ear for the proper pronunciation and not hearing it from everyone, she again emphasized "THHHH," and had them repeat the date a few more times.

Before class started, Maria's seven-year-old daughter had been rattling on in perfect English to another child; she then talked to her mother in Spanish. I thought about something I'd witnessed the previous afternoon at the Denison Post Office. I was in line behind a Spanish-speaking woman who was sending an express package of photographs to Mexico. The woman's daughter, about age ten, translated for her mother as the postwoman explained, in English, the sixteen-dollar cost. The clerk paused occasionally to allow the daughter to translate. The kids who were born here or came when young rapidly picked up the language.

Some whites in Denison and elsewhere were bitter that the newcomers weren't learning English, invoking a fear that America would have colonies of perpetually non–English speaking citizens. But it simply wasn't true. In all the years I'd been reporting on culture, never had I met kids of immigrants born here who didn't speak English. Their parents were another matter. I once was on the conservative radio talk show hosted by Bob Grant in New York City on WOR-AM, talking about immigrants. I'd discovered through a database search that his Italian grandmother had never learned English. So when Grant went on a jag about immigrants setting up a culture apart, I invoked his grandmother. "You're right, she didn't learn English," I recall him saying. Grant melted, and I owned him after that. The kids learn English. The parents often do not.

But some do. And it was a monumental task. I'd first come to Georgia's English as a Second Language (ESL) class to observe, but she instantly recruited me to tutor, and I found myself teaching English. For three nights every week in the ensuing school year, I would sit at a table in this room. I intellectually understood that it was difficult for an adult to learn English, but I wasn't prepared for reality. Simply pronouncing the date was supremely difficult for these learners. Georgia wouldn't get to contractions for a month—about as foreign to these Spanish speakers as my trying to learn Mandarin Chinese.

* * *

The road that led Georgia to be standing before the ESL learners began when she was four years old and living in St. Louis. Her grandmother had given her an album of Spanish folk songs. Little Georgia, of German extraction, danced and sang to the record. Then her father, who worked for a farm implement company, was transferred to Mexico—Mexico, Missouri, a town about ninety miles west of St. Louis. Mexico's schools had just inaugurated a pilot language program, and in third grade Georgia began taking Spanish. She was so fluent that when she went to Iowa State University in Ames, she was given credit for twenty-one hours of Spanish. She was a double Spanish/history major.

Georgia met her husband, Kent, at Iowa State. When they graduated in 1972, she taught for one year in Coon Rapids, and then the couple moved to Denison. Kent worked for an insurance agency while laboring on the side at a family farm with his brother. Georgia became a secretary, then taught one year at a nearby school district but stopped when her daughters, Beth and Rachel, were born. Georgia and a friend opened a day care facility at a Denison church so they could be with their own children. In 1986, when her daughters were old enough to attend school, Georgia began teaching Spanish at Denison High School.

In the early 1990s, there were a few hundred Latinos in Denison. It seemed like a dramatically large number, and many whites grumbled. But others got together and formed a cultural diversity committee. The town had some experience with immigrants: in the 1970s, a few locals had helped bring one hundred Laotian refugees here after the Vietnam War ended. This seemed like a similar situation. No one then knew the Latino population would increase tenfold in the coming decade.

The self-imposed goal of the committee was elemental: Could the city make the demographic change work? The starting point would be to teach the new arrivals English. Members approached the woman who could help, Georgia. Could she give an evening class in English as a Second Language?

God wants me to do this, she thought that night after being asked. It wasn't as if Jesus appeared to Georgia. It was how she lived her religion—by doing, not talking. Being Lutheran didn't mean just going to church on Sundays. Could she change the lives of the newcomers? And could she have an impact on those in town who viewed the Latinos with disdain?

Georgia was excited, but she also was worried. She'd never taught ESL. To teach white high school kids Spanish was one thing. But it was a different matter to teach adults a new language. In addition, Georgia had her two young daughters. But she would have help from one other teacher, and they would teach only one night per week.

The committee also went to a man best able to recruit students: Joe Chavez. Joe was among the first Latinos to arrive in Denison, in 1963. For years, he and his wife and six children were the entire Latino population. Joe, who had taught himself English, was eager to assist. He had rental properties that were occupied by Latino newcomers, and he knew many others. He urged them to attend the class scheduled to be taught by Georgia and the other teacher.

"I tell them everything is possible in this culture. They can be a doctor or a lawyer or the governor of Iowa," Joe recalled of his prodding them to learn English.

For that first class on a Monday, Joe made signs that read,

BIENVENIDOS A LA TIERRA DE OPORTUNIDAD

"Welcome to the land of opportunity."

When the class began that first night, some twenty-five adults showed up—roughly 10 percent of the town's Latino population. All were men—at that time there were few Latinas in Denison. Georgia wouldn't see women in her class until 1999. As the community matured, the men brought their families north. By the time I showed up, the class was at least half female.

The first day went rough but well. After a few weeks, Georgia saw that one night a week was not enough time for the students to immerse in English. So she upped the class to two nights. Another revelation was that many of the adults were either illiterate or only marginally literate in Spanish.

These were not cosmopolitan light-skinned urbanites from Mexico

City or other major Latin metropolises. They were *campesinos,* meaning peasants, or country people. In Mexico, an extremely race-conscious society, members of the aristocracy tend to have a lighter face. The faces seen in Denison were darker, like the pre-Columbian peoples.

Georgia and the other teacher were unpaid. Superintendent Bill Wright, who grew up in outer Queens in New York City, was keen on assisting. The neighborhood of his youth was diverse, and he thought the change was good. There were just a few nonwhites in Denison when he'd arrived in 1965—one black man and a Latino family. Bill bought books and other supplies for the ESL students, figuring he'd later approach the packinghouses seeking financial help to educate their workers. Bill also set the tone of a totally can-do attitude in the school system with regard to Latino children.

As the first weeks advanced, Georgia was amazed by the intensity with which her adult students wanted to learn English. But there were problems: because of a personal crisis, the other teacher had to stop; and funding from the packinghouses never came through. The largest plant did hire Georgia to teach for an eight-month stretch but then dropped the program.

Georgia worked on regardless, alone and for free. She started at seven o'clock in the morning with her high school students and ended with the adult Spanish speakers at nine o'clock at night. Then she went home to be a mother, grading papers in bed until nodding off with her husband, Kent.

At the time, Georgia was also studying for her master's degree in education, which she earned in 1996. She was inspired to focus on what is known as the whole language technique, which delays instruction in grammar. This method has students listen, read, and speak the language; after they get comfortable with it, they take apart its grammatical structure. Georgia learned that ESL should ideally be taught daily because the English language is so difficult. Most native English speakers don't realize that it's among the hardest major languages on earth to learn (the others include Mandarin Chinese, Japanese, and Russian). Children readily adapt to language, for the part of the brain that absorbs it is still receptive, but in most adults, this receptivity has disappeared.

There must be constant reinforcement if progress is to be made. Of

English, Georgia said, "There are two languages—the one read, the one spoken. All the slang terms, and accents, English has it in spades. There it is right there. We can't eradicate slang from our speaking. When we don't use slang, we sound formal, so priggish."

Someone who learns the language by reading will not be able to speak English well—if at all.

Daily study was out of the question, given that Georgia was a one-woman language school. And her students were working grueling hours—even if they wanted to, it would be difficult for them to immerse themselves. But Georgia upped the class to three nights per week. And she had an idea: she'd recruit non-Spanish-speaking townspeople to tutor. These volunteers didn't have to know Spanish. It was merely important for the students to hear English and talk one-on-one with native speakers in a setting where they would not feel embarrassed or inhibited.

"How are the classes going?" fellow members at Our Savior Lutheran Church would ask. Some would add, "Is there anything I can do?"

"Yes," Georgia replied. "Come."

"But I don't know any Spanish."

They found it difficult to believe that this was actually preferable.

The cliché image of midwestern Lutherans is one of hardworking people who are conservative yet nonjudgmental and will reach out to help others. It may be a stereotype, but it has a lot of basis in reality. Georgia built a pool of volunteers from the church, including one woman who was not happy that the immigrants had come to town. Georgia realized there might be an added benefit to the volunteer program: perhaps some residents could be educated by the Latinos. It would be a rare chance for the newcomers to meet whites. There was little interaction between the races in any setting. A common refrain around town in 1994, one that would continue a decade later, was the belief that the Latinos preferred being apart or were somehow sinister in their view of whites.

"They're talking about me!" was the reaction heard from some whites who saw Latinos in the grocery stores. The Latinos would be ripping away in Spanish, an utterly exotic tongue to most locals, who imagined they were being talked about. Most likely, the Spanish speakers were discussing which brand of products to purchase, but it's human nature to be self-absorbed and assume the worst in such situations.

After volunteers came from Our Savior Lutheran Church, some signed on from Zion, the other Lutheran congregation. At first there was a core group of some fifteen people. Some were Monday night people, others came on Tuesday, others all three nights.

The woman who was so disdainful of the Latinos but who had stepped forward to help began laughing and talking with the immigrants at her table. She would see her ESL learners in the grocery store and now stopped to chat with them. One bridge had been built. But this was uncommon. Many whites still shunned the newcomers and would never volunteer.

In those first years, Georgia was asked to give talks to groups. At one women's organization, Georgia began her presentation by explaining how hard it was to learn English. A woman in the front, of German heritage, sat with her arms in folded defiance.

Georgia thought: *Oh boy, we're having fun here, aren't we? Education is happening!*

Georgia went into the process of ESL, and the woman in front never uncrossed her arms. Georgia asked if there were any questions. The woman uncrossed her arms and shot up a hand.

"That's all fine and good," the audience member said. "But when are they going to learn to speak English?!"

The woman went on to relate how her grandparents came to Iowa from Germany, that her grandfather announced they were going to speak English, "and that's what we always spoke after that."

"Of course, she wasn't born then," Georgia noted, "so she doesn't have a clue. Grandma and Grandpa spoke German for the next ten years after that. I hear, 'They've been here for three years, why aren't they speaking?' Our perception of what our ancestors did is forgotten. It's so long ago. A lot of them didn't learn. You don't speak English just because you breathe this air. Because if you want to say, 'I had the worst day of my life, I need some comfort, this is a problem,' you aren't going to speak English if you only have ten words in your vocabulary."

Georgia mimed a person suffering a heart attack.

" 'I think I'm going to die here, sweetheart! Hey, let's try to conjugate this verb. Now what was that vocabulary word in class?' Since they don't know how hard it is, they can't empathize with anybody who must do it.

My mother, whom I absolutely adore and is living in Florida, she's not as sympathetic toward them. She'll say, 'Well, they should just learn English.' I'll say, 'Mom, they're trying.'"

Georgia reasoned with her mother, who had taken a French class in college.

"It was the worst experience of her life. My mom's a smart woman. And she had this wretched French teacher who apparently went too fast and didn't give any practice. I said, 'Mom, just transpose how much fun you had there to trying to live your life in this country. It's ten times harder.'"

No matter. Georgia always lost this argument.

Georgia had her own doubts. Was she doing the right thing in her teaching methods? In the midst of her own self-questioning, on one of her worst days, she was at a service at Our Savior Lutheran Church. They were shaking hands in brotherly and sisterly love. A woman she shook hands with asked, "Are the classes still going on?"

"Yes."

"You must be doing a terrible job. They still aren't learning English."

The woman was joking, no? Georgia wasn't certain. It struck deep.

"It was one of those days where I thought, 'Jeez, what am I doing!?' I felt awful. They might think I'm just a bad teacher because I'm obviously not converting everybody to English."

Then she would walk into the classroom and see the eager faces, and she worked harder.

*   *   *

It was now one week after I had begun volunteering. Georgia had been teaching the class for a decade, missing only the winter term in 1997 when she was recovering from open heart surgery. I'd been in town long enough to see that Latinos were living apart. In the *Denison Bulletin & Review,* the local newspaper, pictures on the sports pages of high school teams featured almost only white athletes; there was one Latino track team member. The only team with any substantial Latino representation was soccer. Latinos never came to public meetings. Whites saw Latinos as they drove around, in the grocery stores, at Wal-Mart. But there was virtually no interaction, save for inside Georgia's classroom.

It was cold and raining, and turnout for class that night was about one-third less than usual, yet all the people at my table had shown up. The single women were all shy. I learned Mina had been married in Mexico and was now happily single, after Jesús kidded with me in Spanish about being a single guy seated at a table with five women.

For reasons of cultural gender etiquette, I talked mostly with Jesús in my bad Spanish; the couple spoke virtually no English. I learned they had four children—one remaining at home, a sixteen-year-old daughter. They'd come to Iowa from California five years before, first living in Marshalltown, some two hours to the east on the Lincoln Highway. Marshalltown is also a packing town, with a reputation for roughness, the prime reason they had moved to Denison just three months earlier. Their daughter was in constant fights in school, and they feared for her safety. Jesús and Maria had heard Denison's schools were great and that violence was not tolerated. Denison was a bit of a dream come true. But the work was hard, Maria said. As she spoke, Jesús rubbed his hands. He endured the pain because he had been making only five dollars an hour driving a tractor in California, and his wage in the packing plants was double that.

Seven o'clock approached. Georgia as usual wrote that day's lesson plan on the overhead projector:

1. We are reading the dialogue aloud.
2. We are practicing with names and places.
3. We are using small words.
4. We are practicing with ownership.
5. We are matching answers and questions.

At seven o'clock sharp, the class read each line aloud as a group, then copied the material in notebooks. They again group-repeated the lines, after which Georgia called on students at each table to read them. Jesús would occasionally raise his hand, and he struggled with the words. The women almost never raised a hand. Georgia would then pick; it became a joke that Mina was usually the one called on.

There was great trouble tonight at my table with the word *dialogue*. Georgia worked through the plan, getting to the nut of the night's lesson:

"small words," pronouns. She illustrated how pronouns work by having the class repeat this statement:

> We live in Denison. This is our city.
> They live in Denison. This is their city, too.

Georgia stood by one table, and upon uttering *we*, motioned to her group; with *they*, she pointed to another table. She then wrote on the board:

Subjective	Possessives
I	My
You	Your
He	His
She	Her
We	Our
They	Their

"They are all small but very important words," Georgia informed the class. Their eyes were intent.

"*Es difícil!*" It's difficult, Jesús murmured to me as everyone practiced. I urged Jesús on, whispering encouragement.

As the lesson proceeded, I carefully studied the faces in the room. I thought about the eleven dead immigrants found in the grain car one year earlier and the journey everyone in this room had made to arrive in Denison. Each of the thirty people harbored a stunning story worthy of a film. It could have been any of them who had died in that grain car. And there are a hundred other ways they could have perished, been raped, or been beaten on the trek to Iowa. I knew a little about what they had been through.

* * *

It was the summer of 1984, and the Cold War was not yet over. President Ronald Reagan had drawn a line in the coffee fields of Central America. The U.S. puppet in Nicaragua, Anastasio Somoza, had been overthrown by the Sandinistas, and Reagan didn't want to "lose" El Salvador to factions he deemed "communists." The United States was pumping in a half-billion dollars annually to support the country's right-wing government. Some 75,000 Salvadorans were killed in the war—many slain by the death squads whose members were from the Salvadoran military.

Michael and I had met some Salvadorans given refuge by a church in Sacramento, California, where we worked for a newspaper. The church was part of the Sanctuary Movement and the underground railroad, comprising a mix of religions—Quakers, Lutherans, Mennonites, Catholics, others—that was smuggling and harboring refugees threatened by the death squads.

Rather than stop with the local story, we decided to travel to El Salvador. We first went to Arizona and Texas to interview the movement's leaders. We then purchased one-way tickets. The travel agent asked why we didn't get round-trip fare—she believed that Michael was joking when he replied that we were going to walk, swim, bus, and otherwise find our way home by land. A Salvadoran family in Sacramento we had written about and photographed had a member—Elisia—who needed to escape, and we were to meet with her and an underground railroad member who would help her get out.

El Salvador was a blur: evening in the guerrilla-held town of Suchitoto amid bursts of machine-gun fire, the road out filled with land mines. Villages of mud huts where women ground *maíz*, corn, on stone mortars. The killing fields of *El Playon*, the lava beds where skulls with bullet holes in the foreheads lay scattered by the score from the work of the death squads, and nearby buzzards perched awaiting new bodies. The refugee camps, fetid and rife with misery, filled with children and their haunting eyes.

We met with Elisia and her two cousins in the plaza in the city of Santa Ana. It was tense—soldiers watched—and Elisia didn't trust the sanctuary member. They decided to make the journey without help, then stole away, lost in the crowd.

We were scheduled to connect with Jim Corbett, the cofounder of the Sanctuary Movement, in the Mexican state of Chiapas. We crossed the Rio Paz into Guatemala, where we made the six-dollar bus ride north with Salvadorans. Getting into Mexico was difficult. The Rio Suchiate defines the frontier—it's known as the River of Death. We had serious problems but got across.

When we had our rendezvous with Jim, we learned there was a death warrant on him put out by the military governor. Jim was known as *El Famoso*, the "famous man," in Latino circles, for he was often in the media speaking against U.S. policy: he defied Reagan by openly declaring he was smuggling refugees. Jim had checked into a hotel under an assumed name. He was here to scout new routes; a week and a half before, a dozen Salvadorans had been shot at the notorious Huixtla roadblock operated by Mexican *migra*, immigration.

In the coming days we slept in "hotels" that cost three bucks a night, never staying in the same place twice. Jim feared our having an "accident." In the previous year, five local nuns and a priest working with refugees had died in "accidents."

"Let's just hope we don't get caught," he said.

We navigated mangrove swamps by boat as Jim charted a new route along the coast. It was amazing watching Jim, then fifty and with a gray goatee. He suffered from rheumatoid arthritis, his hands and feet painfully deformed, yet he ran on the jungle trails like a deer and never uttered a complaint. Jim, a former rancher, often went alone into the Arizona desert to herd goats in search of peace. He was motivated to help refugees by his deep Quaker faith.

We ended up near the remote shark-fishing village of Puerto Madero, where Jim had heard that a huge prostitution slave camp had sprung up. He wanted to go in and check it out. We asked, Wasn't this dangerous?

"Yes. If anything will save us, it will be by directly going in."

Jim said that by boldly entering, the camp operators would assume we must have some connection with the U.S. government. He said it was akin to being a Roman during the Roman Empire. We'd bluff and act as if we owned the place. This would be our last act before fleeing Chiapas.

"You ask questions or do the heavy things two hours before your plane leaves," he said of what he had learned of surviving Chiapas.

It was late in the day when we entered the compound. Puerto Madero was a tiny village. Yet this camp had over a hundred women. Jim said these camps were used as holding areas for women to be shipped to brothels to the north in Mexico. I could now identify Guatemalans and Salvadorans by appearance and accent, and all the women were from these nations. As Donna Summer's "Bad Girls" played on a jukebox, we

ordered Corona beers. Most women were afraid. But Beatriz, a Salvadoran, told us we were the first white men ever to enter the compound.
Beatriz whispered and confirmed what Jim had heard: Mexican *migra*
brought Central American women captured at the checkpoints here and
were paid a bounty by the owners.

Jim offered to help, but Beatriz didn't trust us. As he implored her,
night was falling. We were pushing our luck. We left without her, walking
out like Romans. We caught a plane to Mexico City, where Jim met con-
tacts using tactics out of a spy novel. There were code names, a meeting
where Jim had to carry the newspaper *Uno Mas Uno* under his left arm to
meet a contact with a Band-Aid over his left eye. None of this was paranoia: two Mexican government agents were following us, and we had to
lose them several times.

It was a high-profile family we'd be smuggling: a doctor, his wife and
baby, and a few others. The doctor had death threats against him because
he had treated refugees in the camps. We got this family as far north as the
city of Obregón using the Roman ruse with *migra* in several situations—
migra didn't mess with dark-skinned people traveling with whites. Then
Jim had to get back to Tucson.

Just 250 miles from the U.S. frontier, logic would dictate that the Mexicans should want to let the Salvadorans go, get out of their hair, and
enter the United States. But it was here that the Mexican government was
most serious about catching them. Word was the U.S. government was
applying pressure on Mexico to stop the refugee flow.

Another underground railroad member met us at the safe house in
Obregón—a man we'd later firmly believe was a U.S. Justice Department
mole. The next day he fell "ill" and couldn't drive, or do anything else.
Suddenly the lives of the doctor and his family fell into our hands: we
were now the smugglers. Things were complicated by a new roadblock
just north of town. Michael and I went to check it out, playing stupid
gabachos, white guys, looking for the airport. These were like no other
migra agents we'd yet seen—they had machine guns and were supremely
mean-looking. The Roman trick, we felt, wouldn't work. We couldn't risk
trying to take the family through. We called the big editor at our paper
seeking advice. He blew us off.

"Figure it out," he said. Click.

We were on our own.

We looked at a map and decided to try a dirt track that headed deep into the Sierra Madre. It was risky, but it would circumvent the roadblock. The next morning I took the wheel. But the map lied: there was no road. I drove the ancient panel wagon miles up the center of steadily shrinking arroyos. As the Sierra Madre loomed larger, I turned left and began heading north, traveling by the sun and instinct over roadless open country parallel with the mountains, dodging the strange flora. Late in the day, a family at a hacienda fed the children; they had horses and had never seen a vehicle there. It was night when we emerged on a road again, and our day ended a dozen hours after it had begun when we reached the Nogales safe house.

The family walked with Michael and other Sanctuary members across the border in the mountains. I went by other means of transportation to lessen the size of the group so as to avoid the chance of capture. Back in Sacramento, we met Elisia's cousins. They told us horrible news: they'd been caught with Elisia at the Huixtla roadblock and had been beaten. At one point while being held, they'd seen Elisia, who had also been beaten and raped. The cousins were shipped across the Guatemalan border minus Elisia. They again tried and made it through. No one had since heard from Elisia. They were awaiting word, but it never came. They never learned her fate.

This began a long period of nightmares for me. What could we have done differently to convince Elisia to take the help of the Sanctuary worker? It ground at me, and I grew to blame myself for not doing whatever more I could have. If she were not dead, at best she was a captive in one of the prostitution slave rings in central or northern Mexico. A Sacramento Sanctuary member scolded me for my second-guessing. Elisia was like a soldier in a war, she said, and not everyone made it. Get over it and move on, she snapped. But I wasn't getting over it.

The U.S. Justice Department then busted the Sanctuary leaders in Tucson. U.S. attorney Don Reno was prosecuting Jim Corbett along with nine nuns and priests. In the trial, Reno accused Michael and me of smuggling. I believe his information was based on phone taps and the informant. But my part in the smuggling operation had happened on foreign soil, and there was no jurisdiction. Michael had supposedly lifted the barbed wire separating the United States from Mexico, when one of the women got snagged.

"Welcome to America. Welcome to democracy," Michael allegedly uttered, according to court testimony.

Michael's "crime" happened on U.S. ground. Reporters called to ask me about it (Michael was then in the Philippines covering the revolution freelance for *U.S. News & World Report*), and I honestly said I knew nothing, that I had not been present. For unknown reasons, Reno never indicted Michael.

I was beyond academic argument over journalism ethics. I had a sour attitude about what the United States was doing south of the border. I utterly despised the boss who had hung up on us. I harbored anger about a lot of things. Yet the least of our worries were the feds or the boss. We were living rough. Not long after Reno mentioned us in the trial, Michael was photographing supporters of Ferdinand Marcos who were stealing ballots. They opened fire; and the bullets struck his camera bag. He survived only because a sympathetic Filipino hid him in a closet from the thugs who were hunting to kill him.

Earlier that same year, 1985, after Drug Enforcement Administration agent Enrique Camarena vanished in Guadalajara, Mexico, two other Americans disappeared there—Alberto Radelat and John Walker, a writer. The newspaper sent reporter Mike Castro and me to cover the story. At that point, the bodies of Radelat and Walker had not been found, and details were sketchy. After a week of digging for information, just before we were to leave, we retraced their steps on the last night of their lives by walking to each bar they were known to have visited. We were a strange pair, a young *gabacho* dressed in jeans with a middle-aged American Latino in a blinding white sharkskin suit and tie. At a bar named Carambas, a man with a lightning scar across his face struck a gong as we entered. The final bar was our most important stop, for it was rumored to be a drug kingpin hangout and a brothel: the instructions of how to get to it were that when the road ended, you kept going.

We parked and walked, talking about the wisdom of what we were doing. I didn't tell Mike Castro my real motive: a faint hope of finding Elisia. This sounds crazy now, years later, but I was not thinking rationally, for I was more than a bit posttraumatic stressed from the El Salvador project and a lot of other things that had happened in the 1980s. It was less than wise to go into the bar at midnight where Radelat and Walker likely met their demise in a place where no one who could help would hear us scream. The most important attribute of being street smart means knowing when not to go in.

We went in.

A huge man patted us down for guns. The operation was full of Salvadoran prostitutes. None were Elisia. It was not the place to ask questions. In fact, the Roman ruse was quickly wearing thin. We felt a growing bad vibe. Mike and I looked at each other and, without words, exited.

Years passed. Jim Corbett died of natural causes in 2001. I ended up in Denison amid Salvadorans. While what I was doing in Denison transcended just the story of the Latino immigrants, what had happened two decades earlier might have been one reason I had come to town. I can't say I was searching any longer for Elisia. Time, after all, had gone by. But I was searching for something. Georgia was surprised that I rarely missed a night, and that when I did it was only because of conflicts with meetings at city hall.

One snowy night, one of the Salvadoran men in class came up to me. William Galicia was twenty-five, and could have been one of the five-year-old children we'd seen in the refugee camps. He'd heard I'd been to his native land. In my terrible Spanish and his rough English, we talked about life in El Salvador today.

I knew that it was a destroyed nation. As the war wound down, the U.S. Immigration and Naturalization Service had deported undocumented Salvadorans. Many of the repatriated were hardened Los Angeles gang members who set up gang operations on Salvadoran soil. These were men who in many cases had fled north because of the war and U.S. shenanigans, and were being sent back educated in American-style street thuggery. There was now stunning violence and carnage, with no political purpose.

"No, no," William told me that snowy night, "I am not from San Salvador. San Salvador and the cities, oh, it is very dangerous. You die."

William lived in a village in the state of Ahuachupán near the Rio Paz and the Guatemalan frontier, but there was no work for him in his trade as a mason. He had to travel to San Salvador for work and constantly dodged violence, the *mareros*, bandits; the *pandilleras*, gangsters whose faces are covered with tattoos.

Once three *pandilleras* burst into the apartment of his neighbor, and they shot the woman dead. Another time he was sitting on a bus bench. He motioned how a woman was seated right next to him, to his right. Four men came up. They put a handgun behind William's head and shot the woman dead.

"Boom. Boom. Boom. They shoot her. *Increible,*" William said, using and pronouncing the word *incredible* in heavy Spanish, "In-cre-eee-bleh."

"It was *increible*. I see much blood. Step in much blood. There is a big window from there to here. I like it here. Nothing happens. It's safe."

William flashed a big smile of contentment. Did the legend of the white buffalo and the Ghost Dance portend that William and other Latinos come to Denison? Who knows. But their being in town, at least those from Central America, was perhaps restitution for the U.S. meddling in their countries over the decades of the twentieth century. William was safe for the first time in his life, oddly in the very nation that did much to ruin his native land. He deserved to be here. Is this a liberal perspective? Perhaps. But that night, as I looked into William's eyes and had a flashback to Elisia and the starving children in the refugee camps, it seemed to me to simply be a human viewpoint.

*　　*　　*

There was a lot of geopolitical history underpinning the story of Latinos in Denison. But there was also some local history that applied, as Michael Williamson and I discovered the first time we set foot in town. That winter day, Michael stood on Main Street holding a 1903 postcard of a Denison town scene. He wanted to replicate the shot, a before-and-after image. We picked out the city hall and other buildings. But on the east side of the street, a massive wooden church was missing. All that remained were concrete steps leading to a vacant lot.

The next day, I asked Joel Franken about the missing church.

"Did it burn down?"

"No. People don't like talking about what happened to it. There's some dark stuff around here."

It was the first of the secrets we'd learn about Denison.

SECRETS

Those who named Iowa's ninety-nine counties after the state's creation in 1846 appear to have been scrambling for options as settlers streamed in, having gone through the usual collection of presidents and such. In 1851 the county that would later have Denison as its seat was named after William H. Crawford, secretary of the U.S. Treasury from 1817 to 1825. Crawford County was wilderness—there was just one white family living here, and an unknown number of Sioux, who were doomed to eviction or extinction. No one appears to have consulted any of them about the name choice.

The first treaty that took Iowa Indian lands was signed on November 3, 1804, with the Sac and Fox nations. This treaty, a year after the Louisiana Purchase, dealt mostly with Illinois territory, but it included a slice of the western shore of the Mississippi River. There was no legal white settlement in what would become Iowa until a treaty signed on September 21, 1832, that ceded a 50-mile strip along the Mississippi River. In the mid-1840s, additional "purchases" were made from the Sac and Fox nations as far west as the Des Moines River. The Sac and Fox peoples, who had once lived to the east on the Great Plains and had battled other tribes on their way to Iowa, were moved to a reservation in Kansas. In 1846 Iowa became a state.

Jesse W. Denison was a Baptist preacher from New York State who had traveled to Iowa and saw that there was profit to be made. In Rhode Island he convinced investors to put up $51,000, with him as their agent, to secure a large block of Iowa that would be subdivided and sold to settlers. The enterprise was called the Providence Western Land Company.

But there was a problem: the Iowa land stolen from the Indians was, by federal decree, reserved for veterans. The largest parcels went to those who had fought in the War of 1812 and the recent war against Mexico. Each veteran was entitled to "land warrants" of 160 acres. There were different warrants for other veterans: anyone who had fought in an Indian war got 80 acres, and thirty-two other classes of veterans got everything from 10-acre to 120-acre warrants. Abraham Lincoln was awarded 40 acres near Denison, for fighting in the Illinois "Black Hawk War" (really a massacre) of 1832. He never set foot in town.

The Providence Western Land Company would claim land in the name of a group of eastern veterans: at least 182 veterans signed on with the company, according to *Iowa Public Land Disposal* by Roscoe L. Lokken. Some agreed to sell their warrants to the company for sixty cents an acre, others for about a dollar. The veterans never visited Iowa.

Jesse Denison, however, was behind the curve. Upon returning to Iowa in 1855, he traveled the eastern and central parts of the state and found similar schemers had beaten him there. Denison apparently wanted to locate in the east, where the soil was most desirable—the land was flatter and received more rainfall than did western Iowa. If he'd shown up six weeks earlier in some places, he could have scored. On October 30 he wrote the money men back East: "I knew there was a great rush into this state, but the extent of it is almost incredible."

Denison pushed west. On May 23, 1856, he wrote his people in Rhode Island that he'd found 23,040 acres on the Boyer River where he believed the transcontinental railroad would be located—the more or less east-west river provided a rare flat course for tracks through the hills of western Iowa.

There were shady dealings going on at the government land office in Council Bluffs, regarding the "register," the federal agent in charge of the land disbursement. According to Lokken: "Denison, who apparently had a 'way' with officials, formed an acquaintance with the register. . . . In the evening 'after tea and after dark' the register took him to the office and gave him all the information he desired."

Denison was granted the first hearing the next afternoon, ahead of a crowd desperate to stake claims. He set up the town that bore his name before he left the office—though he later promulgated the myth that the new residents chose the name by popular acclaim. The Denison town site between forks of the Boyer River had been the dividing line between the Sac and Fox nations and the Sioux, some of whom were still present.

Advertisements were inserted in eastern newspapers, and fliers were circulated. Local historian F. W. Meyers, in his 1911 book *History of Crawford County Iowa*, wrote, "It was evidently the same old story with which we are familiar today, by which the lands of a score of states have been exploited by pretentious advertising, by flamboyant circulars, and by rather rash promises of quick and golden returns. Many of our older settlers claim to remember the pictures of an imaginary Denison, a larger city than it is today, with wharves, and with steamboats riding at anchor upon the broad bosom of the Boyer." Then as now, the Boyer River was knee-deep at best during summer, navigable to nothing larger than a canoe that sometimes had to be dragged over mud flats. As for the city in 1856, there was but a crude cabin present as winter set in.

The settlers in the first decade were native-born Americans from New England, of English and Scottish extraction. The first immigrant group was from Sweden. These Swedes bought land for three dollars an acre north of town, in Stockholm and Otter townships, in 1867, the year the railroad made it to Denison.

The first members of another immigrant group arrived on August 13, 1870, an event that Denison duly noted in a letter to the Providence Western Land Company headquarters.

Dear Sir:

Before going out this morning to show lands, I thought I would drop a line to say that I have sold 520 acres at $6 an acre to some leading Germans, three of them, and that a fourth one is here now wishing me to go out and show him some land. They are to pay one-fourth cash when a deed is ready for them, advancing $100 on the contract, and are to give a mortgage in return. The lands are 10 miles from town on the head of Buffalo Branch, or Big Creek, and about four miles west of the Swede settlement at the head of the Otter.

These Germans have been brought here by John Ochs of Davenport, father of the agent employed and appointed by the state legislature to Europe for the purpose of encouraging emigration to Iowa. The father came here with the three Germans. His son, the state agent, will be here the first of September with a number more of foreigners, espe-cially Germans, as he is a German—the low Dutch.

Respectfully,

J. W. Denison

The next batch of Germans must have been impressed because Germans poured in. On October 5, 1870, the *Denison Review* wrote that a dozen new German arrivals were spotted coming up from the depot, "which adds so many more to the population of Crawford County." The article went on to say, "The Germans are one of the most industrious and frugal class of people on the face of the earth, and Crawford is one of the most fortunate counties in the state in securing a German settlement within its borders."

The Germans, of course, spoke German. *Die Denison Zeitung,* a German edition of the *Denison Review,* was launched in 1879. The Germania Verein, a society to promote cultural and social events and perpetuate the German language, was founded on April 1, 1881. It raised $7,000 to construct an opera house at the corner of Main Street and what later would be called First Avenue North. Across the street would later come a German-language newspaper, *Der Denison Herold.* To the north of the opera house was built the German Methodist Church. This intersection was a mini Germantown. Some nearby towns took German names; north of Denison was the city of Schleswig.

On April 17, 1886, the German Brotherhood was formed, with membership restricted to German Army veterans. The German Lutheran School was created in 1887. The German Mutual Insurance Association sold fire, lightning, tornado, and windstorm insurance to German farm families. By 1910 there were 1,650 members and a risk valuation of $6,228,425. There were so many Germans that it was felt a larger opera house was needed. In 1914, the 775-seat Deutsche Opernhaus Gesellschaft von Denison was completed at the corner of Main and Broadway, the building that would later house the museum named after the most famous Denisonite of German heritage who was born here on January 27, 1921: Donnabelle Mullenger, who later changed her name to Donna Reed.

In official accounts and newspaper articles, there was apparent harmony between the Germans and others. Then war erupted in Europe. Still, with news coming over about the war between Kaiser Wilhelm II and the rest of the continent, there was no sign of anti-German sentiment in Denison. Then the United States entered the war on April 6, 1917.

There had been much public resistance to the war, which continued after its declaration. It was seen as a European problem. President Woodrow Wilson whipped up enthusiasm by stoking nationalism. A week after the United States joined in the war, Wilson formed the Committee on Public Information (CPI), a propaganda agency. Among its goals was to convince Americans that Germans were bad, "Huns," and that there were numerous spies among the German immigrant pool.

The United States mandated that during the week of February 4, 1918, unnaturalized German men had to register with the government and give their fingerprints and photographs. They couldn't change their residence without notifying the police and postmaster. In Denison, Postmaster J. T. Carey complied. American flags were plastered all over the downtown.

The CPI recruited Americans to watch "enemy aliens," meaning not just unnaturalized Germans but citizens of German heritage. This was done through defense councils that were ordered to be set up across the nation.

These councils served two purposes: to raise money for the war and to incite a fierce sense of duty to monitor communities for sedition and treason. The first was necessary because of the sale of war bonds and stamps, to raise money to loan to the Allies. (This need for money is one reason that Wilson stoked nationalism; in private, he admitted it was a cynical ploy to enlist support.) The second reason was a brilliant propaganda move, given human nature that a certain number of people enjoy exerting power over others. It would give a sense of local ownership to the nationalism that was called patriotism.

The Crawford County Council of Defense was organized, chaired by Judge James Perry Conner, who later became a U.S. congressman. By the time of the appeal for the third war bond in April 1918, hundreds of men showed up for a Council of Defense meeting in the new opera house, now shorn of its German name. The county was assessed $470,000.

It would take some convincing to get people to open their wallets. Local men were fighting overseas, which stirred passions, but there was a growing tendency to bring the war home by demonizing "enemies" that could be seen: the German-speaking people in Crawford County. Judge Conner apparently tried to head off scapegoating at that April meeting. He said that both of his grandparents were German but that the old Germany of art and culture that they represented had been replaced by a different Germany; in other words, the bad Germans over there were not the nice Germans in their midst.

The men over the age of eighteen were told to fill out a "loyalty pledge card" that had the signer list assets and liabilities. Each man was expected to buy bonds according to his wealth. A date was set in which all businesses in town would close and the bonds would be sold.

Iowa governor W. L. Harding issued an edict: "English must be the medium of instruction in all schools." His order further declared that "English [be] used in conversations in public places, in the trains and over the telephone . . . let those who cannot speak English or understand English conduct their religious worship in their homes."

Leslie Shaw had many meetings with former President Theodore Roosevelt, in whose cabinet he had served; the two men shared a passion for the war and a hatred for the "German menace." In April, Shaw spoke at the Omaha Chamber of Commerce in a visit from back east that also included a stop in Denison. The *Omaha Bee* reported that Shaw said,

This country was the ultimate aim of the Germans at the outset of this war. We cannot at the present time talk of peace, we cannot dream of peace and the man who dares to do so is either a fool or a traitor. For 30 months, men, your wives, mothers, daughters, sweethearts and your homes themselves have been protected from the Germans only by the English and French fleets. . . . It is a case of go on, or go under and there is only one choice for real Americans. . . . This is no time for bunkism. This is a time for action.

Action took on dark forms. Later in the month Shaw spoke, the Denison School Board complied with Governor Harding's edict and voted to cease teaching German beginning the following school year. This was not rapid enough for some citizens. One weekend not long after the vote, a mob broke into the Denison School's Central Building. The mob gathered all books in German, piled them in the school yard, and set them afire. On the blackboard someone scribbled, "No more German."

A sign was nailed to the mailbox of a Crawford County farmer on April 23. "C. M. Pederson, worth $30,000, bought $250 worth of bonds. Slacker." A fired farmhand was arrested, his motive being revenge. M. A. Minty was a cobbler in the town of Charter Oak west of Denison. Minty talked of the International Workers of the World Party, the IWW, or "Wobblies" (union organizers). He also accused some American soldiers of thefts in Sioux City.

"One of the citizens proceeded to baste the fellow and somewhat disfigured his face," the *Denison Review* reported. The article ended with an admonishment, but it was not aimed at the thug who had attacked Minty. Speaking of the beaten man, the last paragraph said, "The people are not disposed to stand this kind of behavior and the sooner it is understood, the better."

Minty was arrested and brought before the military committee in Denison, then sent to Council Bluffs for federal prosecution. Across America, people were given twenty-year prison terms on sedition charges, often for nothing more than belonging to a union. There was hysteria over anything German. There were zero acts of sedition or espionage. German-speaking terrorists were not going around sabotaging the war effort.

Meanwhile, a new command came from Washington for an additional $480,000 from Crawford County. Two hundred members of the Crawford County Council of Defense met on June 16, 1918. Among the actions taken was an order that each resident purchase War Savings Stamps based on their property value. The committee also adopted a resolution that said, in part,

Whereas, believing that the use of all foreign languages and particularly the German language, affords an easy opportunity for the spread of German propaganda, and thus tends to promote insurrection and sedition ... in accordance with our patriotic duty in the premises, all persons in Crawford County are hereby warned against using any foreign language, and particularly the German language, in conversation in public places, or on trains and over the telephone lines of the county, and the various telephone companies of the county are hereby requested to disconnect the telephone of any person found persistently refusing to observe such proclamation.

A key word is *warned;* there must have been reluctance to be more hard core on their German neighbors. The order was interpreted so that older immigrants who had not learned English could still speak and read in German.

Some rural non-German residents from Dow City, some ten miles southwest, grew upset with what they viewed as permissiveness in Denison. On October 6, 1918, scores of citizens from the southwest section of Crawford County drove into town. One account related that one hundred automobiles came, with five hundred people. This group was joined by several hundred Denison citizens. It was a Sunday. The mob gathered in front of *Der Denison Herold.* A fire was set behind the newspaper plant, but it was discovered and extinguished, according to one of the two editors of the paper, Henry C. Finnern, in a diary of his life written shortly before he died in 1957. Finnern wrote,

Molestation of German people brought on street fights as well as disturbances in business places by the so-called "super-Americans." All of this led to the day when mob rule took hold in Crawford County. Law enforcing officers, such as the county sheriff, the city mayor, and the city police were absent for some reason, all seemingly informed as to what was going to take place in Denison. So the mob ruled the city.

Then, as later with the Spanish speakers, the town was split. Back then, the town's elite were largely from British lands, while the Germans made up the working class.

The *Denison Review* reported that Reverend Barker, pastor of the Baptist church at Dow City, addressed the crowd. Barker said that the people from his part of the county wanted the anti–foreign language order of Governor Harding obeyed. He condemned the County Council of Defense for not having done their duty. The reverend urged the mob to remain peaceful, but warned the German paper and Denison's leaders that he wouldn't be responsible for what might happen if *Der Denison Herold*, then the only paper in town publishing in German, did not cease doing so. People cheered. Finnern also addressed the mob:

> I mounted a truck in the middle of the street, introduced myself, and then proceeded to address the crowd. Letters from high state and national officials were read proving to any level headed citizen that the paper was doing valuable work for the government in these critical times, that the paper and its publishers were striving to spread among its readers the importance of winning the war.

Someone shouted that they should hang Finnern. Cries went up that the newspaper plant be destroyed. Others said that wouldn't be necessary—they should break in and demolish the German type.

Sears McHenry, a member of the Crawford County Council of Defense, addressed the crowd. He announced the immediate creation of a committee. The committee huddled with Finnern who suddenly saw the wisdom of agreeing to cease publishing in German, starting the next day. Finnern announced this to the mob, which "loudly cheered." He later wrote,

> Fearing for my own life and the destruction of the business building and contents, I probably chose the better way to save the day at least partially. . . . In my business career October 6, 1918 will rank as the darkest day.

Some days later, a procession of a dozen or so cars of the same men from Dow City drove to Schleswig, to the north, brandishing shotguns and rifles, determined to "change the name, stop the speaking of German, and make the people into good Americans," wrote Larry Grill in his self-published book, *Schleswig in Iowa.*

Mayor Jimmy Schultz waited for them, alone, by a flagpole. He welcomed the Dow City men and then listed all the Schleswig men who were fighting in the war and those who had purchased war bonds. Schultz asked: Did they have this much patriotism in their community?

"As the mayor spoke, the men from Dow City began to notice that from every window, every doorway, over every fence and from every alley, there was a gun barrel pointed at them. . . . He thanked them for their visit and wished them a pleasant trip home," wrote Grill. The mob left without incident.

In history that was not covered by the newspapers but has been passed down orally, other citizens went to the German Methodist Church and commanded that it stop holding services in German. Rumors suggest there were threats to burn down the church. The name was changed to the Second Methodist Episcopal Church in early 1918. There must have been deep resentment, for the congregation disbanded and sold the church. The building was moved by freight train to the town of Hull, in northwest Iowa. The newspaper did not cover this event. It seems to have been moved in 1918, for Nathan Mahrt has a photo of the church present early in the year; in a later photo that year or early the next, it is gone. Thus, the church was not there for Michael to photograph eighty-five years later.

* * *

Shame rapidly set in. By 1920, one newspaper was declaring things back to normal without specifying what had been abnormal about 1918. Special editions celebrating the town's history in the 1940s and 1950s give simply oblique references to the anti-Germanism.

Akin to the burning of the German books, memory had been erased. Most contemporary residents didn't know this history, and those who did didn't like talking about it. Even among old people who told other elaborate stories about this era passed on by their parents, memories were short about the German bashing. When it was mentioned, it was whispered. A trip to the Norelius Community Library found just one volume out of what had been dozens from the several German papers that existed.

"All the rest were destroyed," said librarian Joyce Amdor.

One revered German object survived, however. In 1908 German war veterans had organized the German Landwehr Verein. They spent $150 to purchase an embroidered silk flag of a design that was reportedly approved by Kaiser Wilhelm. On it was written,

DENISON UND UMGEGEND
[In the center, an iron cross, inside which is written, "Landwehr."]
1908

In another slice of history not officially recorded, a mob (perhaps the same that came to *Der Denison Herold,* but I could not pin down a date) came seeking this flag to burn it. Bob Ernst, a German resident, hid it by stuffing it in a mattress; it was taken to Colorado, said Mearl Luvaas, an octogenarian resident. Ernst's daughter later donated it to the McHenry House, a museum in Denison where Luvaas is a volunteer. The flag now hangs in an upstairs room.

In the Carroll County town of Manning, just over the Crawford County line southeast of Denison, Michael and I found Arthur (Art) Rix, age ninety-four, who was ten years old in 1918. Manning was a very German town and in recent years has been trying to reclaim its heritage. A German Hausbarn (which served as both a residence and a barn), built in 1660, was disassembled in the Schleswig-Holstein region of Germany, transported here, reassembled, and dedicated in 2000. A sign as you enter town says, "Willkommen." (Yet in a nod to post-9/11 political conditions, the brochure notes, "Flags of Germany and the United States fly together outside the entrance.")

Rix said his father was a partner in a German-language paper, *Der Manning Herold.* His father also was the postmaster.

"Then this war, this patriotism came in. One morning they found the front of the building splashed with yellow paint," he said of the German paper. There were threats. His father and partner then renamed it the *Manning Monitor* and published in English. At the post office, residents came in and got their mail out of locked boxes.

"One of his friends came in and got the *Monitor* out of his box. And he said, 'Vhot is dis?' My dad said there was no longer a German-language paper. And the man threw the paper right in my dad's face."

Such anger didn't get exhibited toward their antagonists. Rix told about an incident at a big saloon in Manning.

"A large group of men, they were accusing one [German] man of not being patriotic enough, and not enough in favor of the war," Rix said. "They followed him out of the bar, and they wanted to know how many war bonds he was going to buy."

It was not an academic question. This demand carried the threat of immediate physical violence.

"So he decided to buy some war bonds."

And the last thing you would do was utter German. "You didn't want to get caught talking it on the street."

He was once fluent in German and spoke perfect English, but he stopped speaking German back then. Now Rix says he has forgotten most of it. He said they had a strong desire to speak English. He felt that today's Spanish-speaking immigrants do not want to learn.

"I don't get enthusiastic about these schools where they teach in two or three languages. My dad learned to talk and write in English. Why can't they? All the German-speaking people, they were doing their best to learn English."

* * *

Rix wasn't alone. In Denison, Germanic residents had the strongest feelings against the Spanish speakers. One woman with a German name commented about their language being stifled, "I wish someone would do that with the Hispanics today." Then she stopped herself. "My kids would kill me for saying that. I don't really mean it."

But did she? There was a volatile undercurrent. Another resident said, with some satisfaction, "It's their turn." At Denison High School, Schleswig kids, most of German ancestry, are often resentful of Latinos, sometimes starting fights. (Schleswig shrank in population, its high school was closed, and students are now bused to Denison.)

Joel Franken, talking about those upset with the Spanish speakers, recalled an old joke: "What is someone called who speaks three languages? Trilingual. Two languages? Bilingual. One language?" Joel paused. "American."

This antilanguage sentiment dates to the nationalism of World War I. Patriotism was equated with not only forgetting other tongues, but being zealously against their utterance. Americans who vigorously promote English-only don't realize that if their children spoke, say, Mandarin Chinese or Spanish as well as English, they would be guaranteed a high-paying job.

The resentment over Spanish being spoken in Denison today is confined to the muttering of Joel's "negatives" when they gather for morning coffee. Many want to believe the high end regarding the population estimate of Latinos, and they uttered "50 percent" in a whisper that was a combination of fear, wonderment, and sometimes anger. Yet they were unlike their counterparts I'd documented in California, who picketed and got in the face of immigrants. In Denison they were not campaigning to harm Latinos by denying them public services or calling in immigration authorities, nor were they moving away in a version of prairie white flight.

Officials were not banning Spanish being spoken on the street, in church, on the phone. There are no mobs surrounding Latino newspapers. But what if there is another terror attack and anti-Arab feelings morph into a general hatred of all things foreign?

If none of this happens, given the norms of the contemporary racial and political climate, there are other ways a community can exert influence over immigrants.

* * *

On August 4, 2003, the Denison City Council had a third reading of "Ordinance #1237 Amending Zoning to Adopt A More Restrictive Definition of A Family." The ordinance would limit the number of unrelated people living in a single-family dwelling to three persons. It's not uncommon to find three Latino families under one roof, and in California I had interviewed people who slept in shifts: if a man had a night job, another house member would use his bed.

Is this a sign of resourceful people? Or was it creating problems related to density that tax police and other services? What was the cultural dimension? In California, ordinances were proposed by anti-immigrant groups that didn't present any other argument than that they wanted to keep America white. They were opposed by immigrant rights activists who called the ordinances racist and unrelated to any issues of health and safety. The answer was in the eye of the beholder.

As I sat down in the council chamber, I figured I'd hear a discussion about Latinos and the scope of the situation. What kind of densities existed here? What were some specific problems and potential cures? I noticed there wasn't a single Latino in the room. The word *Hispanic,* the preferred term in Denison, didn't come up in council discussion. There was some debate that the number should be four people, but the city was modeling the ordinance after one passed in Ames, to the east. Three was the number there.

"A lot of our problems are with a housing density in a zone where the services were not designed to support it," said city attorney D. R. Franck.

Mayor Ken Livingston noted that one citizen wanted to speak. Amanda was white and worked providing job training and care for the disabled. The ordinance contained an exemption for people living in a group home that was part of a designated program.

Amanda was nervous. She told the council that there were disabled people in town who were not in designated programs and lived together to save money. She added that it might even affect four single women who wanted to share expenses. Why shouldn't they be able to do so? She sat down.

The council members talked a bit more. If there were problems, they agreed, the ordinance could be amended later. The consensus was to pass it and get it on the books. The vote was unanimous in favor.

Not once, even in code language, were Latinos mentioned. This had been the case, I was told, about a year earlier when the council had passed an ordinance mandating that all gravel driveways be paved and that no vehicles be allowed to park on unpaved ground. Latinos were parking on lawns, but the cultural aspects were not raised.

The council continued its business. Amanda left, and I followed her outside. She had only recently moved to town and was puzzled by the ordinance.

"When I hear that an ordinance targets people with less income, this concerns me," she said.

"Is it aimed at Latinos?"

"I didn't want to go there in my talk." She looked around the empty street and seemed nervous about this question. "But it sure seems so."

As I ruminated about this inaugural lesson about Latinos in Denison as Amanda walked away, I stared at the vacant lot across the street from city hall that had been the site of the German Methodist Church. City manager Al Roder came out the door. I brought up the lot. Al was relatively new to town. But he'd been told some things.

"I hear they were going to burn them out," Al said.

Compared with what happened to the Germans of Denison back in 1918, the ordinance seemed benign. But was it? I later presented my concerns about it to Mayor Livingston; he didn't see any racial overtones. And besides, he added, "we're not going to go around like the Gestapo. It will be complaint based."

But when I went to Joel Franken, who by then was contemplating running again for a seat on the council that fall, he was less sanguine.

"It's Denison imposing some Midwest values on our guests."

AN AMERICAN STORY I

Der Denison Herold, the newspaper swarmed by the Dow City mob, was forgotten over eight decades later by everyone except Nathan Mahrt. The two-story brick edifice at the corner of Main and North First Street became a café that was a long-time favorite of farmers. Then it was a bar called the North Main Tap. The building was boarded shut in 1982. The roof began leaking, rotting the interior. Dangerous mold flourished.

Nathan began agitating for the city to save it, lest Denison lose yet another historic structure. He found a sympathetic ear in Mayor Livingston, who said, "I don't want to be known as the mayor that tore down Denison." This was not a universally favored sentiment. One day I was in the building inspection department and overheard the inspector talking to city manager Al Roder about the old German newspaper office: "If you want my opinion, a bulldozer should have been used on it."

The city signed on to save the building, but the absentee owner balked at selling for less than $15,000. As Nathan tells it, the owner was well off and had once lived in Denison, but now resided in Texas on a huge ranch.

Nathan telephoned the Texan.

" 'I don't want the building,'" Nathan recalled saying. " 'I'm a third party. My interest is seeing it saved.' I told him, 'I know you got the way you are because you care about $15,000. But now $15,000 doesn't mean anything to you.' "

Nathan asked if the owner had seen the building recently. He had not.

"He asked, 'How bad is it?' "

It was really far gone.

" 'They're going to make you tear it down eventually,' I told him. 'It's on the busiest corner in the city, and it's just sitting empty.' "

The Texan offered to give Nathan the building—free. Nathan replied that wouldn't be fair; he suggested the price be lowered. The Texan agreed to sell for $5,000 to the city. Nathan had a victory: the city would renovate the building and sell it at cost to a private party. There were four or five phases of work, the first being gutting the rotten interior.

One day Nathan's friend Luis Navar stood on the corner studying the building. The life of the native Spanish speaker from Mexico was possibly about to intersect in a financially rewarding way with that of the forgotten native German speaker named Henry C. Finnern.

*　*　*

Luis was born in Mexico in 1970, the oldest of five boys. His father worked as a construction crew foreman building public works projects such as aqueducts. The family moved when projects were completed. They lived everywhere. When Luis was eleven, his father deserted the family. They were in a *colonia* near Rio Bravo, just across the border from McAllen, Texas. Luis had to become a man fast and help support his siblings.

"I was tall and big and so people thought I could do some work," he said.

His first job was rinsing and sorting onions for a produce company; he concurrently got a job cleaning at a butcher's. The bosses gave meat to young Luis, who desperately needed to feed the family. But it wasn't enough. At age fourteen, he was lured with the promise of great wages fishing for *camarones*, shrimp. The camp required an hour-and-a-half canoe ride to reach an island in Media Luna, a Gulf of Mexico bay. Luis had signed himself into servitude: he was required to buy food with scrip at a company store and was always in debt. He worked to eat. And the camp was infested with scorpions and poisonous spiders.

He was trapped, for four months, until he accidentally gashed his foot while fishing. Camp operators wrapped his foot with a rag and took him by canoe to the mainland—and told him he had to come back because he owed them. He hitchhiked to Matamoros, where he was treated at a government clinic; someone gave him 20 pesos for bus fare back to his mother's home in Rio Bravo.

"I still owe the camp owners that money," he said, with a chuckle, of the 100 peso debt.

At his next job, Luis began buying used clothes in Texas and taking them to Mexico City for resale. He had to bribe Mexican soldiers at checkpoints. The enterprise was modestly profitable. This went on until he turned sixteen. His father reconnected with the family, calling from Los Angeles. He began sending money and asked Luis to join him.

In those days, it was easy to cross between Texas and Mexico; the immigration checkpoints were not at the border but deeper inside Texas. In California, the border area was more carefully watched. Luis's father paid $100 to a "coyote," a professional smuggler who illegally moves people across the border. The coyote was creative. After Luis got across the border he and three others were taken in a van crammed with racing bicycles to the beach frontage road near Camp Pendleton. They donned bike riding clothes and helmets, and pedaled like weekend racers up the coastal road, past the U.S. Immigration checkpoint on Interstate 5.

Los Angeles staggered young Luis. It was so big, so rich. He lived, however, in its bowels with his father in Compton, "where they would kill you for nothing."

He purchased fake documents and worked doing masonry and stucco with his father. But then his father's new wife, who was still in Mexico, demanded that her husband return, and Luis was alone in the new land. It was 1985. Luis's fortunes went up and then they'd crash. When work was slow, he'd lose his apartment and live out of his car, sometimes for months. He was thrown in jail several times.

"I didn't steal or nothing. I had tickets, and I couldn't pay the tickets. Sometimes we do stupid things when we're young. Drive without the seat belt or whatever. You don't have enough money for the insurance."

He sometimes stood with a hundred other Latinos at one of the day labor pickup street corners in Los Angeles—Pico Boulevard and La Brea Avenue. He'd jump into trucks and do whatever work awaited at the end of the ride.

At eighteen, he fell in love with Lupita, Lupe, and she got pregnant with Sergio, the first of their four children. Luis meantime heard about the amnesty program in which he could apply for citizenship, and he did so. He taught himself how to speak English by listening and practicing at construction jobs and from radio and television. Their lives were good, and it seemed they would become citizens who called Los Angeles home.

Then came the riots of 1991. They watched the city erupt in flames. In early 1999, when Sergio was twelve, they were living in the MacArthur Park area. Sergio left the house to ride his shiny "low rider" bicycle to get a haircut. Luis and Lupe heard a commotion. They ran to the window and saw a kid pulling a gun.

"Pow! Pow! Pow!" Luis said. The victim had short hair, just like Sergio's. Luis rushed outside.

"The guy was still running with the gun pointed at everybody." Luis leaned down to see if it was his son. "It was one of my kid's friends. I had stomach pains."

The stomach pains intensified. It was time to get out. The family couldn't risk their children dying. That June, Luis made an exploratory trip to Dow City to visit his sister, where she had moved to do field work.

"My sister said there are good opportunities here."

Lupe resisted the move, but Luis insisted. They arrived in July 1999. By month's end, both were hired at Farmland. Luis started at over eleven dollars an hour in the warehouse department as a setup person, who figured out how to ship some of the three thousand items. He'd never before worked in a packing plant, but he learned the job in two weeks—it required a lot of math. The highest-level worker was a Grade 5; he was a Grade 4.

He was the first Latino in the all-white unit. Then came the first lunch hour.

"There was this big, long table," Luis said of the table of big white guys, all with beards. "I sat down to eat. Guys started sitting down, over there, next to me. Pretty soon, the table was full. Then one guy said, 'What makes you think you've been here long enough to eat with us?' I said, 'I don't see Bill Clinton or Prince Charles around here. I worked in the freezer all morning, and I can sit here.' They weren't going to scare me. Some of them cut me off at that point. But most of them, we got along pretty good."

As in California, Luis discovered there were two kinds of whites. He'd run into the racist kind with the lunch table challenger and the other kind when he went to a bank to seek a loan for a house.

"I went to the banker, Jean Heiden, at the United Bank of Iowa, and I had no credit. She talked to me, and I told her I work hard. She gave me a loan for the first house. She told me, 'You guys are going to make this town stay alive. This city before the Hispanics was losing people.'"

The family now owned their first home in America.

"We fell in love with the place," Luis said of Denison. "We had such good pay."

When his quest to become a citizen reached fruition, he had to return to California for the ceremony, but his boss at Farmland would not let him take time off. So he quit or was fired—depending on one's view.

"They didn't care. You're just hands and a number there. Argh. They don't want you to be something else. They don't want you to know about unions, nothing. The job is good. The management is terrible."

He went to California and returned to Denison a U.S. citizen, but unemployed. Under Farmland's rules, he could be rehired after six months. Back in the warehouse department, he ran into a young, angry white man who challenged him to a fight.

"They called me big mouth. I was not going to let them push me around. I could talk back to them."

Luis didn't want to fight, but he had no choice. They fought in a semitrailer, with other guys from the department standing in the door so the managers could not see.

"I lost. He was a short guy. He almost picked me up. I couldn't get at him. I can't fight. But I'm not going to let them believe that. I'm not going to back up. Even if you don't win, you got respect."

This was not the most hurtful incident.

"One guy made me cry. And not because he hit me, because of his feelings, the way he treat me. I went into the coolers and I started punching the boxes to get my stress out. And I cry. I cry because of the frustration of why are people like that. I cry because he hate me like a fucking dog, like a pig."

He left Farmland and went to Tyson Fresh Meats, the beef packing plant. At the same time, he began a contracting business on the side. The family moved up and bought a second house, renting the first out. The new place on North Main Street was a dream home, large and clean. There was one problem: a neighbor who despised Mexicans. There were mean stares, mutterings. Then one day the neighbor blew.

"What divided us was an alley. We did some concrete work, and something was wrong in his mind, and he came over, screaming. He pushed on the door, trying to get in the house. He's nuts. He doesn't like us."

Lupe was ill in this period, and her blood pressure shot up; she then suffered an attack of Bell's palsy. Fearing for her health, the family rented out the house next to the anti-Latino neighbor to get away. They moved into a third house that Luis owned with his brother, José, who had recently left town for a job in Georgia. There had been a fight between two other men at Farmland, in which one of them broke an arm. Both combatants knew they'd be fired, and they begged José not to say anything. He complied and told the boss he saw nothing.

"Then one of the guys backed up and said we had a fight, and I broke my arm. And José saw what happened."

José was fired.

"He was just a witness. He didn't fight. He liked his job. He was doing very well in this town. They're just mean."

He also saw discrimination against others. One day he was at a car repair shop on North Seventh Street, which was closed to through traffic because of construction. As he watched, he said a Denison police officer simply turned away white drivers who didn't have business on the street, but each Latino was asked to produce a driver's license.

Luis now talked on the porch of the third home he owned in Denison. His youngest child, aged four, played nearby.

"This one is a Denison boy," he says of the child, who was born in town. "These guys are going to make this town their life."

Luis, a slightly heavy-set man, laughs when I tell him that at age thirty-three, he is a *viejo*, an old man. But he is not, really, despite his life's experiences. He's a very happy man, prone to philosophize and eager to learn. In fact, he had just purchased his first book in English, *Distant Neighbors: A Portrait of the Mexicans*, by Alan Riding.

Luis was now at a crossroads. He'd been doing construction work on the side while he worked at Tyson. Now he wanted to go full time, be his own boss, and quit the beef plant.

Nathan and Luis met not long after Luis moved to town. They'd bonded over a common interest in construction, for Nathan was an able builder in addition to his other three jobs. Luis had great admiration for

Nathan's abilities. When someone talked about one of Nathan's projects to save a dilapidated house, they remarked the work involved was almost impossible. "For most people, yes," Luis said. "But not for Nathan."

The friendship grew deeper when they began discussing women and children. One day Luis left his house in a state of confusion and sought out Nathan. Luis had wanted his son Sergio to do an errand, and he had refused; Lupe came down on the side of Sergio. What was it about America, Luis asked, that made women do this?

"I told him there was nothing cultural about it," Nathan said. "It was primal, a mother and child. Get used to it."

These conversations continued. Amid this, Nathan went to Luis after the city bought the German newspaper building, advising him to bid on a contract to gut the interior so restoration could begin. Luis called city hall, and Mayor Livingston invited him in to discuss the bid. The meeting would happen in one week. Luis was nervous. He needed the job to go independent, and he had never before met with an American politician.

"They are fixing up many buildings here. I hope to get some of that work."

PART TWO

FALL

WILLARD'S DIARY

PRAIRIE PASSIONS

CONCERNING THE OLD MAN

The old man stood out from other elders, not because he was black and had a full head of froth-white hair, but because he was always surrounded by youths who walked respectfully with him as he made his way along with the assistance of a cane. They plied the old man for stories and advice. The attraction was not just his wisdom, but his zest for life, embodied in his laugh. The old man was always laughing. He had the laugh of a man who had seen things, yet had not been made ancient by them.

The writer observed how some white people reacted to him and used the term "Uncle Tom." One day the writer was with Kate Swift and expressed his puzzlement.

—A lot of people call him an Uncle Tom. He's no fool.

Ms. Swift's reply came fast.

—Neither was Uncle Tom.

He'd spent most of his eight decades living on the Great Plains, and he had often been the only black man, or one among a handful of black folks, in the towns in which he dwelled. In 1908 in Denison, the newspaper wrote about the sole black resident who had just died, and it referred to him as a "good darkie." By the late 1950s, there again was just one black man in Denison. He owned a popular steak and chicken joint near the courthouse, and whites called him "Nigger John."

The writer wondered what it was like for him to have spent a life in white small-town America. The writer didn't know how to approach him. Then one afternoon the old man took care of this problem: he ran into the writer and announced,

—I hear you're a writer, and you're going to help me write my book!

And then the old man laughed, then laughed some more. He told the writer he had many stories to tell.

Some days later, the writer paid the old man a visit. It was a windy day that promised rain. The two sat in a room. The old man told about an early job as a porter on the Union Pacific Railroad.

—Oh, I can tell stories about that. Oh, there are things that happened.

He was one of the few blacks in his hometown in the 1920s and early 1930s, and he was sometimes a minority of one in the towns in which he'd later lived. There were tales of discrimination, but he always ended the stories with the disclaimer,

—I always looked at it as their problem. Not my problem.

Seldom was the racism overt in modern times. The Midwest is not that kind of place. It is subtle. When he moved here, he looked at forty houses and finally bought one for $18,000, then a big price. The neighbors were friendly, as were others.

—Later they were saying to me that other people [their friends] were saying they didn't want to live next to me, but you proved them wrong.

The old man meant years later.

—That's the kind of place this is. They won't tell it to you. But they think it.

The writer had to bring up what he'd heard. There was no other way to ask.

—Some people call you an Uncle Tom.

The old man looked startled.

—I've been called nigger. I know that. I can handle that. But Uncle Tom . . .

He paused.

—That hurts.

The writer realized it was the first time he'd heard this sentiment. The writer felt horrible and suddenly realized a new dimension about the town. There was a truth in this understanding, but he didn't yet fully grasp it. The conversation evolved. The old man's children were successful, and, looking back at his life, he declared that he was happy.

—Me, a little old black man. A little old black man from Kansas, with discrimination and all that, rising up to the high stratosphere of society.

The writer asked if white people were secretly resentful of Latinos moving in.

—Oh, you picked up on that.

And then he laughed.

—There's a few people doing the good neighbor thing. But they're minuscule.

The writer and the man talked for hours, the afternoon melting away as the expected rain began softly falling. The snow would come within weeks. The Sioux would have called this time of year the Drying Grass Moon. There were some native grasses in the distance outside the window. It was tallgrass prairie, big bluestem and Indian grass, now brown and thick and nearly as high as an average woman.

The writer was drifting after so much talk, focused on the grass, and he imagined the buffalo that would have long ago roamed the distant hills. His thoughts turned to a nap awaiting back at home, but he regained focus, and they discussed the old man's book, which he'd not yet begun to write. The writer offered words of encouragement and then was about to leave. The old man announced he had one more story.

It was a time when the old man was a young man, in the 1940s, when he was a freshman at the big, elite university. Out of thousands of students, there were just seventeen blacks. He was involved with sports. He also belonged to a fraternity in which he held a position as an officer and had to meet with the officers of a sorority. At the first meeting, when everyone was new to each other, introductions were made. There were three women in the room, and as the first two spoke and told of themselves, the old man fixated on the third woman, who was white.

—This woman was beautiful, and she had the longest blackest hair all the way down to here.

The old man reached around to his lower middle back.

—Oh, she was the most beautiful woman.

When the woman introduced herself, she utterly ignored him. This took the other women aback. They asked what she was doing. She paid them no mind, and told of herself. The woman had come to the Iowa college straight out of high school from a town in Mississippi, then under Jim Crow. She talked about her family's cotton plantation.

—She grew up with slaves, I mean, black servants and such, and she was taught from her birth days not to like blacks.

He said the two women admonished their sorority sister.

—She didn't even look at me. She looked away like I wasn't there. The two other women said, "Aren't you going to introduce yourself?"

The black-haired woman got up and left in a huff.

The old man now looked out the spattered window, not at the grass or trees, or the vanished buffalo, but at the dark sky from which the cold rain now came with fury.

—I thought to myself, "I'm going to fuck her."

The writer took this to mean the old man wanted to do something to get her goat. But the old man meant it literally. His eyes came back to the writer.

—So I was as nice as could be to her. The next time I saw her, I introduced myself. And she looked away.

The old man laughed deeply. He called her the "Dolphin Queen" because she was on the swim team. The old man told how he started working on the Dolphin Queen. He waved his hand like a roller coaster through the air, to signify the passage of time.

—Each time I saw her, I was nice.

He again formed the imaginary roller coaster in the air.

—Time passed.

His hand traveled slowly, and there was soul in this movement.

—Then it got so she'd say hello.

The hellos went back and forth, and his hand in the air marked this passage of time. Then came a night when the fraternity and sorority held a dance.

—So I went up to her, and asked her for a dance. She said she didn't feel like dancing. So I went away.

The old man again traced the roller coaster. There was another dance. No luck. She wouldn't dance with him. Then another dance came.

—This time, she tells me she can't dance to the song that was playing. You know what this tells me? That if another song comes on, she might be open to dancing. So when another song came on, I went up to her. We danced.

The hand again slowly rolled. Another dance was planned.

—I called her and asked her to be my date. That meant she would be with me. She said, "yes." We went, and we had a nice time.

At the end of the evening, she was nervous. He was too wise to make a move.

—I thanked her and left her.

The hand curved through the air.

—There was another date, and another. You know what that means?

The writer nodded knowingly as the older man answered his own question.

—You're eventually going to have sex.

But he was in no hurry. The hand moved through the air a few more times. The writer was patient as the old man continued the story. He got to the night when it happened.

—So we had sex.

He smiled but did not laugh.

—Oh my, did we have sex. She was beautiful, that long black hair. Oh, what a sweet memory. I was young and full of cum. Oh, was it sweet. We went out for a while. She really loved me.

The old man paused. He stared at the writer, who was absorbing the story. The old man raised his hand for the last time, gently caressing the air as if he were running his hand over the curves of the woman's body.

—She asked to marry me. I didn't ask to marry her. She asked me.

With that, he dumped the Dolphin Queen, whose real name he never used in the half-hour of telling the story. Then he sat back and savored his memory; he saw unasked questioning in the writer's face.

—I was proving something to her.

It was time for both of them to go. The writer and the old man went out the front door. There was a steep set of steps. The writer held the door for the man, who moved slowly with the help of a metal cane. He paused, tapped his calf with the cane. It made a metallic clink. The leg had been amputated for some unknown medical reason.

—Bet you can't do that!

He laughed as he again struck his fake leg.

The writer let the old man go down the stairs ahead of him.

At the bottom, the old man looked back at the writer. His face was wetted by the rain.

—And you know the hell of it? I can't remember her name.

CONCERNING THE COUNTRY WOMAN

The writer saw numerous abandoned farmhouses when he drove rural roads. In some places the only sense that humans possess this earth is the corn. Yet working farms remain, along with isolated still-occupied former farmhouses far outside town now rented to nonfarmers. This is clear because of the lack of implements cluttering the yards or because the barns have been torn down.

Who chooses to dwell so far from town? And why?

One day the writer was interviewing someone in town as a woman approaching middle age eavesdropped. This woman insinuated herself into the conversation, and wondered why the writer would choose to live for any period of time in Denison.

—It's boring here. I'd like to leave.

This woman was unlike others her age in town. She was thin. She had the movement and talk of someone younger. The writer learned she was single. Her daughters were grown and had moved away. The woman lived to the east many miles out in the country.

Not long after, the country woman and writer again ran into each other. Phone numbers were exchanged. That Friday she rang.

—I'm having trouble putting up my Christmas tree. Could you come help me get it up?

That evening he drove out to the realm of gravel roads and desolate houses. The woman's was among the most isolated, at the end of a long drive and atop a hill that afforded a grand view of the Great Plains. The stars were thick. A strong wind blew. It was cold enough for snow. The door opened. The woman had a margarita in hand. There was no electric light. There was substantial illumination, however, provided by candles in the kitchen, living room, bathroom, in the bedrooms whose doors were open. She offered a margarita or a beer. He chose beer.

She gave a tour of what had once been a farmhouse. She dwelled here alone with dogs, one that growled constantly and kept a distance from the writer. In her bedroom, a cool blue electric light glowed over a pool of water the size of a cooking wok, set atop the dresser. She delighted in showing how waving one's hand over this device caused the water to send smoke billowing into the room. They took turns making smoke.

The bed appeared freshly sheeted, made up as perfectly as in a hotel. They retreated to the kitchen, where he drank the beer and she made a new drink. As the blender whirred, she stood facing the machine, back to the writer. He noted that her pants were exceptionally tight. As his eyes moved up her legs, what met his sight was as well formed as someone half her age.

The writer asked about the tree.

New drink in hand, she took the writer to a room where a five-foot artificial tree lay on its side. The plastic needles were snow white; it was not at all attractive. The "trunk" was a metal pole as thick as a broom handle, and therein was the problem: the stand was designed for a real tree with a trunk at least as thick as the stout end of a softball bat.

Sipping her drink, the woman issued a challenge.

—You're not going to get it to stand up.

It would work, the writer assured her.

They dragged the tree to the living room. He wrapped the bottom with cloth and gaffer's tape and put it into the stand, cinching down the wing nuts. The tree toppled.

—I told you you were going to have trouble.

The writer swigged beer. Did she have any pieces of wood in the garage? No. The writer had an idea. On the way up the drive, he'd noticed a group of trees behind the house, next to the stubble of a corn field. He explained that if they got fallen branches of varying thickness, he could cut them and wedge them around the base. She doubted the efficacy of this plan, but they put on coats and with a flashlight went into the night.

The wind howled off the prairie. The stars were rich and sharp as they entered the grove of burr oak. The writer studied the movement of the country woman as they searched for fallen branches. He shivered. Fifteen or ten years before, he would have been moved to hold her against the cold and kiss her. To hell with the morning. The writer looked back at the house and the dim light coming from the candlelit panes, the blue glow coming from the window to the right where the bed awaited. But he sensed a want on the part of the country woman that was far deeper than anything that might occur atop that freshly sheeted bed. He did not know what fragility lay beneath the country woman's want. The only certainty was that he could not shatter it. The house seemed now shrunken against the expanse of the night. The prairie had swallowed every mortal thing about the writer. He felt very alone.

She inquired, over the roar of the wind, if they had enough sticks. He rapidly finished searching, and they carried their bundles to the warmth of the house. The writer used a hand saw to cut lengths; these he wedged into the stand and succeeded in getting the tree to remain upright. The country woman wrapped a blanket around the base. She then turned on a blue floor light aimed at the ugly tree. It suddenly became a thing of beauty.

The woman made another margarita and sat on the couch; the writer, now on his second beer, sat far opposite. The writer learned her story.

She'd moved to town a few years before from a different part of Iowa. She'd been married, to the father of her daughters, and that man was terrible. He beat her, and she left him not long after her second daughter was born. She'd raised her girls and fell in love with a farmer who lived near the Illinois border. They lived together but were not married. He farmed several thousand acres. They worked together. She drove a tractor; they raised pigs and cows, and grew corn. She talked dreamily of their life and marriage plans. Then the man had a farm accident and died.

She was very sad talking about the lost man.

Her friends have told her she has to move on from the death, which happened years ago. She tried dating other farmers, but they were jerks. One drove a Harley, and he talked more to himself about the motorcycle than he did to her. She last had a farmer boyfriend in a brief relationship that had ended a few months earlier.

—I made a decision last month. Get a new boyfriend or another dog? I got the dog.

The country woman was now inebriated, her words slurred. She talked of her first husband and the rotten men she has known, and the rotten men a lot of rural women have to put up with. She brought up the story of Dixie Shanahan, a woman in the town of Defiance just south of Denison. A month previous, Shanahan had been arrested on a charge of murdering her husband, Scott. Shanahan was charged with blasting him in the head with a shotgun when she said he attacked her, then hiding his body in their bedroom for sixteen months. At the time of the killing, she was pregnant with their third child. Scott Shanahan had been twice convicted of domestic abuse.

—Did you hear what went on?

The country woman had talked with a cop over drinks and learned that the husband starting having sex with Shanahan when she was thirteen; the girl had been adopted by Scott's parents. He got her pregnant and in anger threw Shanahan down a flight of stairs, causing her to miscarry.

—And she didn't touch any steps.

After blowing Scott away, she shut the door on the room. And there Scott remained.

—She told her kids that was the stinky room. She kept pushing air fresheners under the bed. There were dozens of them there.

Scott was not exactly missed. No one in that town, far smaller than Denison, inquired why he was not seen around. Four people showed up at his funeral, and one of them didn't want to be there.

—He deserved what he got.

This was a common feeling of country sisterhood—bake sales were being held in Defiance to help raise money for Shanahan's defense. (She was later found guilty of second-degree murder and sentenced to at least thirty-five years in prison; one problem was that the jury found her claim of self-defense hard to believe, for an autopsy showed that Scott had been shot in the back of the head.)

Scott, to the country woman, was an extreme example of the crop of men she had to choose from. It was hard even to have fun. The country woman used to go to bars in Denison but gave up on that. There was too much gossip. A few nights before, she was at a public dinner event.

—I ran into a guy I knew who was with four of his friends. They asked me to go with them to a bar after for a drink. I wouldn't go. By the end of the night, I'd have fucked them all.

This is the kind of tongue wagging that would have occurred from those who saw them, but it would have all been in their imaginations.

—I've been a lesbian. I've been in a porn flick, with a woman lover. You wouldn't believe what I've done.

She laughed about her fictional sex life that was gospel to the tongue-waggers. The worst of the gossip came from the wives of the merchants and lawyers and other elites who live in Uptown, as the old downtown is called because it is atop the hill overlooking the Boyer Valley. It is unlike the Route 30 business district below, lined with the usual American assemblage of fast food chains, auto dealers, and hotels.

—They all think I'm trying to steal their husbands.

She burst into laughter, saying that none of those men appeals to her. She had contempt for the wives, whom she viewed as smug and with an inflated sense of self-worth and beauty. Most of them were likely frigid, she added.

The writer had heard all manner of sexual hearsay. A sheriff's deputy told him that the hot gossip had him fucking a woman atop a picnic table at the Farmland plant in broad daylight on his lunch hour. The only thing unusual about the rumor was that the woman was his wife. Usually the rumors dealt with sexual twistedness—trios and quartets, old men and women getting it on with high school kids. People believed each new story. It was usually so fantastic that about the only thing the writer didn't hear was someone doing a walrus. What were people gossiping about him?

The country woman noted that people who need to make up such tales aren't getting any action. Denison was a town of incredible sexual frustration. To be a single woman and over the age of twenty in Denison was a curse, she said, pausing to sip her drink.

—So I stay home on Friday nights, and drink.

Save for the writer's presence, she said this was a rather common Friday night. She keeps the blender going and hangs out with her dogs. She told the writer she prefers their company, but she contradicted herself: she's lonely and would like a man in her life.

—I used to have guy friends to talk to. Like I'm talking to you. I want guy friends to talk to. But everyone is married.

A woman friend suggested she try Internet dating. She scoffed, fearing a psycho. The writer noted that dating is different in one's forties. He suggested that at this point in life, perhaps there is no ideal love.

—But I had it once.

She spoke with a faraway look, and seemed to be thinking of the dead farmer.

The writer was curious. Why did she choose to live in a rural place, so far out in the country? Why didn't she simply leave?

—And go where?

—Wouldn't you be happier in a bigger city?

After all, the first words she'd uttered to the writer were, "It's boring," and that she'd like to leave. But she said the big city scared her and she couldn't afford to live in one. These sounded like excuses. The Latinos were different. They could explain why they'd come to Iowa. The coastals call this flyover land. But the edges were simply never-fly country for some whites here. The writer pursued his questioning, and the woman continued trying to explain. Here she can have as many dogs as she wants. Each morning, she takes them for a walk. They run down the corn rows. The summertime soybean fields were her favorite. She spoke with reverence of the beans, which don't grow as tall as corn and you can stand amid them and see over their tops.

—When the wind blows, it's like the ocean in the beans.

She spoke of the wind rippling across a field like waves hitting a beach.

—You see the wind coming, and then going behind you.

She offered the writer another beer as she went to make a new marguerita. But it was time for him to go.

As he walked to his vehicle, he heard the blender working in the house that seemed even now tinier, but soon he was far enough away so that there was just the whistle of the wind.

CONCERNING THE NIGHT MAN I

A wheelchair rolled over the streets of Denison—often after dark. One heard the whir of the battery-powered motor before seeing the man piloting it. He was in his late twenties, a bit overweight, with short hair, and eyes that were small but intense.

The writer had first spotted him at midnight that very first time he and the photographer visited town. He was in front of the courthouse staring at the street. It was bitterly cold, and the writer wondered what drew him out. The writer announced,

—I want to get his story.

Months later when the writer began living in town, he often took night walks. It did not matter if was two o'clock in the morning, the writer often saw the wheelchair rolling about town, and he came to think of him as the "night man." Once the writer stood behind the night man in line at the twenty-four-hour Hy-Vee Supermarket. The night man was purchasing three Reese's Peanut Butter Cups, a Coke, and some other candy, for a total of $4.70. On his key chain were the words *"United We Stand."*

Most commonly, the night man was in the shadows. When rolling along the street, his eyes seemed intent on propelling himself forward, but he never seemed to go anywhere in particular.

One evening, the writer had dined at La Estrella with Kate Swift. They were walking home, and Ms. Swift was being extra friendly. She had a man in her life, but he wasn't around. She suggested the writer come to her house.

—I've got an empty bed.

The writer pretended not to understand. She further suggested what could happen on that bed. The writer shook her hand and left the confused Ms. Swift. The writer, unable to write, paced his quarters that night. There are many passions, and he was too wrapped up in his own to be thinking of the one Ms. Swift had in mind. Or was he? He now felt desolate and needed to walk. The writer wandered the dark streets. He traveled the blocks to the house of Ms. Swift. A light was on. He paused and studied the glow in the window. He continued walking. It was one o'clock in the morning.

In the business district, the writer spied the night man. The chair was wheeling down Broadway, and the night man's face showed both contentment and a certain passion that was not evident when the wheelchair was out by day. There was something about the dark that made the night man come alive. The writer had a sudden line of questioning. Yet he did not approach. It didn't seem right to invade the night man's world. He watched the chair until it was no longer visible, and there was only the faint whir of the motor.

The writer walked home to his chamber. He could not sleep.

THE LAND

A grid of country roads surround Denison. Many are unpaved, either gravel or dirt. On the latter, signs warn,

CAUTION
MINIMUM
MAINTENANCE
ROAD
LEVEL B SERVICE
ENTER AT YOUR
OWN RISK

Unpaved roads are rare on the eastern Great Plains, but this part of Iowa is relatively remote and underfunded. Where gravel roads intersect, there is a timeless feeling. One could expect the appearance of 1930s cars. There is also a sense of freedom on these roads; they seem endless.

Most roads march in a straight line up and down the steep hills, platted without regard for topography. There are grand views at the rises. The earth undulates to the west and the Missouri River, the route of Lewis and Clark. It doesn't take much imagination to see the prairie as the explorers and Indians must have viewed it—unbroken, growing, burning, and regrowing, as it had for ten thousand years since the last Ice Age.

But little native prairie remains. Some of it's being restored, as are 145 acres near the East Boyer River that the city of Denison purchased to sink deep wells for its water supply. The reason for choosing native grasses was not solely environmental political correctness; there was no better cover to protect the water source when the river flooded—the deep roots held the soil unlike any other plant could. This is not the wussy grass of a suburban lawn. Tallgrass prairie species are stout, almost woody, and one has the sense of an ecosystem as special as an old-growth forest.

Other remnants of prairie grass are found along railroad rights-of-way and the edges of the Boyer and its tributaries. The branch creeks are deeply eroded as a result of runoff, with 15-foot sheer earth walls cut as if a slice of chocolate cake; one can occasionally find buffalo skulls or pieces of horns protruding from the ancient alluvial deposits.

Walking the prairie evokes the time of the Sioux. A late summer walker disturbs grasshoppers by the hundreds with each step; the sound and movement are as if waters are parting ahead in anticipation of one's passage. The bottomland trees are mostly cottonwood. On a summer day with a slight breeze, the leaves clatter like thousands of tiny clapping hands. It's a sound of the West, and of water.

But it is not prairie grass that defines Denison. For the town of Denison to exist in the economy of the twenty-first century, pigs must be slaughtered and processed at a maximum rate of 9,400 per day. Iowa raises more hogs than any other state, and one-quarter of all pork produced in America comes from the state. For swine to exist, corn, and not prairie grass, must grow. For corn to grow, soil is required.

Iowa is the epicenter of the corn and soybean belt because it has the greatest concentration of Grade 1 soil, the top rank for crops. Iowa has 26 percent of all Grade 1 land in the nation, according to the National Resources Board. The next highest is Illinois, with 15 percent, followed by Minnesota with 12 percent; Missouri, 9 percent; Nebraska, 8 percent.

One source of this great soil deteriorates with each passing year: the deep humus that remains from ten thousand years of prairie grass growing, dying, and decaying.

The other major factor behind the premium soil is glaciation. Iowa was covered by a series of glaciers anywhere from 1,000 feet to 1 mile thick, depending on location and varying theories. These masses of ice ground Canadian bedrock as they marched south. Glaciers are soil-creation machines; as they travel, they pulverize rock. This mineral-rich soil is called loess (pronounced "luss"), a German word for glacial deposits in the Rhine River Valley. Most of the Midwest is covered in loess, but it's especially deep in much of Iowa.

There were four major glacial periods in Iowa from about 2.5 million to 10,000 years ago. It was really the same glacial mass that moved down from the north, retreated, then came back, but these successive fingers of ice did not return to the same areas. The first two, called the Nebraskan and Kansan, covered almost the entire state of Iowa. The Kansan added loess atop the Nebraskan. The Illinoian period lasted from some 150,000 to 130,000 years ago, but the glacier touched only eastern Iowa. The final glaciation, the Wisconsin, lasted from 31,000 to some 10,000 years ago and stopped north of Crawford County. This explains why the hills are so steep here: they were not worn down by this final ice attack. The glaciers are responsible for a unique landform west of Crawford County: the Loess Hills. These run in a narrow band north to south along the Iowa border with the Missouri River and were created when till, mixed with runoff, drained from the glacier to the north and spread out over a plain where the Missouri River is now located. Winds carried this dusty loess and deposited it to create the steep-sided Loess Hills—they were really dunes covered by grass and now many trees due to the cessation of prairie fires.

There are other reminders of the ice besides soil. Walking in the bottom of ravines coming off the ridges around Denison, one finds rounded granite rocks ranging in size from engine blocks to those of Humvees, left by the Nebraskan and Kansan glaciations. These misplaced igneous rocks in a land of sedimentary deposits were carried down from Canada. There's an unwritten tradition in Denison: residents love to wrest free large glacial rocks with bulldozers and place them on their front lawns. The largest in town is a 15½-ton bright pink granite behemoth in front of a home on North Twentieth Street.

With the existence of good soil, two other factors influence corn in Iowa: a relatively long growing season due to the state's latitude and water, which is affected by longitude.

Denison lies at the 95th Meridian. In the eastern United States, longitudinal lines are of no consequence, but on the Great Plains, each degree farther to the west has an impact on life and commerce. In his well-known book *Beyond the Hundredth Meridian: John Wesley Powell and the Second Opening of the West,* Wallace Stegner wrote of the critical dividing line of the 100th Meridian. When one drives across the country from the east, a sign isn't needed to mark the transition. The land suddenly becomes drier; rainfall slackens because of the effect of the rain shadow of the Rocky Mountains. But the 100th Meridian is merely the most remarkable point of demarcation: there is a slight change with each degree one moves west from the Mississippi River. At roughly the 98th Meridian (in eastern Nebraska), the tallgrass prairie gives way to that of the shortgrass, which is more drought tolerant.

Denison is some 300 miles east of the 100th Meridian. About a third to half of that distance to the west, in Nebraska, irrigation in the form of rolling sprinklers is required to grow corn and soybeans. Denison is affected by the Rocky Mountain rain shadow, but not all of Iowa falls under its influence. The state receives most of its rainfall from storms that come from the south, out of the Gulf of Mexico.

"Southeastern Iowa has more rain than the rest of the state," according to *A Geography of Iowa,* by H. L. Nelson. "It is closer to the source of our moisture. From southeast to northwest the rainfall decreases in amount."

Iowa is divided into three rainfall zones. Crawford County falls inside the driest zone, with an average twenty-five to twenty-eight inches of annual rainfall. Central Iowa gets an additional five inches; an extra eight inches fall in eastern Iowa, which is at the 90th Meridian.

Water is destiny. It equals power. In Iowa, simply put, corn has a better chance of thriving in the east, especially in dry years. That means a more certain economy for farmers and towns. A sense of how water affects population and political-cultural influence comes from examining the size and density of a line of Great Plains states proximate to Iowa, from east to west.

State	Square Miles	2000 Population, U.S. Census	People per Square Mile
Indiana	35,867	6.11 million	170.5
Illinois	57,914	12.48 million	224.6
Iowa	56,272	2.92 million	52.3
Nebraska	77,354	1.71 million	22.3
South Dakota	77,116	756,600	10.0
Wyoming	97,814	494,423	5.1

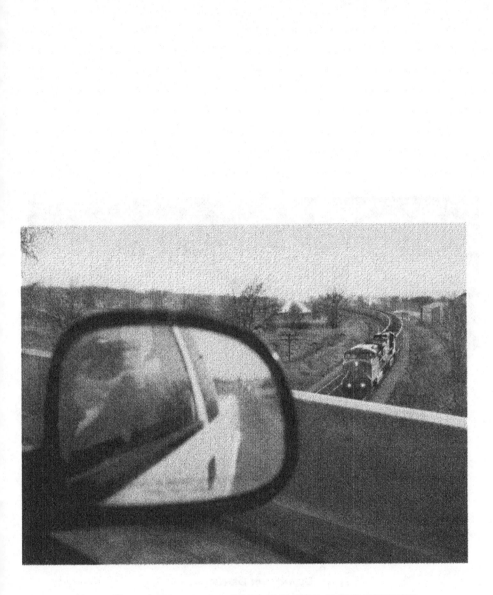

Union Pacific coal train, grain elevator in the distance,
where eleven immigrants were found dead
in a sealed railcar.

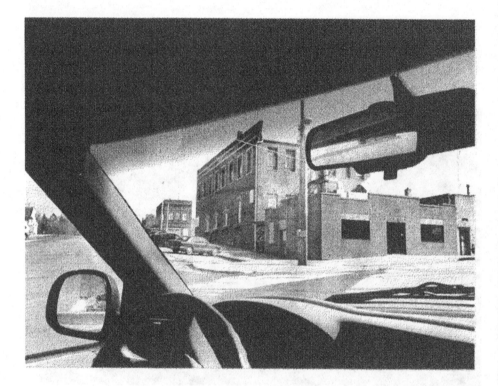

Downtown Denison.

TWO-HEADED PIG, CRAWFORD COUNTY COURTHOUSE.

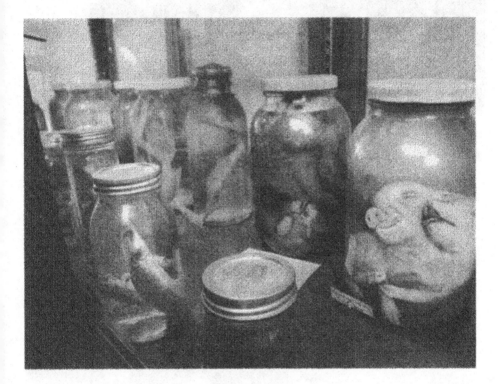

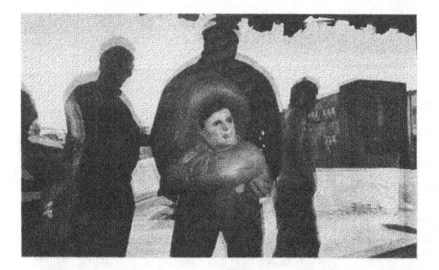

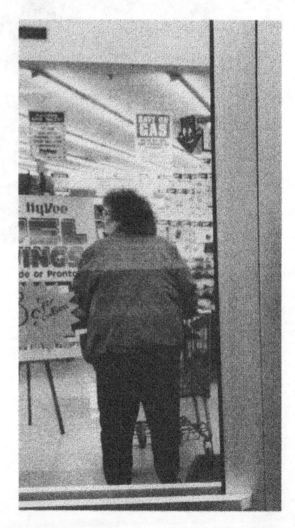

Window display, Latino business.

The Hy-Vee Supermarket.

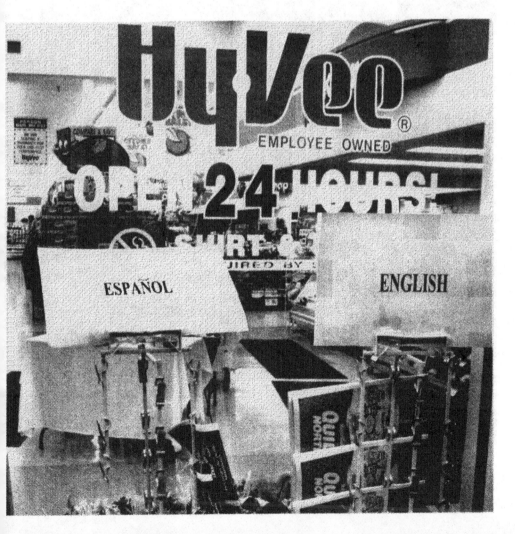

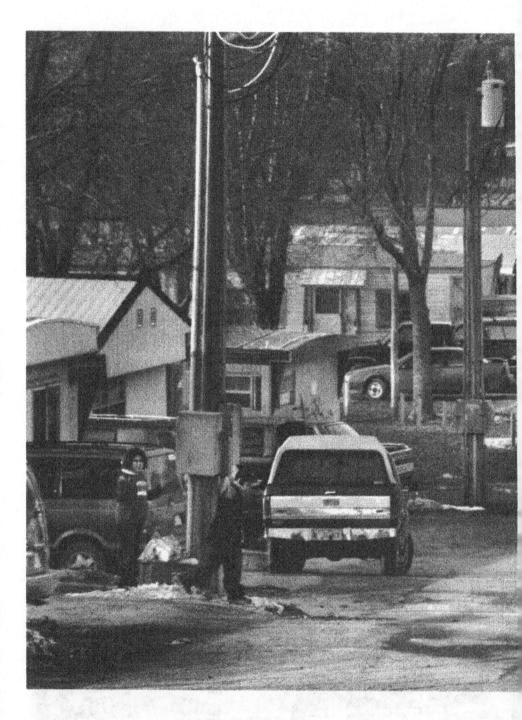

TRAILER COURT.

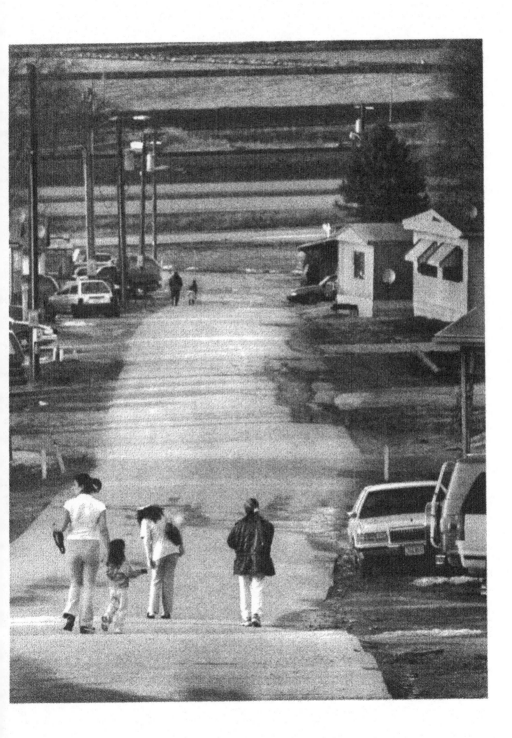

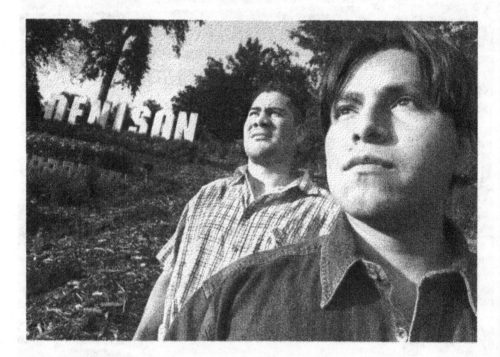

Juan Escobar and William Galicia.

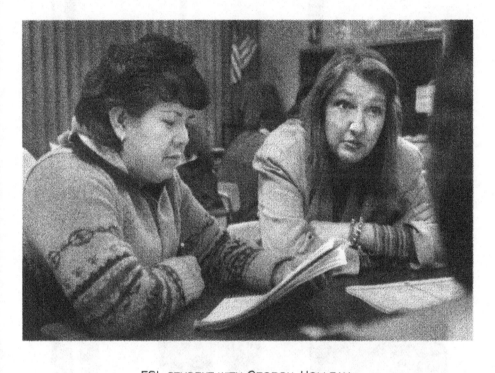

ESL STUDENT WITH GEORGIA HOLLRAH.

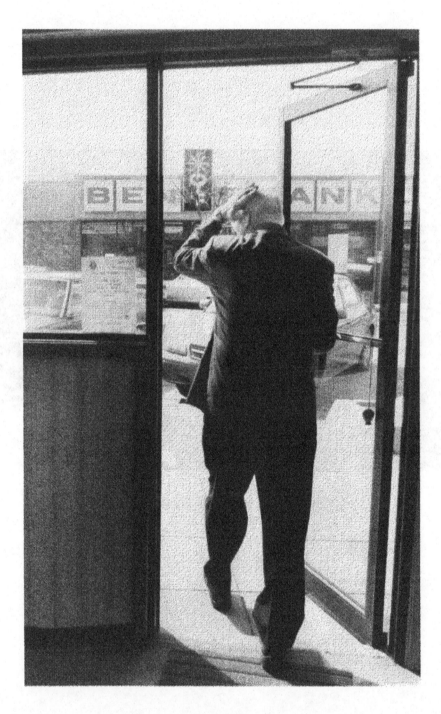

DICK KNOWLES.

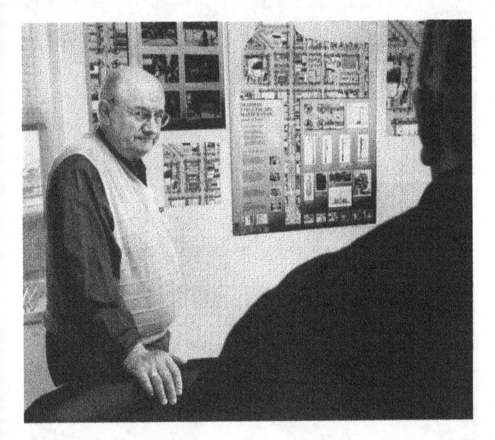

MAYOR KEN LIVINGSTON AND DRAWINGS FOR THE STREETSCAPE
REDESIGN OF DOWNTOWN DENISON.

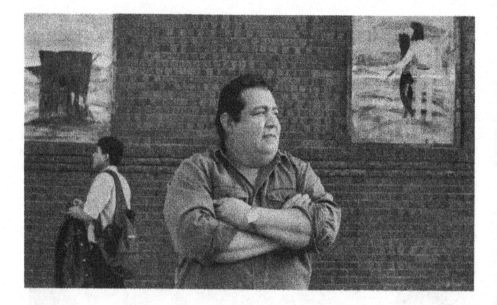

Luis Navar, *Der Denison Herold* building.

Nathan Mahrt.

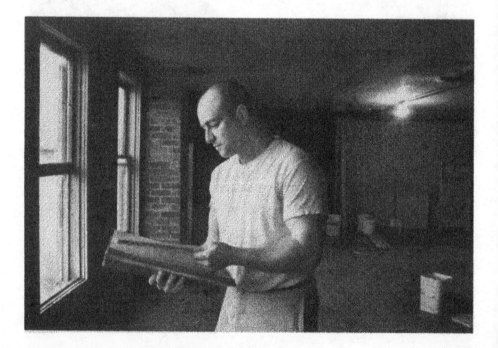

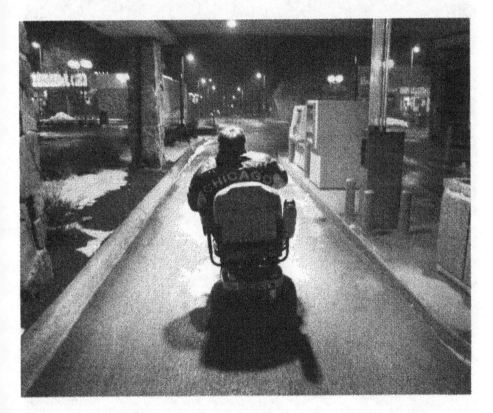

THE NIGHT MAN.

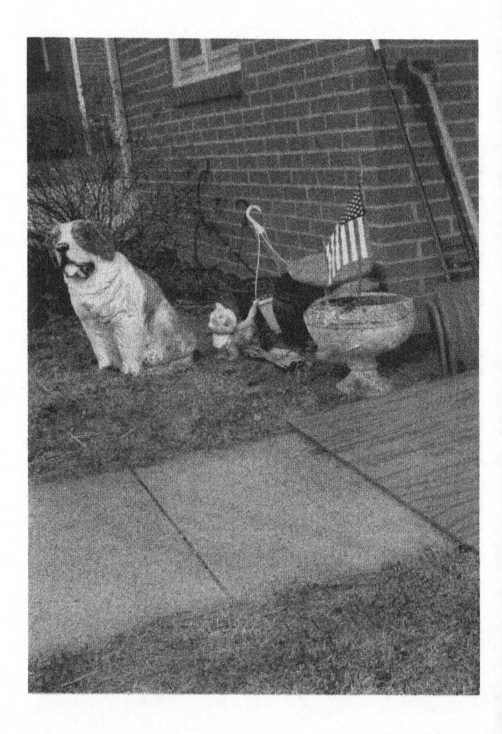

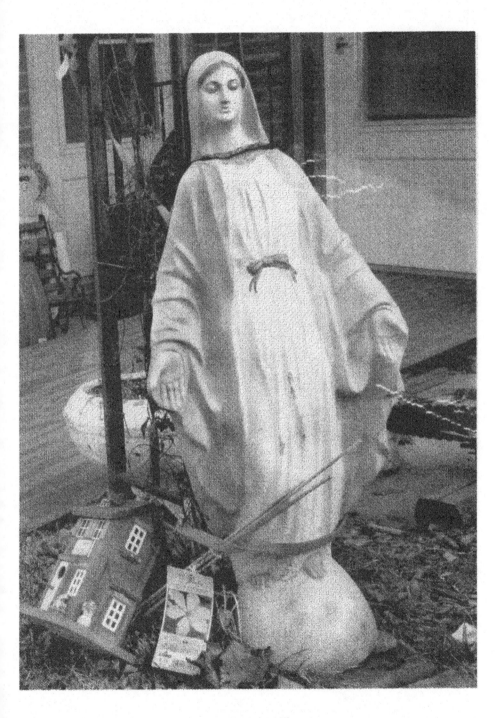

Lawn ornament.

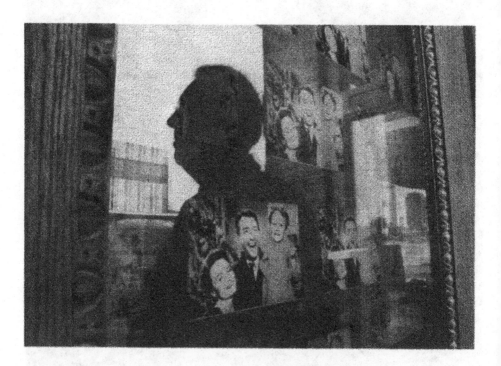

JOEL FRANKEN IN FRONT OF THE DONNA REED MUSEUM.

Western Iowa is more desolate. Crawford County, for example, has 23.7 people per square mile compared with 37.1 people per square mile in rural Jefferson County in southeast Iowa. The western part of the state is less politically powerful than the east. Eastern Iowa has more population and more wealth. Could it be due to those eight fewer inches of rainfall? Crawford County engineer Paul Assman pointed out a fundamental reality when asked about this: "All new wealth comes from fields and mines. Unless you have that, everything else is value added and service. When I talk about fields, I mean fields of fish in the ocean, fields of oranges, fields of corn, and so on. The wealth comes from the land."

This is something most Americans have forgotten—that a service economy or high-technology workers cannot exist without wealth coming from the earth. For all the talk of the "new economy," the health of a town, a state, and a nation really comes down to some very old economic rules. In Denison, this means farmers plant corn, others feed it to pigs or cows, and then people work in a factory that slaughters and cuts up those pigs or cows.

There is one high-tech firm, Professional Computer Systems, in Denison. It creates and manages software for nonprofit rural cooperative and municipal utility companies, programs involving billing and customer service. PCS is quite successful—it has some forty workers with salaries ranging from $30,000 to $60,000—but if not for corn and pigs and cows, there would be no business, for a majority of its clients are Midwest rural cooperatives. If corn and pigs were no longer driving the economy, there would be no Denison, no infrastructure to support PCS and its employees.

As a measure of the influence of water, people in Denison speak with disdain of the *Des Moines Register*. This paper does a miserable job of covering the area, the opposite of how it treats the eastern state. Western Iowans identify more with Omaha and view it as the bright light on the horizon. Omaha, of course, is a river town and its metropolitan area has 717,000 residents, over a third of the entire population of the state of Nebraska. Denison residents are Iowans in geographical name only, for they live at an end of the road of sorts.

There has always been a frontier mentality about Denison. A first-time visitor expects it to be populated and run by an oligarchy dating to its pioneer founders—families with names like Denison, Laub, McHenry, or Shaw. But they don't exist. Either they made their money and left, or they built empires that their children inherited and the children bailed out. Nathan Mahrt said they fled to urban centers, usually Chicago or the East Coast, where they constituted the new money.

Was there something in the nature of the land that made them leave? Was it what they once called "prairie madness," caused by boredom and desolation, a natural result of living in the Great American Empty, the difficulty of life on the drying land as one neared the 100th Meridian?

Today most white children of Denison citizens leave after high school. Principal Steve Westerberg said, "Most kids can't wait to blow this popsicle stand when they graduate." Besides pork and beef products, Denison's biggest export is young people. Nathan said that out of his class of 133, just two others besides himself live in Denison. Nathan too left for a while, for college and then to serve a stint in the U.S. Marines. He'd tried law school but didn't like what it would make him into. He was drawn home, but to survive he worked three jobs: one for the city utilities, one as a U.S. Customs agent inspecting packages for United Parcel Service, and one as a substitute teacher. Amber, his wife, was a nurse. It was hard getting by despite all this labor.

"I could make $60,000 in another town," Nathan said. "But I know a millionaire, and he's not happy. I wouldn't have a life."

Opportunity is relative, and the Latinos who were coming had a different view from the white high school kids blowing town. What the whites viewed as horrible underpaid work, hacking at meat, Latinos saw as a golden chance at a new beginning.

No matter where I turned in Denison, white people young and old muttered about how they hated living here. "It's boring," was a common refrain. I found no Latino adults who talked this way. They embraced the town. Latinos are about the only people eager to move into rural Iowa. In the 1990s, some 40 percent of the state's cities lost population. Iowa has the most people over age sixty-five of any other state except Florida. Sixty percent of Iowa's college graduates leave.

But are the Latinos, as Nathan says, a continuation of what Denison has always been, really—a place where one comes to make it, only to move on, as did the founders and their children? Nathan felt the children of the immigrants would follow the same pattern. Or was there something distinct about the Latinos that would lead them to create a new society on the Great Plains?

UPTOWN

When Jesse Denison arrived one late summer day in 1856 on the hilltop site for the city that would bear his name, only tallgrass prairie blew in the wind. Not a single tree existed. The few pioneer families in Crawford County had settled in rare bottomland groves of cottonwood and black walnut. It seemed insane to plat a town atop a hill, exposed to winter wind and snow. And water had to be hauled from the river. But a country person to this day will advise, "Always build high." If you build low, you eventually get flooded. Jesse Denison must have had an eye to the future. Historian F. W. Meyers cut Denison some slack for the misleading advertisements depicting a bustling metropolis.

"It is very possible that in his mind's eye, he saw the Denison that was pictured [with] busy streets," Meyers wrote in 1911.

To begin the process of replacing grass with a city, Jesse Denison constructed the Denison House, a lodging quarters for himself and workers. It was a crude building with neither a ceiling nor plastered walls. The Denison House was strictly for survival and was only useful for him to begin the real work.

For Jesse Denison, the first order of business would be business. To lure settlers so that the Providence Western Land Company would profit, Denison knew he needed a mercantile store, which he proceeded to construct—a ten- by sixteen-foot frame building. A small amount of goods to be sold were brought overland by wagon. Because Denison planned on being busy selling land, he hired a store manager.

The manager "proved incapable or dishonest," Meyers wrote. Denison was not a merchant and was unable to properly oversee the manager. The store was a miserable failure.

Casting about for the right person, Denison discovered Henry C.

Laub, a settler who had given up on farming and had opened a store in the nearby town of Deloit. Denison convinced Laub to take over the operation, sweetening the offer by trading his failed store and its goods for an inconsequential plot of land Laub owned a mile outside town.

Laub's opened in 1857, filled with goods brought by ox team from Chicago. He and a partner opened two other stores in the county, but he wound up $78,000 in debt. He dumped the ineffective partner. A problem was that settlers had little money, and Laub extended credit while they established farms. Laub hung on. As the settlers began to sell grain and hogs, they squared up with Laub. In three years, Laub paid off the debt.

Jesse Denison was consumed with selling land. Laub was consumed with creating a city. He was a shrewd merchant and a Republican, but not the laissez-faire kind common today. He knew that for his store to flourish, he had to think of things far larger, fostering a climate that was conducive to creating a city that people wanted to live in. By community building, his store in turn would profit. Meyers wrote,

> Mr. Denison had now interested and allied with him the most active business intellect that ever came to Crawford County. The things which Mr. Laub did for the upbuilding of this town and county are almost past belief. He was interested in everything. He built houses and stone buildings, contracted for the erection of bridges, built schoolhouses, supplied the courthouse with wood, was interested in the manufacture of brick and built the first telegraph line from Boone to Council Bluffs.

The town grew around the Laub store, and by 1868 there were some 300 residents. That year, *Turner's Guide to the Rocky Mountains*, published to sell ads to towns seeking newcomers and promote western migration, wrote of the city of Denison:

> The business of the place is represented by three dry goods and grocery stores, one hardware store, one furniture store, one drug store, two saddle and harness shops, two boot and shoe shops, two hotels, one blacksmith shop, one wagon shop, one saw mill, and one flour

mill. One physician and two lawyers, all highly ornamental but not extremely useful, grace the town.

Laub eventually had thirty-two stores all over western Iowa. He built the brick two-story Laub Block, at the corner of Main and Broadway in Denison, a stunning mercantile operation when it was completed in 1873. With the Laub Block, Denison now resembled a real city. But it was legally only a township, with lesser status and ability to control its destiny. It was the only county seat on the entirety of the Chicago Northwestern Railroad line that remained unincorporated. There was a move to seek cityhood.

The streets were dirt, and there was no thought of changing them, but there was interest in creating sidewalks. An improvement association was formed in 1873. Along with a handful of other men, Laub put up his own money and formed a subscription committee to pay for the first sidewalks. History seems in hindsight to be an inevitable march forward. Civic improvements in later years are taken for granted, and citizens forget that infrastructure did not just materialize—someone had to plan for it and pay for it. No matter the time in history, there are always people opposed to paying, and so it was with sidewalks. Meyers wrote,

> The opposition to incorporation came from three sources, those who felt that it meant increased taxation on general principles; those who feared that additional sidewalks would be ordered in; and those who felt that incorporation would mean added regulation and added license for saloons.

Laub sold his stores in 1874 to concentrate on construction and community activities. That year, Laub headed a commission to hold an election for incorporation. (A vote on cityhood had failed in 1870.) The 1874 measure also went down in defeat, 66–44. Laub came back in 1875 and this time incorporation passed, 116–55. Denison was now a city. Lingering bitterness over sidewalks appears to have cost him; he made a bid to become the first mayor, but lost. Yet he was later successful in other electoral arenas: he was a county supervisor, the sheriff, and a member of the state legislature.

Laub lived in a mansion just north of Shaw's. (Today it's a funeral home.) He was proud of what had been created from his hard work. Nathan Mahrt possesses a scrapbook owned by Laub: it contains original black-and-white photographs of Denison's mansions—but also of street scenes and schoolchildren—glued in a book the size of typing paper turned sideways.

The first photo is of Laub's home on Broadway: a Victorian house with gingerbread trim and a long porch. The street is dirt, yet there's a sidewalk. Five years before his death at the age of eighty-six in 1910, Laub wrote in fountain pen at the front of the book,

RESIDENCE DISTRICT

This is one of the oldest residence streets in Denison. The first houses were put up about thirty years ago. This street has recently been paved and the whole front is in a much more presentable condition. Broadway extends over a mile in length. This book was made up in 1905.

The next seven pages are pictures of Victorian mansions owned by the town's aristocracy. Laub wrote their names beneath. These founders were now late middle-aged or elderly, and they were living well forty-three years after Laub and others organized a military regiment to chase marauding Sioux Indians. In the photos, streets bustle, homes gleam. There are electric and telephone lines. Everything is new, and the photographs emanate energy. Viewed through the prism of Laub's book, one gets a sense of an America on a never-ending march to prosperity.

Indeed. It was the dawn of the American Century. The Indians had been defeated after nearly three centuries of war. As the frontier was in the last days of closing, there had been a policy of "continentalism," that the United States should not expand off the North American continent. That changed with Theodore Roosevelt who, in the administration of President William McKinley, had been instrumental in getting the United States to declare war against Spain in 1898. The reason was the sinking of the battleship *Maine* in Havana harbor, though the cause of the sinking was later found to be the explosion of the ship's boiler in an accident. Spain had nothing to do with it. Now, one of Denison's own, Shaw, was working for Roosevelt, the man instrumental in setting America on a course to be a world power.

On the ninth page of the picture book, Laub wrote,

Residence of L. M. Shaw, ex governor of Iowa and Secretary of the Treasury of the U.S.

Roosevelt wanted the United States to control the world's seas. Vital was the construction of the Panama Canal. In 1903 U.S. gunboats carved off a piece of Colombia to create the nation of Panama. On May 11, 1904, Shaw signed the largest check up to that point ever issued by the U.S. government: check number 4860 for $40 million, to pay the French company that had started the canal.

Shaw still held title to the house pictured in Laub's book, and he had planned on coming home. But the world had changed for Shaw, and for America. Shaw's Iowa law reference books remaining in the library of the Denison home probably seemed rather inconsequential as he put the $40 million check in his pocket and boarded a train in Washington to personally deliver it for deposit at J. P. Morgan & Co. in New York City.

Shaw was just entering middle age, and Laub was an old man. One year after Shaw wrote out the big check, Laub was content to write in the scrapbook about his corner of the United States. His accomplishments didn't make national headlines. His priorities for Crawford County were evident by what he wrote beneath a picture of students streaming out of Central High School:

More money is spent for education alone than most counties have for their whole county tap.

"Tap" seems to mean budget. Laub's ego is not present. He doesn't mention his role in creating an environment that prioritized education over limiting taxation. Nor does he mention how much of the downtown that he built, including two business blocks. One picture shows a few dozen wagon and horse teams parked on Broadway, shoppers crowding the sidewalks. Beneath the picture of his first business block, he wrote,

Corner of Maine & Broadway. Denison's & Crawford's busiest place; over 50,000 people trade in Denison each week.

A person had trouble navigating the sidewalk on a Saturday afternoon. Denison was no longer a frontier but an established and growing city. As the American Century advanced, it must have seemed to Laub as he lived out his final few years that the town would continue to grow and become a regional metropolis. Why would it not? It was situated amid the richest farmland on earth, and its trajectory seemed limitless.

* * *

On a Saturday afternoon a century later, a person could lie down on an Uptown sidewalk and nap undisturbed. But he or she would dare not do so in the Wal-Mart parking lot across the East Boyer River, where the big roads in and out of town intersect.

The decline of the Uptown business district, to be fair, predated the arrival of Wal-Mart in 1991. While Wal-Mart did harm, there were many other factors. The early 1970s was the last good period: Uptown had a three-floor Montgomery Ward, a JCPenney, and lots of shops. But there was steady slippage. By the 1980s, it was clear that there was a serious problem.

Crawford County had lost a lot of small farms. According to the U.S. Census, the number of farms peaked in 1900, when there were 2,649 in the county. By 1950, there were still 2,437. But shrinkage continued and intensified in the farm crisis caused by high interest rates and ruined land values in the 1980s. Census figure show the pace:

Year	Number of County Farms
1964	1,909
1969	1,794
1978	1,590
1982	1,511
1987	1,339
1997	1,107

No more recent data were available, but locals say the loss has continued. Farms grew to a thousand acres or more, the largest encompassing some 30,000 acres. In the early days, there were large farm families; the families grew smaller as the farms grew larger. Denison had been the mercantile center for all those families, plus hundreds more from surrounding counties. "Going to town" was an event, a ritual.

In addition, the habits of Americans had changed. People shopped differently. The concept of distance was transformed.

"I sat up on the hill behind Cronk's and watched them pave the Lincoln Highway," said Mearl Luvaas, the octogenarian resident. "They used horses for some of the work." He was uncertain of the year, but it "was sometime in the 1930s. In those days, Omaha was not a one-day trip. It would take two days, and it involved some tire repairing and such."

Because of improved roads and cars, the drive from Denison to Omaha now took an hour and a half. It was a day trip.

One merchant spoke bitterly of the white-collar elite, who happened to be the 125 teachers. (After the two large packing plants, the school is the third largest employer in Denison.) Uptown shopping by teachers dwindled after the 1980s. Teachers mostly live in a suburban-like neighborhood of tract homes called Fort Purdy, and they drive through Uptown on their way to Omaha. There they patronize big-box stores, sip lattes at Borders, buy organic foods at the Wild Oats Market, perhaps have a sushi dinner, and come home at night. Blue-collar workers, both Latino and white, remain close to home and frequent Wal-Mart.

"You know what saved Uptown?" Nathan Mahrt asked. "Hispanics. They pay cash. Talk to any of the merchants. The Hispanics don't shop in Omaha. The teachers are the worst. The teachers have to go to Omaha to buy a two by four."

"Everything is better out of town," added Amber, Nathan's wife, about the attitude of the teachers. "It's getting out, getting to the big city."

Most of these weekend escapees are not transplants. Many were born here, and Amber says there is a stigma: "If you grew up around here and stayed, you are a failure." Going to Omaha for a day makes them feel better.

Latinos, however, were not exactly breaking down the doors of all Uptown businesses. Many stores didn't provide products the newcomers wanted. The needs for specialty items such as food were met by Latino entrepreneurs.

By 2004, there were between sixteen and twenty Latino-owned enterprises, ranging from a western apparel store, a women's and children's clothing shop, four food markets, an auto repair operation, to three restaurants and a bakery. Many were fragile businesses. Some were like their counterparts in Latin America and were hardly more than street vendor–like operations set up in storefronts to serve friends and neighbors. The owners, who worked long days, were "buying themselves a job," as one white merchant put it; they might earn as low a salary as they would in the packing plants after seventy-plus-hour weeks. It was a nascent business community, not yet strong enough to lead an economic transformation of the city.

Several businesses, however, were thriving. The most successful was Reynold's Clothing on Broadway, owned by Brett and Troy Gehlsen, sons of the founding owner. When I stopped in seeking T-shirts, Brett suggested I go to Wal-Mart.

"We sell what they don't," Brett said. "I go to Wal-Mart for my kids' underwear." Reynold's sells large sizes that Wal-Mart does not carry and specialty clothing like Carhartt jeans and Rockland work shoes.

"We're not going to compete with them, duh," Troy said. "We have better merchandise than Wal-Mart. We give customer service." Troy said their store provides dry-cleaning at cost. And they'd just lured in a woman who did clothing alterations in her home, to an upstairs office. Now when someone buys pants that need taking up, she's right there. Troy added that Wal-Mart has helped them: "They increased traffic from the west part of the county."

He says people shop Wal-Mart and figure they need something else, and come up the hill: "It hasn't hurt us. They go there, get their basic needs, and come here. While they're in the city, they say let's go to Uptown." (The Family Table Restaurant down on the Lincoln Highway also saw its business increase, said owner Steve Harris; people who drive in from outlying towns to shop at Wal-Mart then come in to eat.) Still Troy worried. He looked out the window at the street empty of people. The town needs foot traffic.

"I asked my dad, how did you all make it when there were four men's clothing stores here? He said we all did okay. Let's face it. It's never going to be what it was pre-1970. That's impossible. But we have to try. We're for anything Uptown."

The problems facing Denison are like those facing thousands of cities large and small all over America. Desolation has taken hold of many downtowns. It's as if there was a motion picture rolling, dating from the days of incredible bustle to something that resembled Archer, Texas, in the Peter Bogdanovich cinematic black-and-white adaptation of Larry McMurtry's novel, *The Last Picture Show*. Would Denison end up like Archer, with wind blowing dust down Broadway to be swept by a lone boy?

Denison had gone through three major periods following its founding in 1856 and was now on the brink of a fourth.

The first era began when the Native Americans were driven out. It encompassed the pioneer times and the post-pioneer years in which men like Leslie Shaw came to the frontier and became rich through hard work. Their mansions were built between the 1870s and the turn of the century. Yet even the poorest European immigrants were relatively wealthy, given that they'd come from countries where land ownership was a dream. They worked hard, but they had title to 160 acres of Iowa soil, the best temperate cropland in the world. The expansion of this wealth ended about the time Shaw went to Washington, coinciding on a larger scale with the waning of Jefferson's agrarian ideal and the ascendancy of the industrial and imperial age.

The second phase of Denison's history was a decline that began at the turn of the twentieth century. Mechanization, a process that accelerated after the Great Depression as farm prices plummeted, changed farming. Men with tractors could farm larger acreages. There were fewer people on the land. Denison did not need to be as large a city as it had been. The desperation of this period was marked by violence. Iowa was a center of the radical farm movement in the 1930s. Banks were foreclosing on land, and across Iowa people formed "Farm Holiday Associations" to stop the sales. In early 1933 there was a foreclosure sale at Joe Shield's Denison farm. Fifty sheriff's deputies and state agents, wielding clubs and axe handles, were attacked by a crowd of a few hundred. Farmers grabbed the clubs and beat the officers; the sale was halted. Governor Clyde Herring declared martial law in Crawford and nearby counties. Machine-gun nests were set up around town. But the foreclosures continued, and the farmers lost.

In the post–World War II period, Denison's leaders realized that the town had to reinvent itself, and it did so by becoming "The Meat Empire," the motto before the title of the Donna Reed movie was painted on the water tower. Instead of shipping hogs and cattle off to Omaha or Chicago to be slaughtered, entrepreneurs brought the factories to the fields. These plants butchered, packaged, and processed the meat near where the animals were raised.

Denison actively courted the packers; it was no accident that they came. Andy Anderson did an inversion of what Henry Ford had done with the automobile when he founded Iowa Beef Processors, or IBP, in Denison in 1961. Anderson brought the assembly line to the meat industry. But it was, as has been said, a disassembly line. Packinghouses before Anderson had cut up a cow in one spot, moving workers around; a plant might process 200 head a day. Anderson moved the carcasses on a line, with workers doing specific cuts as meat passed, and his plants processed 1,600 head per day. In days of old, cows were shipped in halves or quarters, to be cut into steaks by distant butchers. IBP pioneered "beef in a box," ready-packaged steaks preferred by chain grocery stores, which were then just emerging.

The city invested millions of dollars in its water plant to create water of exactly 8.6 PH, or 7.5 grains hardness, required by the plants so that the liquid in canned hams and other products did not discolor. (The water is slaked with lime, and then it's precipitated out.) Farmland Foods now uses about one-third of the 3 million gallons treated each day. Denison and towns that landed packing plants thrived, although they were forever changed. Denison was no longer a farm town but a blue-collar city. Locals grumbled about the newcomers—they were white but were viewed as a caste below. The wages, however, were fantastic—there was a $2 million payroll. In 1966 the *Wall Street Journal* reported that Denison's retail sales had increased 50 percent from the time before the plants, to $15 million annually, "and the downtown area has many new and just remodeled stores."

Yet some rue the day the packing plants came. To them Denison made a mistake, unlike the city of Carroll immediately to the east. They were identical in the 1950s. Carroll, however, sought different industries. It landed a Pella window plant, a company that sold homeowners' warranties, a warehouse, a telemarketer, and a jet engine fuel systems firm.

Combined, they provided nearly 2,000 jobs. It was a "clean" town, and residents didn't mind telling visitors they were better than Denison, a "dirty" town where animals were killed and Latinos lived. (There is a pecking order among Iowa towns. Denison considers itself far better than Missouri Valley to the west, a languishing river town; nor is it Ida Grove to the north, seen as in more desperate straits.)

No matter, Denison's choice had long ago been made.

Then came the third era: the uncertainty of the 1980s and the farm crisis. Economic difficulty was deepened with the busting of the union at Farmland Foods when the 1982 strike was lost. The prestrike starting pay was over ten dollars an hour. In 2004, it was about the same. If salaries had kept pace with inflation, the rate should have been well over twenty dollars per hour. There was less money to go around. The packing plant impact on local retail sales noted by the *Wall Street Journal* in 1966 had atrophied.

Farmland Foods, a farmer-owned cooperative, was in bankruptcy when I came to town. In late 2003, it was purchased by Smithfield Foods, the world's largest pork processor. Smithfield controlled nearly 30 percent of all pork production in America, according to published accounts. (Smithfield was viewed with fear by independent farmers, for unlike Farmland, it often worked by contract. In some cases, the "farmers" did not even own the hogs, but were in effect livestock sharecroppers.) The second-largest plant in town, with some 400 workers, was Tyson Fresh Meats, formerly IBP.

Farmland, as a cooperative, was not likely to close, short of bankruptcy. There were not the same assurances with a distant corporation. A CEO eager to make a stock option bonus could decide to close the plant with the wave of a hand. Denison's leaders knew about other one-industry cities with steel or textile plants. People didn't have to travel but a few miles in any direction to see their future if the meat plants downsized or vanished. Iowa and nearby Nebraska are dotted with towns of shuttered storefronts, dead houses. There are winners and losers among cities in modern America, and on the Great Plains they are next door to each other.

And, at best, wages would forever be substandard. Plant employees live a hand-to-mouth existence. A sense of this can be found in the statistics from Denison's elementary school: 65.2 percent of the 743 students got reduced-price or free lunches (over half were free) under the federal program for low-income families. A majority of these kids were white.

Andy Anderson and imitators automated the process as much as possible, and the unions were busted. There is no day soon coming when this industry will again have robust wages.

"The United Auto Worker learned how to run a robot, and can be paid well," said Denison pharmacist Craig Whited, who once worked at Farmland. "There's no more efficiency to be gained in the meat plant. You still have to search for the gland in the neck to cut it out. No machine can do that."

This third era was also the time of Wal-Mart. Denison, like so many other places, was hit by the world economy and changes in trade policy and technology that allowed the importation of cheaply made foreign goods that were then sold in big-box outlets. Because of low wages, its vehement anti-union policy, and the way it strong-armed suppliers, the giant retailer was able to undercut competitors that paid workers better and could not dictate price to suppliers. If not for national economic policies, Wal-Mart could not threaten local business. But because Wal-Mart chose to locate in Denison, it helped the town by adding to the tax base, and the jobs, no matter how poor the pay, contributed to the town's survival.

It was an evolution not yet complete. City officials said Wal-Mart had hit a specified level of sales, which meant that it was eligible to be replaced by a Wal-Mart supercenter. This was only talk, a rumor. In Denison, however, it became the hot topic among merchants, a fact. These supercenters sold groceries and large items such as tires. When the company built these giants, it closed nearby normal-sized Wal-Marts. One fearful scenario was that the super-Wal-Mart would go to a nearby town, and the Denison outlet would close, as had 150 Wal-Marts around America since the chain began building its megastores, according to Ken Stone, an emeritus professor at Iowa State University. Many of these dead Wal-Marts had grass growing in the parking lots. Whatever Wal-Mart might decide would present a tremendous challenge.

It was now time for the fourth era, the post–meat empire Denison. The city had to rapidly evolve, finding footing in an economy of uncertainty.

It also had to find its way in dealing with the cultural transition; its success with this question was tied up in its economic fortunes. Because there were so many Latinos, they created an economic force that would affect the white residents. One culture could not succeed without the other.

* * *

There had been a moment of great hope in 1965, the year a new university opened its doors in Denison—Midwestern College.

Education Facilities Laboratories had received a Ford Foundation grant to create an idealistic model for a four-year liberal arts education. The goal was individualized instruction. Many students were bright and ambitious but for whatever reason might not have achieved the best grades in high school.

The college was constructed on a hill east of Denison. But by 1970, it was out of business. Among the reasons were underfunding and the cessation of college draft deferments. Midwestern had opened when the East Coast colleges were filled to capacity and men were seeking schools elsewhere to avoid the Vietnam War. If the school had succeeded, Uptown certainly would be different today, with bookstores, youth-oriented shops, coffeehouses.

Talk of doing something to boost Uptown intensified after the school closed but never went anywhere. Meanwhile the Sixties became the Seventies, the Eighties, and the figurative wind bringing in dust was blowing stronger. By the end of the Nineties, Denison's leaders were alarmed.

Some leaders saw hope in the Latino influx. But there were communication problems. When approached by the chamber of commerce, some Latino business owners thought it was an extortion racket like they'd experienced in Mexico. Other Latinos were embarrassed to come to public meetings, fearing their English was not good enough. Others were like parents of all races: too busy raising their children to become involved. And others were apathetic or were here just to make money and go home. A significant portion of the Latino residents, however, loved Denison. There was great untapped energy in the community.

But Denison could not wait for that day a decade or more in the future for this energy to mature. Uptown was hurting *now* from the impacts of a global economy, lifestyle patterns. Any city that could adapt and hang on might someday be okay. Why? There was no other choice. A plus for the future of Denison was the crowded and expensive nature of the American coasts. As the nation's population grows, many will have no choice but to come inland if they want to buy a home or have good schools. Also, the time of Wal-Mart, as that of every other merchandising era, would also pass. Everything big eventually fails.

Choices had to be made, now, however, if Denison would make it to this fourth phase. Something risky had to be done. The town needed a new Henry Laub who could see the big picture and have a bold vision. Would anything work? Who knew? The latter-day Laubs had to at least try.

* * *

Bill Wright graduated from Midwestern College in 1969. He'd enrolled as a self-described C student, not quite ready for college. But he was bright and ambitious. By the time he graduated, he'd excelled. He faced a choice. Should he go back home to New York City? He missed its diversity. He recalled a conversation with his mother when he'd first arrived.

"How is Denison?" she asked.

"It's so white!" Bill responded.

Bill knew that if he went back to New York, he'd be one tiny person in a teeming megalopolis. He asked himself: Could I have any impact there? The answer: possibly. In Denison, the answer was a definite yes.

Bill didn't participate in the Sixties as the decade was experienced on the coasts. But he'd absorbed the ethos of wanting to change the world. He decided to stay and change this corner of it. Bill married Marilyn, and he became a teacher at Denison High School. The couple moved into a trailer in 1970. He made $6,500 annually at a time when his students upon graduation would go into the Farmland plant and earn $10,000 to $12,000 cutting up hogs. He taught, raised his children, became an assistant superintendent in 1988, and at night and on weekends worked toward a doctoral degree, which he earned in 1993. The following year he was named superintendent of the Denison Community School District.

Bill had an infectious positive outlook and used his job as a platform for change. He grew involved in community activities such as helping create the Donna Reed Center. Then Bill turned his attention to a pet issue that dated to his arrival in 1965: rejuvenating Uptown. Now, decades later, Bill's path was about to cross with others who could help make this vision happen.

*　*　*

Paul Assman was one of fourteen children in Earling, south of Denison. He was born in 1960, but his youth was a throwback. His parents ran their farm old school, growing or raising all of their food; his mother made soap using bacon grease and lye. His was a tale of hard work of a man who came from an impoverished background to become an engineer. He built dams and other projects all over western Iowa for a private company.

In 1993, there was a great flood in Denison when the Boyer River overspilled its banks. By 1998 Denison had landed a grant to build a levee for protection, but as a condition of the federal money, the city had to hire an engineer to oversee planning. Paul was looking for a change, and he took the job of project impact manager.

At that time Denison had no city manager, and all officials were part time. Paul discovered that no one was really thinking about the big picture, so he took on all manner of jobs beyond that of an engineer, including economic development.

"I was dubbed the first unofficial city manager. There seemed to be a lack of continuity, a lack of direction."

Paul was a local, but he was able to stand back and see Denison in the big picture of the movie called the United States.

"You talk about amber waves of grain," Paul said rhetorically about the image of the middle of the country to those on the edges, in one of his typical observations. "I see waves of change in the Midwest. Socially, culturally, economically, this is a beast of its own."

He talked of his German forebears who had arrived in the late 1800s, and how they worked to make their 160-acre farm thrive. He rattled off the tonnages of lumber and building supplies that arrived in Denison in those days.

"A hundred and fifty years ago, what an exciting time that must have been. They were building houses. They were building churches and bridges. They were building a country."

He paused.

"Now we're dismantling."

Paul ticked off surrounding towns, naming the years when hardware, grocery, and other stores closed. He painted a bleak picture. And as he looked at Denison, he worried it might end up the same way.

"We needed to provide a path, a yellow brick road," he said of his mind-set in 1999. This drew snickers. "When I talked about the yellow brick road, people thought I meant Oz. But we needed somewhere to go."

His prime idea was to create an 800-acre lake on Otter Creek, a branch of the Boyer north of town. He pointed to Lake Panorama to the southeast, with hundreds of homes around it. The nearby towns are booming around that lake.

"I think wealth has to be created from within. It's difficult to attract the golden goose. What separates us from the surrounding towns? We're a meatpacking town. There's only just so much you can do with that. People are looking for things to do with their money and leisure time."

There are few lakes in western Iowa, and the Otter Creek Lake would draw people seeking second homes from Omaha. The problem: it would cost between $20 and $30 million to build the dam. That wasn't realistic at the moment. Paul was at a loss. Then he attended an economic development conference in Des Moines. One of the speakers was Martin Shukert, a former planning director for the city of Omaha, who now was a partner in RDG Crose Gardner Shukert, a consulting firm. Shukert talked about the decline of Midwest cities, and how this drift could be stopped.

"I sat there and thought this guy has to be talking about Denison. As soon as his presentation was over, I went up to him and said, 'I want to talk to you about coming to Denison.'"

Paul went home and convened a handful of community leaders, among them Eric Skoog, the owner of Cronk's Cafe, and realtor Doug Skarin. Eric and Doug were enthusiastic, but others had doubts. Maybe the time was not right. But when would the time be right? There was cajoling and more talk.

"So we brought Marty out," Paul said. Shukert explained they had to be proactive and set priorities. A start would be a detailed study to determine the city's options, which would cost $25,000; the study would take place over a two-year period.

After debate, it was agreed that the study would be done by Shukert's company, but only if it didn't sit on a shelf. The city would pay a third, the city-owned utilities company another third, and the rest would come from the Denison Chamber of Commerce and the Crawford County Development Corporation, a county agency.

There were focus groups involving some 300 citizens, leaders, and businesspeople. After nearly two years, thirty-eight major goals were defined in the report, *Denison 2020: Building the Wonderful Life.* The title reflected both perfect vision as well as the deadline year for what the city should look like as it matured into the century's second decade.

Among the major findings, business and job creation garnered 100 percent support. And 61 percent identified "multi-cultural integration and acceptance" as the second-most "critical issue" facing the city. Other issues each got between 17 and 22 percent (in ranking, not as a total percentage): retaining college graduates and young families, a better community image, recreational activities, and downtown revitalization. Many felt there was an "over reliance on low-paying jobs." Others felt the city needed a community center.

There was a list of goals, ranked in order. The top three were:

1. A new community and recreation center
2. The revitalization of Uptown.
3. The revitalization of businesses along Route 30, using a Lincoln Highway theme.

"Uptown remains vitally important to all residents of Denison," the report said. "Even for those few who do not use the district routinely, its location in the heart, rather than on the edge of the city's residential areas means that Uptown's health directly affects the value of nearly everyone's property. . . . Denison's Latino population is attracted to the urbanism of Uptown."

Meantime, the first two goals of the Denison 2020 Plan were already unfolding.

Two men involved with the Denison Community Golf Course came up with an idea for the Denison Community Conference Center. The hotel/conference center would be built at the golf course on the south side of the Boyer River. It would also house a new golf clubhouse and a community room that would function as a hall to rent for weddings and other events. If the men could raise $1.5 million in pledges by seeking donations from citizens, would the city pony up $1 million? They were told to go ahead.

Uptown was on the move. In March 2002 Bill Wright was named head of Streetscape, an improvement project initiated by the chamber of commerce. He had sat in meetings years before when people were brought into a room to discuss fixing Uptown: he'd watched the negatives kill plans. When Bill had toured Washington, D.C., he was told that nothing was built without controversy—the Washington Monument, Lincoln Memorial, Vietnam Wall. And so it was in Denison: the indoor municipal pool had been opposed, but now those who voted in the minority against it were some of its most faithful users. Bill had to bulldoze over the negatives. For Uptown, his notion was to cut the negatives out at the start, to get a core group of positives to sign on; this would pull everyone else along.

To sell the idea that included revamping the storefronts that had been "modernized" in the 1960s, Bill recruited Joel Franken, who was still an art teacher, to make paintings of what the storefronts could look like.

"I don't care if we get only four or five of them," Bill told Joel. "That's four or five more than we have now."

Bill met key building owners by "accident" in social settings, floated the idea, and was surprised by the interest. He netted thirteen owners, and Joel went to work. In his vision, Denison emerged as it had looked in the 1930s. As Joel put it, Denison would be "the town that went to its past to secure its future." He used blowups of stills from *It's a Wonderful Life*, painting what the thirteen business fronts could look like. Joel also used the stage-set infrastructure from the fictional Bedford Falls to design lampposts, benches, and signage. It was a classic example of life imitating art.

In addition to the building fronts, with Streetscape, the roads would be narrowed and the sidewalks widened. It would be an inviting pedestrian-friendly environment. Potential employers and residents would realize the city was serious about change and that it was a good place to live and do business. In time, the hope was that stores would fill with shoppers.

Then along came Ken Livingston, whose 2002 campaign vow for the

2020 Plan was to "make it a living document." Ken followed twenty-five years of mayors who did little more than sit in meetings. The mayor's job was part time, but Ken was in his office from morning 'til night. He brought a business mentality. With opposition from some council members, Ken pushed through the hiring of city manager Al Roder, at a salary of $81,500 per year, to professionalize how the city was run.

On August 14, 2002, the city's leaders were ready to present Streetscape at Denison High School. Among the building owners present who signed on were lawyer Bill Norelius; Reynold Gehlsen and his sons, Brett and Troy, of Reynold's Clothing; attorney Michael R. Mundt, who had purchased and renovated the Montgomery Ward Building; others.

Bill and Joel and Ken didn't do much talking. Joel showed his paintings, and they stepped back and let Norelius and Mundt and the others share their excitement for the redesign. They hoped a spark would catch. People mostly listened. It worked: city officials moved forward with the plan. It was certainly a strange mix to make Denison look like its early twentieth-century salad days, a Bedford Falls theme in a city that was now between one-fifth and one-half Latino, depending on whom one believed.

At the dawn of 2003, plans for Phase 1 of Streetscape were being finalized. It was not a done deal. The council had to vote to appropriate the funds in 2004. Streetscape and the golf course project would be expensive. The first phase of Streetscape, if approved, would cost $1.9 million. Construction would begin when warm weather broke, to change Main Street and parts of the major cross street, Broadway. Building owners would be assessed part of the cost, which could cause trouble.

In late 2003, the city council passed, with just one dissenting vote, a measure authorizing its $1 million portion of the golf course community center project—if the backers met their goal to raise $1.5 million. They were still short. The city would own the building and would be responsible for the road, cleaning, and other costs.

Now there was open rumbling, not only among the usual negatives but even some positives. Was the city being rosy-eyed on the true cost of the golf course project? Many felt it would far exceed $1 million. Why would a major hotel chain locate in such a small town? How many companies would choose to hold their conferences in Denison?

The city had limited shots, and a significant number of people thought the officials were firing wide. It was a city that had never before incurred debt by issuing bonds. There was a pay-as-you-go mentality, rooted in conservative farm culture. The state of Iowa authorized a city the size of Denison to carry as much as $9 million debt. With all the projects planned, the city would be about $1 million below this cap.

"Do we have too much debt?" asked city manager Al Roder. "We have prudent investment. We're not broke. If the interest rates were 9 or 10 percent, they would have an argument. But they are 2 and 3 percent." It makes sense to borrow when rates are low, he said. Nothing would get done if bonds weren't issued.

Meantime, more businesses in Uptown were closing. The owners of a television repair service and a shoe shop announced they were retiring, with no successors to purchase them. That meant two more empty shops and one more step to that desolate street scene in *The Last Picture Show*.

As events unfolded, Mayor Livingston convened biweekly meetings at Cronk's Cafe of the 2020 Executive Committee, comprising civic and business leaders, to discuss ways the 2020 Plan could be implemented. The gatherings had a sense of urgency. Their mission was nothing short of saving Denison. In one meeting, a member lamented that the town always seemed so defeatist.

"I hear people say we're just a blue-collar town," Ken said. "They don't strive for the best, just the good enough." He was baffled by this attitude.

"We should stop calling ourselves a blue-collar town," said Eric Skoog, the owner of Cronk's. "Rather, we should say we're a community of hard-working people."

Doug Skarin said doing Streetscape was vital. He dismissed critics who said it would not be a magic cure that would automatically increase business.

"But if the town is fixed up, it might get three or four people out of the car, walking around. If one comes to my building, looks in my window at what I have for sale, and comes stumbling through my door, it's up to me then. I don't expect the city to do my business." Doug added, "The truth is, we have pathetically little to market. We need to talk about that."

Another problem was burnout. In one meeting, the group discussed how it was the same thirty or so people who always volunteered. Doug said that for a committee of four people, two will come forward, and for the other two, "you have to get them liquored up to do it." In a later meeting, Doug also noted the talent pool was shallow in a small town. The wrong volunteer can be disastrous. "Guys, if you haven't seen some nodding heads, you haven't lived here!"

The ideas flew that fall in the meetings dominated by questions. Could the town remake itself into a city that would thrive in the complicated economy of the twenty-first century? Could it make the cultural diversity work? Committee members felt they had to do something. To even be neutral meant defeat—doing nothing guaranteed failure. Was this similar to the struggle of Henry Laub in the 1870s when he tried to pull the community together for sidewalks and the incorporation vote twelve decades earlier? No minutes of those meetings exist, but if not exactly walking in his shoes, these figurative sons of Laub were evoking his spirit.

"This is no small challenge," the mayor said at the end of one of these contentious meetings. He looked gravely at the faces of about a dozen men and two women in a conference room at Cronk's. "You're talking about the future of a community here. This is a behemoth monster you are dealing with."

*   *   *

A cold rain fell as I walked up Main Street at four o'clock one afternoon that Halloween season. I was on my way to meet city manager Al Roder. As I came upon a storefront two doors down from La Estrella, I noticed a woman standing in the window display area. I cocked my umbrella high enough to see the establishment's name: Joleen's Boutique. The woman couldn't see me, for her face was covered by a foot-wide strip of long brown paper that she was taping to the glass.

"GOING . . ."

My eyes fell to the remaining words on the eight-foot roll:

" . . . OUT OF BUSINESS."

I went inside. A Latin couple was looking at high-end women's clothing while the thin woman worked in the window. I introduced myself, but before I said much more, she spoke.

"Wal-Mart is the ruination of small-town America," said Joleen Grau, fifty-three. Joleen then talked with the customers. When they left, she tried to remain stoic, but her eyes wetted.

"It's very emotional. I know all my customers by name. It's personal. I deliver clothes to older folks. I break down so many times. I'm going to miss my customers. When you've done it for as many years as I have, you have everything into it. Here I am in midlife crisis. I don't want to go work for somebody else."

Joleen paused with a renewed welling of tears. She would hold a sale to sell out all stock. In a month, on November 30, it was over for her after seventeen years. Joleen's Boutique began in 1986.

"The first seven years, each year kept climbing. I put everything right back into it."

Joleen invested in more stock. She labored hard and studied fashion merchandising. She took classes in cosmetics, and after a long day in the store she'd make house calls until eleven o'clock at night to serve working women.

Then something changed.

"The last ten?" she asked about the previous decade of business. "Tough, tough, tough."

It started in 1991, when Wal-Mart opened. But Joleen recognizes that a combination of factors contributed to her hard times. Wal-Mart was not the entire reason, but a piece of the puzzle of her destruction.

"My customers don't want the same things they can buy at Wal-Mart," she said of how she adapted and stocked high-end clothes. Yet some of her business went to the big box down on the highway. She had to find another niche. She opened a new line of expensive baby clothes, for instance. "Grandmas want better quality."

A slow decline continued. Joleen ticked off other reasons. The farm economy was still shrinking. Demographics were an issue. Most Latinos shopped at Wal-Mart because of price, yet when they came in, they paid cash. The problem was she wasn't seeing a large number of Latino customers. It was a combination of bad luck: Wal-Mart, the loss of farmers, and the fact that some one-third or more of the city's population was suddenly not a significant customer base.

That wasn't all. In her early days, she saw many teachers, but as the 1990s dawned, that traffic slowed.

"Last Christmas, I was in the Hy-Vee, and I heard people who used to be my customers talking about going to Omaha to do their Christmas shopping. I was standing right there; they had to see me. That hurt."

The past few years, she was working on the narrowest of profit margins. "The real killer this past year was I had to put a new roof on."

And then the taxable value of Crawford County real estate skyrocketed. She was paying a third more in taxes, despite the city of Denison cutting back on its share of the take to soften the sting. It was a result of the artificial escalation of real estate prices across America because of low interest rates and a stock market mentality toward housing that seemed like fiction here. Coastal prices had infected the prairie. No matter that local property really was not worth more.

Joleen was not upbeat about Uptown. I asked about the plan to revitalize it. Her anger focused on Ken Livingston.

"I don't like our mayor," she said firmly through gritted teeth, but she said no more. "I'd better shut up about that."

Hers was a widespread feeling. Joleen didn't consider herself a negative but a realist. To Joleen, their mayor was crazy, foolishly spending tax dollars like a man suffering from prairie madness, leading them on a road to financial ruin.

LA MAESTRA II

Georgia Hollrah held up the cardboard cutout image of the *bruja*, witch, silhouetted against a yellow moon: the *bruja* rode a broom, wore a pointy black hat, and had a big wart on her nose.

"Is this a picture of a beautiful woman?"

"No!" the class of English learners replied in unison.

"No, it is not. She is very ugly."

Georgia wrote the word *witch* on the blackboard. She used other Halloween icons such as an orange cardboard jack o'lantern to teach words. Halloween, also celebrated in Latin America, was a good lesson tool.

"She is a witch, and she is riding a broom."

The class was asked to repeat words, and then each student had to repeat them at the six tables. At my table, we went around, and the students said them fairly accurately, but when Jesús's turn came, he stumbled.

"Why-yyych."

"Close," I said. "But it is 'witch.'"

"Why-yyych."

Jesús's mouth struggled to get around the word. Minutes before class had begun, he'd scrambled to finish his homework. Maria, his wife, had hers done. Across from the couple, Mina sat quietly with her completed homework set neatly on the table. I peered at it. There was just one error, amazing because she'd been in the United States only some three months. She'd written, "I no work." I told her there are two ways to say it; Georgia had taught the class about contractions the previous week.

As the clock ticked toward seven o'clock, Mina repeated, "I do not work. I don't work. I do not work. I don't . . ."

Mina was always days ahead in her workbook, with answers filled out in pencil with precisely executed letters. She was seeking work and in the meantime attended the morning ESL class held by the Lutheran missionary. On paper Mina was advancing rapidly. Yet in any real-world situation, she was terrified of speaking, and had trouble understanding, English. Even when I talked very slowly, using words she'd been learning in class, Mina often did not understand.

I could relate. Basically Mina was me when I had spent time in Mexico and points south. I knew a lot of words, and a bit about how to construct a sentence. But my adult brain's language center had atrophied to the size of a dried pea and didn't fire rapidly enough for me to communicate well. Being a guy and American, I forged on regardless, blundering and butchering the language. *Mi Español es muy mal, no?* Ha. Ha. Being a woman and Mexican, Mina wasn't going to blunder or bluster, no matter how much I gently prodded and told her it was okay to make mistakes.

"That is how you will learn," I often repeated. "Don't be shy."

One day when I ran into her shopping at the Hy-Vee Supermarket, she understood me talking in English, but replied in Spanish. I understood her Spanish, but replied mostly in English. Save for my male bluster that came out in mangled Spanish, we were equals.

"*Necisite practicar!*" I said in ungrammatical Spanish as we parted.

How to break through so she could make it to the next level? I didn't know the answer. When I went to Georgia to inquire, she did not either. I was beginning, in a very small way, to understand what Georgia had been going through for ten years. These were people who put in stunning effort to learn, but whose progress was slower than the proverbial advance of a glacier.

I was starting to comprehend Georgia's frustration, though she never exhibited it. I'd now been sitting in the thrice-weekly class for one month. My table had faithful attendees: Jesús and Maria, the two other Marias, Mina, Virgen. Jesús caused the most frustration, though I of course kept this hidden. He always sat to my right, and I worked with him more than any of the others.

Georgia put aside the cutouts of the witch and other icons, and the class started reading material about goblins. We English-speaking tutors then practiced with the students. When it came time for Jesús's turn, he absolutely crashed saying the word *ghost.*

"Gop-sst."

"*Es difícil, sí!*" I said. "But *otra vez,* try one more time. 'Ghost.'"

"Gop-sst."

I didn't want to make him feel bad, so after a few more attempts I gave up and went on to a new word. That night in the Shaw Mansion I wrote in my journal,

He absolutely could not get "ghost." He seems like he's never going to learn! It's frustrating.

The weeks passed as the nights grew colder. The class peaked at forty-five students, with far fewer when the weather was bad. Sometimes there were four other adult English-speaking volunteers, other times just one besides me. Georgia also used high school teens from her daytime Spanish class; she made it a requirement that they come a few times each term. But the high school students were often shy around the adult Spanish speakers, and their usefulness was limited. Georgia lamented that in the past few years, she'd lost the pool of ten or so faithful adult volunteers. That fall I was there, one woman in her seventies came most nights. I could see the class was vastly more effective when there was an adult at each table.

I wondered why Georgia didn't recruit new volunteers but learned she'd done this numerous times in the early years. How many times could one beg? She didn't want to come off as the town scold. There also was the disdainful reaction from a significant number of townspeople. No matter how much she reasoned or explained, their ears were closed. Her way of dealing was to shut herself off. It's one reason she didn't subscribe to the *Denison Bulletin & Review.* Readers could anonymously telephone and have their bleats transcribed on page two in a column called "Sound Off." Anti-Latino diatribes occasionally appeared. These would ruin not just her day but a week of her life. Why subject herself to such negativity?

One night I mused aloud to Georgia that it would be nice if some corporation or entity would at least donate supplies.

"I don't know if I want the help. I am so used to doing it with nothing."

Georgia was, however, a tremendously upbeat person, the ultimate positive. To preserve her attitude, she chose to pull into her own little private Iowa consisting of her family and church and teaching.

"It's my faith. I really, really rely on it. I tend to focus on the positive things and shut everything else out. It's all you can do."

If the day teaching was rewarding in a way akin to eating a good lunch, the night teaching was a three-course meal. This was because the students were so grateful. The joy of these nights was measured in increments. "Did you see! Marilou raised her hand tonight!" Georgia exclaimed after the students had all filed out. Or that so-and-so spoke a few words at all.

On the Richter Scale of an America that measured success by stock options gained, or the size of one's trophy home, or the tonnage of one's SUV, the needle for Georgia was not deviating much off centerline. For her, though, the microblip of Marilou moving forward was an 8.0 event. Georgia lived on a teacher's salary and in a home not much larger than a bungalow, but she was a rich woman. One could see this the night Francisco the baker gave her a pudding cake, or when Mina gave her a card and Georgia hugged her so hard that she lifted tiny Mina off the floor.

But the disappointments were profound. Halfway through the term, Jesús and Maria didn't show up one night. The chair to my right remained empty the next few classes. Then Mina told me that Jesús was too frustrated to continue, and the couple had dropped out. I was depressed. I wondered how Georgia felt, but I'd already learned not to talk with her about these defeats. They were just too personal.

* * *

Georgia wrote on the overhead projector,

1. We are looking at symbols.
2. We are practicing with special verbs.
3. We are reviewing the conversations.
4. We are listening.

It was now November 24, and there was black ice on the streets. Only a dozen students were present, the lowest turnout so far this year—but Mina, Virgen, and the two Marias were at my table.

Georgia held up a big cutout of a colorful turkey.

"What is this?"

"Turkey!" someone shouted.

"Who likes turkey?" Only one hand went up.

"Who likes it with *mole?*"

Most hands now shot up.

Georgia held up an image of a pumpkin.

"What is this?"

After the answer, she held up a cutout of a pie.

"This is pumpkin pie."

On the overhead, Georgia wrote:

Thanksgiving:

We give thanks to God. And to our families and friends.

Turkey	Pumpkin pie
Pumpkins	Pilgrims

Speaking in Spanish, Georgia explained about the Pilgrims: "They came to this new country, and they were ignorant of how to survive. The Indians helped the Pilgrims, and they gave thanks. They came for a new life here, and liberty. But it was different from the conquistadors in Mexico. The Indians were different than the Aztecs. There were no large cities here, they lived far apart. It was very, very different."

The class was keenly interested. There were many questions.

"Were they Spanish?" Juan Escobar, from El Salvador, asked.

"No, they were English. They were different from the Spanish. And the Indians were different from the Indians in the south."

"Different than the Maya?" someone asked.

"Yes. Very different."

That night, I took a small group of the better English speakers to a separate room for a more advanced lesson. In the group were Juan and Virgen and Antonio. They continued to pepper me with questions about Thanksgiving. They wondered where it happened. How far away? I drew a crude map. I depicted Boston and Plymouth Rock. Then I showed Iowa, Mexico, and Central America. And as I tried to explain it more deeply to these people hearing it for the first time, who had the blood of

Cortes and K'an Hok' Chitam and Moctezuma II, it sounded absolutely crazy to me.

The next night at the end of class, the exercise was for the students to write down in English what they would give thanks for on Thursday. The students read them. A very Indian-looking man with a ponytail who worked killing hogs raised his hand.

"I am thankful for my health. I am thankful for my job. I am thankful for my family. And I am thankful for my teacher."

*　*　*

Two nights later, I was at Georgia's house with twenty-some members of her and Kent's family. The kitchen bustled. There were three turkeys, a ham, ten casseroles (Iowa is casserole country, and there was the ubiquitous canned green beans smothered in white sauce), a diced potato and cheese dish, freshly cut celery, cranberry sauce, gelatin molds, four cheesecakes baked by Georgia and Kent's son-in-law, Mark, and pumpkin pie.

Mark is married to Beth, the couple's oldest daughter. She is a teacher, pregnant with their second child. Mark was about to become a pharmacist. Also present was Kent's sister Jane and her husband, Lance. They farm in Madison, Nebraska, and he also runs a seed store. It was the presence of Kent's father that dominated the eyes of the room. He had terminal cancer and did not have long. When he gave thanks for the meal, there was solemnity.

While all heads were bowed, I glanced up. These were Americans sent straight from central casting to represent a prototypical Iowa/Nebraska family. I thought of something Georgia told me about the 1980s, when Kent and his brother lost the farm, begun by their grandfather, during the farm crisis. The family didn't respond by imploding. They grew tighter. Among many cutbacks to save money, they canceled all magazine subscriptions. And then the couple faithfully made a weekly pilgrimage to the Norelius Community Library with their daughters to spend an evening reading; this continued even when they got back on their feet. They were strong because they were a family.

I ate seated across from Lance. Madison is also a meatpacking town. Jane had told me all the things their school system was doing to integrate Latinos. In Madison's high school, a Latino couple was crowned homecoming king and queen. It sounded as if Madison was a bit ahead of Denison, for its immigration wave had begun earlier. I wondered aloud about what I was seeing with immigration in the Midwest versus California. Perhaps religion played a role. I also wondered about religion in the Midwest versus the South, where one saw radical conservative evangelicals. Lance said people are just as religious in the Midwest, with the critical difference that "people aren't judgmental here. They might pray for someone, but they would not be judgmental."

He felt this helped attitudes toward Latinos. Even if some religious people harbored resentment, it was against the culture of the Great Plains to openly exhibit it.

But was this good or bad? I didn't know. Hidden resentments can erupt, as they did against the Germans in 1918.

* * *

St. Rose of Lima Catholic Church in Denison had a significant Latino membership, Catholicism being the predominant sect in Latino culture. There was a separate mass held in Spanish, Father Edward Murray said. And some twenty of one hundred students in the K-6 elementary school run by the church were Latino.

But the most outreach was being done by the Mission Board of Our Savior Lutheran Church, of which Georgia was a member. The church funded Pastor Bo Brink as a missionary; he also spent time to the north in Storm Lake, a town that also has a large immigrant population. Brink had previously been stationed for twenty years in Venezuela.

Our Savior also funded the Oficina Hispanica de Información on Broadway in Uptown. The office helped with translation, job searches, medical problems, and generally welcomed the newcomers.

At the quarterly meeting of the Mission Board that fall, eight people sat facing each other across a table. It was a white group with the exception of Pastor Bo, who is Latino. The first order of business was to discuss why they were still such a white group. Pastor Bo and Georgia headed the committee to diversify, and in her report Georgia said that a huge setback had been their loss of a man who worked at Farmland. Some white guys were harassing Latinos, Georgia said, and when he stood up for them, he was fired. The problem is finding someone fluent enough in English to help organize. Some Latinos would like to help, she added, but "it would be hard for many of the people who would want to, to be able to follow this conversation."

"We need this board to look more Hispanic," said Pastor Daniel Vogel, of Zion Lutheran Church in Manning. "If we keep it as our goal, it will happen, even if it takes ten years."

A budget report was passed around:

WESTERN IOWA MISSION COMMITTEE

Beginning balance as of 7/11/03	$606.42

Receipts

Cash donation from office (10-06-03)	100
Interest from checking (July, August, Sept)	.09
Our Savior donation (08-14-03)	200
Our Savior donation (09-23-03)	200
Lutheran Church extension fund withdraw (08-26-03)	500

TOTAL RECEIPTS	1,000.09
GRAND TOTAL	$1,606.51

The expenditures were then listed, including a part-time salary:

TOTAL EXPENDITURES	$1,506.79
Balance as of 10/10/03	$99.72

They were doing a lot with little. A local company had issued a challenge grant of $800. The board decided to hold a pancake dinner to raise funds.

"We'll sell $800 in pancakes," Mark Gray said, confidently.

"How do you say 'pancake' in Spanish?" someone asked Georgia.

"*Panqueque.*"

"Pan-Kay-Kay," a unison of voices responded.

Georgia then gave a report on her class.

"There are fifty to fifty-five enrolled. The largest turnout has been forty-five. We average thirty-five people a night."

One-third had continued from the previous year—the rest were new.

She lamented that there were so few adult volunteers. If there were more, she'd like to regularly break out the more advanced students in a separate room, so they could progress more rapidly. The meeting ended. Heads bowed as Pastor Vogel gave the closing prayer: "We thank you for bringing these nations to this nation. These folks you have brought to Denison, we hope that you bless their lives and let us continue to help them."

AN AMERICAN STORY II

Four companies were in line to bid on the city contract for gutting the mold-infested interior of the former *Der Denison Herold*. This was Phase II; Phase I had been "tuck pointing," or regrouting the exterior brick. Luis Navar's meeting with Mayor Ken Livingston had gone very well. If he got the job, he'd quit the beef packing plant.

Luis went to Nathan Mahrt for help. Nathan was adept at costing out construction projects, and he looked over the job. Luis was thinking of playing it safe, bidding low.

"I told Luis, 'This isn't Los Angeles where there are four other Hispanic companies bidding.' These guys are going to have to bring equipment over from Nebraska, and pay their guys fifteen dollars an hour. I told him they'll bid $20,000 minimum. You need to bid $15,000, and you'll get it."

A week later Luis told me he had slept on Nathan's advice.

"Yeah, that's what he says," Luis said of Nathan's telling him to bid $15,000. "But I need some work."

Luis was sick of toiling in the packing plant. He decided to go lowball to ensure he got the job.

Of the four companies, two had studied the dirty work involved and withdrew. It wasn't worth it to them for any price. One bid came in at $25,000. The bid by Bravo Construction, the company owned by Luis and named after his hometown city in Mexico, was for $9,000. Luis became the first Latino contractor ever to do any work for the city of Denison.

"I wonder how much these big companies make," Luis said, marveling at the other bid. "These companies, they don't care, everything inflates. A profit of five grand in three weeks, that's plenty I think. If you bid $20,000, you'd make $15,000. It is worth it to me."

The job went fast that November. I walked by the building as Luis's two main workers, Alfredo and Angel, hauled out rotting beams and crumbling sheetrock. Then one day I walked past and stuck my head in the open door. The interior was stripped clean.

"They said you must have good people working for you, because this thing, it's clean," Luis said of what he'd heard from Mayor Livingston and city manager Al Roder. "I told them I don't have workers. I have friends working with me. Alfredo, he came from California. He'd been working for me for five years in California. He get to this country just seven years ago. He does everything, from concrete to brick, A to Z. Now he's a maestro. He can teach me things. He is very expensive now. But he is worth it. And Angel, he's not afraid of work."

It was a good job for Luis, albeit not as profitable as it would have been had he listened to Nathan. He had proven himself. He quit the Tyson plant.

PART THREE

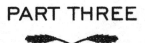

WINTER

WILLARD'S DIARY

PART I: THE NIGHT OF THE TEMPLETON RYE

AL CAPONE'S WHISKEY

The snow began in the afternoon. It stung exposed face flesh. Whiteout conditions existed on the Lincoln Highway. East of town, a truck driven by a Latino whipped around in circles and skidded off the road, stopped from rolling over only by a barbed wire fence halfway down an embankment. In town, cars spun out on streets rutted a half-foot deep with powder.

The phone rang at the writer's residence.

—It's in.

The caller invited the writer over that evening.

Months earlier, the caller had told the writer about Templeton rye. Templeton is a town twenty-four miles southeast of Denison straight as the prairie chicken flies. It had been a center of bootleg activity after Prohibition began on January 16, 1920, when the Eighteenth Amendment to the U.S. Constitution became law, banning alcoholic beverages. This was no rotgut white lightning. It was a special recipe based on rye, not corn mash. Templeton rye quickly gained a reputation as a fine product. Three trucks filled with kegs left Templeton per week, according to Lam Schwaller on the town's web site.

Al Capone was a customer, according to the web site, as well as Denison resident Harry Hass, age eighty-four, who used to swim in the water tanks for the Chicago, Milwaukee, St. Paul & Pacific Railroad in the nearby town of Manning. In the summers of 1931 and 1932 Harry and his swimming buddies watched over the rim of the tank as locals who sold to Capone filled Chicago-bound rail cars one-third full of corn, then put in a layer of whiskey barrels, which were covered with more corn.

Capone's speakeasies helped stave off foreclosure for many farmers-turned-bootleggers at the dawn of the Great Depression.

The Templeton web site implies that the bootleg era ended with the repeal of Prohibition. But Templeton rye is still being made in the region, using the same recipe handed down from father to son to grandson. The writer's source said it was easy for him to get.

—I can make a call, park my car over by city hall, and when I go out there, there will be a bottle in a plain brown bag on my back seat. It costs $25 for a quart.

The writer wanted some.

—I'd like a bottle.

As the months passed, the writer heard additional Templeton rye stories. Kate Swift said that in her youth, a man left a bottle in a bag on their doorstep every six months. People waxed on about its wonderful qualities. Some contemporary distillers gave it away for free to friends, a labor of love. There was great pride that it was of the exact quality that had been sold in the Al Capone era. It was a secret known to few outsiders, and the writer was eager to learn it. So it was with no small amount of anticipation that night that the writer pulled on rubber boots, bundled in storm clothes, and headed into the blizzard.

The source lived about a mile distant. The writer slogged on foot through the snowdrifts in Uptown, devoid of vehicles, into a residential neighborhood. As he walked, he realized that he'd been cocooned in a growing solitude that paralleled the plunging thermometer to below-zero depths the previous week in a winter of record snow. He had not set up any interviews. And until the source called, people had not been contacting him either. One woman explained that this was common to a Great Plains winter. People pulled inward when the weather grew this extreme. The writer quickened his pace. He had both socializing and Templeton rye waiting at the end of his snow march. He was glad when he spied the source's home, postholed through drifts to the front door.

The writer shed clothing. The source fetched a brown paper bag concealing a bottle.

—It came to me on another snowy night. I had put the word out. My source was at a party. He said come out to the truck with me. He's the direct source. With the other source, I had to go through three people. That stuff is twenty-five a bottle. This is free.

The writer insisted on paying, but the source said that was impossible. The distiller finds joy in making the whiskey, and gives it away in case he ever gets busted, the logic being that he could escape prosecution because there's no profit motive.

—His still is dismantled and put away. He brings it out and makes it for about one week each year, so it can't be traced.

The source pulled the bottle and held it to the light. Clear glass, no label. The whiskey was the hue of the lightest maple syrup. The source studied the bottle with loving eyes.

—It was a recipe that was handed down.

Another man, a prominent Denison citizen, was in the living room. The house's owner ceremoniously opened the bottle. The writer put his nose to the rim. A rich fragrance pleasured his sense of smell; it resembled an alcoholic cream soda. The source poured the 180 proof Templeton rye into three clear plastic cups to a depth of about one's pinkie finger.

—You will sip this for an hour.

The writer put the cup to his lips. It was strong, sure. Yet it was the smoothest whiskey he'd ever consumed. He could feel alcohol being absorbed by his throat before it struck his stomach. It left a taste that mimicked the odor.

The men sipped and had delightful conversation. Though the writer had been doubtful such a small bit of whiskey would last an hour, the source had been correct. By the time the hour had passed, the writer was toasted. But he didn't feel drunk. It was reminiscent of a marijuana buzz. He poured some more.

It was late. The writer donned his boots and coat, and with the bag containing the Templeton rye crooked under an arm, he headed back into the storm. It was what locals call a "twenty-four-hour snow," and the fury had not lessened. Nearly a foot of new snow had fallen since his arrival.

The writer thought of the snows of his youth as he moved slowly up the center of the road using a tire track left by a four-wheel drive. He heard the scraping of distant shovels. There was talk coming from the unseen shovelers, and occasional laughter rode the wind. When the wind shifted, all was quiet, the street locked in a hush. The writer was happy yet at the same time felt unsettled desolation.

In Uptown a man was hunkered over the door of La Estrella; the sound of a key turning the lock closed was sharp in the cold air. The writer recognized the man as the restaurant's manager.

—Miguel, you are working late!

—Hello! What is that you have there, my friend? Tequila?

—No, bootleg whiskey!

Miguel laughed as if the writer were joking.

A dozen steps later, the writer thought of offering Miguel a hit of the rye. He could then ply the manager for secrets to add to all those he'd already learned about the town. But Miguel was already backing his car out of the spot and, hell, it was snowing too hard. There also was a rush of futility. Perhaps truth was out of the writer's grasp.

CONCERNING THE NIGHT MAN II

The writer moved beyond the merchant district after seeing Miguel, reaching his house. He faced its door. Something about the night commanded that he not enter. Snow blew in sparkling plumes off the steep roof. He set the Templeton rye on the stoop and began shoveling the walk along Locust Street, a most insane act, for the snow was still falling, and even a slight breeze caused drifting. Fifteen minutes later, he looked back. The snow was already several inches deep where he'd started forty feet behind. At this rate—the house was on a corner—by the time he circled the dwelling by coming up the long drive and doing the back sidewalk, the blowing snow would have filled in the first excavation.

He continued shoveling.

This was the first sidewalk constructed due to the efforts of Henry Laub 129 years before. It led to the railroad depot in the valley bottom, the epicenter of life in those preautomobile days. The writer listened to the past. His cocked ear took in the voices of German immigrants trekking up the walkway to Jesse Denison's land office, speaking excitedly in their hard tongue about this new land at the end of their long journey. His vision took in what existed before Jesse Denison, captured in a block-long mural on Dick Knowles's building next to the Hy-Vee on Broadway, depicting the view from just above this very spot: two Sioux men on horseback overlooking the vast treeless grassland of the Boyer Valley.

The writer reached the corner of Chestnut Street. A half-hour had passed. He was cold. Something told him to remain at work. He dismissed this urge to the lingering effects of the Templeton rye; he moved up the walk to go inside.

No, a voice said. He returned to the unscooped snow. *Keep shoveling.*

He cleaned the Chestnut Street walkway, stopping often to stare—at nothing. He was lost now in the white dream of the night. As the pioneers said of winter prairie evenings, according to a story written by Leslie Shaw, "Sometimes we sit around the fire and think. And sometimes we just sit around the fire." Not a single vehicle had journeyed on either street, and not a single light burned in the pane of any house within sight. There were just the street lamps and the snow swirling against their halos, the stark limbs of trees bearing burdens, and the sound of the aluminum against concrete. He became mesmerized by the rhythm of throwing each shovel's load. Reaching the end of the sidewalk, he was now at the long driveway, which he started scooping. Again he halted to consider the warmth of the house.

Keep shoveling.

He was bone-cold, and his arms were tiring. Perhaps an hour had passed since he'd set the bottle on the stoop. He didn't have a timepiece but reckoned it was midnight.

Between scrapes, the writer heard a faint whir. He wrote it off to his imagination. It resumed. The writer went down the drive to investigate. Up the block he discerned movement over the roof of a parked car. Stepping out from where the curb was submerged in white, he saw that it was the night man. His chair was bogged in a drift. The night man was pushing buttons, but the chair wouldn't move.

—You okay?

—I don't think so.

The writer was mindful not to condescend. Years earlier, after being rebuffed by the blind and others with infirmities, he'd learned to be cautious about offering assistance. So he now addressed the night man with forced lightness.

—You need some help?

—Yeah. Uh, maybe a little.

—You heading up this way?

—No, I live that way.

The night man pointed down Chestnut Street.

—I'll push you.

—I live too far. If you could just help a little bit of the way.

—I'll get you home, man.

—No, it's too far! Just a little way, that would really help.

The motorized wheelchair wasn't meant for manual operation. There was no place for the writer to securely grip the device. The night man threw the arm rests back, and they protruded like skyward-pointing arms at a two o'clock angle. The writer gripped these, but when he pushed too hard, they flew upright. There was still enough power remaining in the batteries, however, so that the force of the writer's careful thrust combined with that of the wheels was able to move the chair.

—I think my battery is low.

—We'll get there.

—It's a long way. I really appreciate this.

—It's no problem.

The night man wore a medium-weight jacket and a heavy pullover logger's cap. But no matter what he had on, he would be cold. The actual temperature was now zero degrees Fahrenheit. The wind chill? Ten or twenty below? Why was he out on such a bitter night? The writer knew. But he had to ask.

—Where you coming from?

The night man mumbled something indiscernible. The writer knew he'd come from nowhere. It's likely he'd been outside for quite some time, inching along. An outsider might consider his being out that night an act of supreme stupidity. But the night man had no choice. For months, the writer had been wondering how to approach the night man. And now here was his opportunity to learn his story.

—Where do you live?

—My mom's. And my dad's.

The night man volunteered that he'd like to rent his own place. Rents had risen here, as they had nationwide during the boom times, even though Denison was hardly riding the escalator of prosperity. It was difficult for him to find an apartment that he could afford on his government disability payment.

—Why'd the rents go up so much here?

—Greed.

The nation was wealthy, or so went the official line from Washington. The recovery was underway and all was well, the *Wall Street Journal* told the writer a few days previous when he'd purchased the paper at the Hy-Vee.

They moved through the first intersection.

—You like it here?

—Yeah.

—Think you'll ever move away?

—No! I don't think I'd like a big city.

The chair moved forward a few feet.

—Even though I know it would probably be better for me.

—I see you in the library a lot.

—Yeah.

—It's nice they have those computers.

—Oh, I wish I could have my own computer at home!

—You can't afford one?

—No. They're so expensive. My mom works at McDonald's. She's a cook. My dad works over in Carroll. He drives a truck. Oh! I'd like to work. I fill out applications. They never say why, but they never hire me.

The writer suddenly was overcome by guilt. Why was he questioning the night man? He had long desired his story. But now that they were in forced company, it was wrong to have it. For once, he had a useful purpose in town. His job tonight was to get the night man home—no more, no less. The writer ceased inquiry.

They'd come one city block. The course had been slightly downhill. It was also made easier by the passage of a few vehicles hours before that had somewhat packed the snow. Now a long upgrade lay before them, and no vehicles had driven this section of Chestnut Street. The snow was much deeper, and the motor was not assisting as much as it once had. The wheels were bogging, despite the writer's straining and the night man using his arms to push on them. The chair's arms repeatedly jumped up. The writer sweated profusely; Templeton rye exuded from his pores.

—My low-battery light just came on.

The writer stepped ahead of the chair and used his feet to kick a path for ten feet. He then pushed the night man this distance, repeated the process. The upgrade became Everest. The night man also struggled, using his upper-body strength to jostle the wheels and rock the chair when it became stuck.

—I owe you.

—Nah. We're gonna get there.

A few more feet. The writer was in front, kicking away snow.

—I really appreciate this. I'd have been out here all night.

—Someone would have stopped.

The night man laughed a sad laugh, a laugh peculiar to this era in America. The writer had heard it a lot in the previous two decades in response to questions when he talked to working-class people; it was a laugh not of cynicism but of defeat.

—It's a small town. People aren't friendly?

Again came the laugh.

—A lot less friendly than you would think.

The men fell silent as the process repeated ceaselessly, the writer kicking snow, pushing, kicking, pushing. The writer now had to pause because he was out of breath. As he rested, he stared at the darkened homes and wondered about the lives behind the doors. He thought of James Joyce's first published book, *Dubliners*, a story from this work, "The Dead," about a husband and wife, Gabriel and Gretta, and the shattered truth of their long married lives, discovered by Gabriel after a family holiday party. The story ends with Gabriel staring at the shell of his sleeping wife on their bed, a woman he realized he really did not know, and then his gazing out the window at the falling snow. Joyce wrote,

> His soul had approached that region where dwell the vast hosts of the dead. He was conscious of, but could not apprehend, their wayward and flickering existence. His own identity was fading out into a grey

impalpable world: the solid world itself which these dead had one time reared and lived in was dissolving and dwindling.

And the snow fell all over Ireland, on the bogs and waves, churchyards and graves:

It lay thickly drifted on the crooked crosses and headstones. . . . His soul swooned slowly as he heard the snow falling faintly through the universe and faintly falling, like the descent of their last end, upon all the living and the dead.

The writer thought of lost loves, one from the recent past who now had three simultaneous lovers on the distant coast. He was not sad or jealous. The writer thought of the country woman to the east lying on her bed, her wants and those of others he knew in town, all the Gabriels and Grettas who clung in asexual desperation in their beds behind the doors, others asleep in the same bed but as far opposite as possible, as solitary as both he and the night man were now. Not far away were homes belonging to couples of which he'd heard gossip—tales of frigidity and loathing, affairs that had been bandaged leading to a never-healed semblance of what once existed. These exposed secrets were the same everywhere, and the writer saw no truth in them. They were simply more visible in a small town. The only difference from the big city is that the couples could not live their false lives anonymously.

He thought of Kate Swift. The last time they had met, they were walking through Uptown. Ms. Swift remarked that, to her surprise, the drugstore filled a prescription that was a month out of date. The writer inquired what had been filled.

—Well, now that you asked, it was my birth control pills.

She looked at the writer with want.

—You put the bait in the water, and see if the fish bites.

The fish didn't bite. Once again the confused Ms. Swift went home alone. An acquaintance in New York City, a man much younger, was incredulous that the writer had not run home with a willing, attractive woman. It was impossible to explain. Kate Swift was very nice, but the writer did not desire a Gretta.

And the snow continued falling. It accumulated on the shoulders of the two men, on the roofs covering the dead in their bedrooms around them, the distant granite mausoleum holding the disconsolate bones of Leslie Shaw. The town was dead. The country was dead. Few here understood the dead; Nathan Mahrt certainly did. And, the writer suspected, so did the night man. The writer's gaze fell on the night man, whose coat and hat had whitened considerably. The night man must have known somehow that he was at the end, for at the start of the following winter, at the age of twenty-eight, he would be dead, after falling ill from pneumonia; he went to bed one night, and his body was discovered in the morning. The writer would later believe the night man had given up, would have been happy not to have been discovered the night of the blizzard and have perished in the snowdrift.

All that was in the future. For now, their eyes locked. Sweat beaded on the night man's forehead from his struggling to help.

—I owe you.

—No you don't.

Blocks remained. They were not going to make it with the system they were using. The writer spied a snow shovel leaning against the porch of a home that belonged to a Latino family. The writer used the borrowed tool to scoop a narrow path in the two-foot-deep drifts. He'd dig the length of a motor vehicle, push the chair, dig the next section. Progress was now faster.

The night man pointed to his distant but finally visible house. Both men now worked in silence. The last fifteen minutes were ones of extreme concentration. The newly shoveled route reached the tiny home. The writer opened the storm door. The night man wheeled in. Nearly two hours had passed since the start of their journey.

—I owe you.

—No, I owe you.

The writer closed the door and hurried away, replacing the shovel on the porch of its owner.

PART II: LUST, LOVE, MONEY, CRIME

NAKED PIONEERS AND COPULATING STALLIONS

The writer was in Denison City Hall studying the first laws written in 1875, the year of incorporation. A quill pen had been used to record codes in elaborate handwriting. Some actions must have upset the social order that November, for these ordinances were entered in the early pages ahead of numerous other offenses.

> Whosoever shall willfully appear in any street or other open or exposed place, or before any assembly of people in a state of nudity, or make a lewd exposure of his or person, or exhibit, sell or offer to see any lewd picture, lewd book, or lewd representation, or utter in any street or other public place, or in the hearing of any family or assembly of people, any indecent language shall be deemed guilty of a misdemeanor.

> Whoever shall willfully let a stallion to a mare or a jack to a mare or jenny; or a bull to a cow in any street or other exposed place shall be deemed guilty of a misdemeanor.

Maximum fine for being naked in Denison:	$100
Maximum fine for an amorous stallion:	$30
Maximum fine for being drunk in public:	$10

The nudity law was still on the books 125 years later when two male workers showed up at the home of a man prominent in town to conduct some business. One of these workers told the writer that the man's wife answered the door. She was buck naked. One of the startled men stated the obvious.

—Uh, Mrs.———, you don't have any clothes on!

—It's okay. C'mon in.

BOOK 'EM DANO

The bar has a small sign with a palm tree on it, above a plain door. The writer thought it was just another of the ten taverns in the town of a dozen churches. (Denison is about one-third Catholic, one-third Lutheran, and the rest other denominations.) But Book 'Em Dano, just down the street from the Donna Reed Foundation, is a topless establishment.

One night the writer opened the door and descended dark stairs to a dim chamber. Men sat at a bar and tables. At the rear seated in a chair was, by appearance, a typical Iowa housewife: fortyish, a bit overweight, round-faced from too much corn-fed pork. The housewife smiled with anticipation. Before her stood a thin blonde, naked save for thong underwear; the dancer rubbed her own body seductively, mounted the chair, and performed a grinding lap dance on the housewife while smothering the face of the seated woman with her breasts.

When done, the dancer hugged the woman, whose hands wantingly clutched the bare buttocks of the worker, who had a flower tattoo on the small of her back. Money exchanged hands, and the housewife went up the stairs to the exit. Behind the pool table, a marker board announced:

DANCING TONIGHT
TOY
ANNIE
SAMMI

There was a big-boned black woman, with glow-in-the-dark green nails and large breasts, who was in the lap of a drunk customer near the dance run, which had one chromed steel pole, a mirror on its ceiling, and a rim of red lights. The other dancer was a dark-haired white woman whose breasts sagged. The customers were an even mix of Latino and white and one large black man. None were recognizable to the writer.

The sag-breasted woman now danced at the pole, watched by a twentyish bearded Latino man wearing a blue bandanna tied pirate style. He was seated at the stage edge, a mix of fear and want in his eyes. Perhaps he hadn't aspired to be here, but he was a single man far from home, with desires that couldn't be fulfilled by women here from his culture—most

Latinas were claimed and pregnant by their late teens—and what were his odds of getting a white woman? So he paid the black woman for a lap dance and stroked her thighs; he paid the blonde and stroked hers. He then retired to a booth and sat, looking sad.

The black woman pranced. No one else was buying a lap dance. She punched the jukebox.

—A cheap crowd!

She went to the bar and put on her clothes.

—It's cold! Turn up the heat!

The barmaid sneered.

—If you worked harder, you wouldn't need the damn heat.

No one turned up the heat.

The black woman sighed. She stripped and climbed the stage, shouted as she grabbed the pole.

—I want to play the pussy song!

Men at the bar yelled encouragement.

—The pussy song by Missy Elliott! Lick pussy, because I don't want dick tonight!

CONCERNING THE TATER-TOT CASSEROLE BOY

On weekday afternoons, the writer was at the Norelius Community Library, studying microfilm reels of old newspapers until he was dizzy. Or he sat at one of seven public computers to use the Internet. One day he sat at Computer Number 5, aware of a patron seated behind at Computer Number 4, talking on a cellular phone. The man was in his mid-twenties, with a goatee, and generally plain looking. He was nervous, tapping the keyboard loudly, talking with a woman with whom he'd been communicating via email over an Internet dating service.

—Me? I'm hoping to get my racing car going again.

Her voice was audible but too faint to understand. The young man hummed nervously as she talked.

Doodoo de da doo, doodoo de da doo . . .

—Uh, I prefer a home-cooked meal. I don't like eating out.

Doodoo de da doo, doodoo de da doo . . .

—Oh! But if I eat out, I really, really like Arby's. Arby's is my favorite.

Doodoo de da doo, doodoo de da doo ...

—I don't get out much. I sit around a lot, play video games. I'm going for a second job. The Kum & Go here in Denison.

Doodoo de da doo, doodoo de da doo ...

—Obviously, racing in my car is my favorite thing to do. Uh, let me see. One of the other things I like to do is I like to go out and dance once in a while.

Doodoo de da doo, doodoo de da doo ...

—Oh yes! I love to cook. Other than racing in my car, that's my next favorite hobby. I make some absolutely great casseroles. One of my favorites is a tater-tot casserole. Oh, it's just amazing!

Doodoo de da doo, doodoo de da doo ...

—I'm one of the bored people obviously. Ha. Ha. I'm going back to my email. Then playing with my video games.

He now stopped humming while she talked; he simply tapped at the keys.

—Believe me, I've met some pretty interesting people! I've heard it all.

Tap. Tap. Tap.

—Wow. I haven't heard that one yet. I've not been that unlucky.

Tap. Tap. Tap.

—I've got two kids. A lot of people don't believe me for having two kids.

Tap. Tap. Tap.

—I'm all right with treating women all right. I've only been dating since I was seventeen. I've been okay with the dating scene. I've just made some bad choices with women. Oh, to tell you the truth, I was never good with the dating scene. Women obviously see something in me. A lot of girls just dated me to get me in the sack. Don't get me wrong, that was okay. But after a while it just got kind of boring.

Tap. Tap. Tap.

—Yeah, I used to have women like that. My second son's mother. I told her you just want to keep hanging on me. It turned out that things didn't work out. And, *woohoo!* Here I am.

Tap. Tap. Tap.

—Ah, you're getting me to blush!

Tap. Tap.

—Everything, except for opera and classical. I listen to anything.

Tap.

—Yeah, I grew up on that stuff!

Tap. Tap. Tap.

—Unfortunately, this town ain't the greatest. It's quiet. That's all I am giving it. It's a normal quiet town. Once in a while we get our shake-ups in this town. The biggest thing is when someone gets pulled over for speeding. Or brushfires.

Tap. Tap. Tap.

—Any idiots? Oh, just myself and my mom. Ha. Ha.

Tap. Tap. Tap.

—I'm actually thinking about getting another dog. A basset hound. I love them. I also would get a pug. I love them, too. Those dogs are cute.

Tap. Tap. Tap.

—Oh, I don't want to. I'd rather have someone to go with. Somebody to snuggle up with at the movies. Somebody like you, I think. That would be if you want to go. If you'd actually like to go, I'd travel anywhere.

Tap.

—That would be awesome! That's a movie I'd like to go see. Great!

The young man wrote directions on a paper scrap, and again hummed, eager for his Friday date.

LOVE ACROSS LINES

The writer talked to the first of three of Larry Peterson's American Heritage classes at the high school. He asked students about interracial mixing in the dating scene. Few kids wanted to publicly discuss this. After the class, three white farmboy types with short-cropped hair came up to him to talk about the Latinas.

—We'd like to go out with them.

—Some of them are real cute!

—But they won't go out with us.

—Do they hate us?

In the second class, a Latina explained to the writer why Latinas didn't date white boys.

—We talk about them, say, "Isn't that guy cute!" But they don't dance to the music we like. And a lot of the girls feel they don't speak good enough English and are shy about this. It isn't that we don't like white guys!

She added that her Latino boyfriend would not be happy to hear any of this.

—He said if I went out with a white guy, he'd kill me.

Several weeks later the writer ran into the three farmboy types.

—Listen, dudes, I've got the answer.

The writer related his discovery about dancing and language; if they tried their music or learned just a bit of Spanish, they might score. The young men suddenly seemed disinterested. It sounded like too much heavy lifting.

A very few white girls dated Latinos in high school. A Latina explained that the school, like so many others, was broken down into preppies, goths, and loners in the white crowd. There were two kinds of Latinos and Latinas: those acculturated (which meant they spoke good English and had good grades) and those who had trouble with the language and got bad grades.

The preppie white girls were not the ones dating Latinos, she said, save for one.

—We went on a field trip, and they sat together on the bus, and they got a lot of shit.

Class lines were involved as much as race. It was the same in the adult world. The town's elite white women did not date Latinos, but some blue-collar ones did. An Uptown white woman explained it was usually a certain kind of woman.

—They are, how do you say, . . . different.

Translation: not very attractive.

One meeting place was the Latino Night Club, a sprawling dance floor beneath the Topko Drug building that pulled in 150 people on weekend nights to throbbing techno and Mexican music spun by dj's. It was the most "happening" scene. One night the writer counted five white women, two in pairs and one alone, who had come to dance and meet Latinos. No white men, the writer excepted, were present.

The white bar scene centered around two establishments: The Pub near the East Boyer River and Prime Times in Uptown. The Pub's lounge patrons were largely twentyish, while Prime Times drew an older crowd. An occasional Latino would show up at The Pub, but the writer never saw any Latinos at Prime Times, and certainly no mixed couples at either establishment.

At Prime Times, the women, in their forties, felt compelled to joke about being lesbians when they tried to pick up on men. But the pickings were slim. The regulars included a pronounced town asshole. One night, the pronounced town asshole talked about getting some action, but he wasn't referring to any of the faux lesbians around him as he shouted to the writer.

—I'm going over to Book 'Ems! Let's go get some titty in our faces! Put our faces in there between them like this.

He slapped his cheeks with his hands, whooped, and roared with laughter.

CONCERNING THE BANKER

A bungalow or a condominium would sell for $300,000 or $400,000 or a lot more in many coastal cities. A small but fine home could be had in older Denison neighborhoods for $40,000 to $60,000, and a modern Fort Purdy suburban tract went for a little over $100,000. A buyer who went ten miles out to one of the dying small towns could pick up a good little house for $20,000 or $30,000. These prices were drawing some people from the coasts.

On the white end, the writer met a high school girl whose father was disabled and whose mother was a social worker; they'd moved here from San Francisco because it had gotten too expensive there. There was a family whose children had gone to Columbine High School in Colorado and who had moved here after the rampage. Another white family came from California; they'd sold their house for big bucks and were flashing it, buying up real estate and causing local tongues to wag because many felt they were acting like fifty cent millionaires.

On the Latino side, just about everyone the writer met came from California if they hadn't come directly from south of the border. Typical was the family who opened a new market, Tienda Mexicana La Jaliscience II, in an empty Hardees on the Lincoln Highway. Some called it "El Hardees" because the sign remained over the rented store. The parents had decided to flee Los Angeles, fearing gang influence on their children, and they'd just purchased a trailer on the edge of town. They *owned* it and were proud. And they were happy with the Denison schools. Their daughter had gone from a D to an A in math in her first term.

One day the writer went to the manager of one of the six banks in town. In the previous month, this banker's firm had granted twenty-eight loans. Twenty were to whites, seven to Latinos, and one to a Laotian family.

—The Hispanics are different than whites. They most often take loans of ten to fifteen years. They do not want thirty-year loans, and they ask about the APY box, which is the annualized rate. The whites don't ask about that. Hispanic, it's a fiscally conservative culture. Some come in and pay $200 per week. They want to pay their houses off fast. It's not uncommon that they pay off early. They are very proud of owning a piece of property. They're not comfortable with a big loan. Often families will pool resources. You'll see two families in a house. One will buy food, the other will pay the mortgage. They do take care of each other. One thing they have that whites don't have is day care. The grandmother takes care of the kids so both parents can work. They aren't paying a hundred a week for that. The family is very strong.

The banker noted that there is an equal default rate between Latinos and whites.

—Even when people go back to Mexico, the payments are made. Others make them.

CONCERNING THE PROSECUTOR

The police chief told the writer that in his twenty-three years on the job, there had been three murders in Denison. One involved a dispute between two men: one went into a bar and blasted his opponent with a shotgun. Then a mentally ill woman killed her baby. The most recent had just occurred: a Latino, distraught over his girlfriend's ending their relationship, shot the woman to death in the Farmland employee parking lot.

—Your chances of being murdered here are pretty slim. They were all acquaintance murders.

There had been two armed robberies, one of them at the Kum & Go convenience store. The officers solved that one rapidly: they followed the culprits' footprints in the snow, which led them to Book 'Em Dano and the robbers.

Some whites talked fearfully about Latinos and crime, pointing to the police log in the newspaper that often contained many Latino names. They talked about the four Latinos who robbed the U.S. Bank in Norfolk, Nebraska, in 2002, killing five people. The crime sent reverberations throughout the Midwest.

The man who prosecutes all crimes in Crawford County said that in any given year, he will handle some four hundred cases. About half are traffic related, mostly drunken driving and driving without a license. A third are property offenses—burglary, theft, bad checks. The remainder are drug crimes or assaults—bar fights, domestics, and so forth.

Six years earlier, not many Latinos were prosecuted. Now they comprise half of all cases. This didn't surprise the prosecutor, because they were likely about half of the community now. He said it's a blue-collar town, and white or Latino, the crimes were similar.

—It's not that Hispanics are worse. The influx is working class, with the problems of the working class. Plus some things that are uniquely Hispanic. A lot of it is cultural.

In Latin America, drunken driving is not enforced, and new arrivals are surprised when they are stopped. In addition, fights are not viewed as breaking the law.

—Things we call assaults are not seen as assaults. You work your differences out on your own. How law enforcement works is different in Mexico. Who really are the bad guys? People who are here are suspicious of law enforcement.

His biggest problem, when a Latino is busted, is figuring out his or her true identity.

—There are lots of fake IDs. There's cursory perusal at the plants. We've never gotten one call from the plants saying, "We've got someone we believe isn't who they say they are." I've seen I-9 forms where the person wrote a social security number on the form that was different than what was on their card. I understand they work hard. I understand what the plants do.

145

OPPOSITION

Dick Knowles, the seventy-seven-year-old retired publisher of the *Denison Bulletin & Review,* was often not referred to by name, but as "our adversary" by Mayor Ken Livingston. If Ken were for something, he felt Dick was automatically against it. In Ken's view, Dick was the enemy, the über negative. If Denison were a western movie, those in city hall wore white hats, while Dick rode into town on a black horse, a black Stetson on his head.

"Negativity? I would challenge you to find a town they would be happy in," said city manager Al Roder of the "negatives" he's seen in a number of Midwest cities where he has worked. "It's easy to complain. But where were you on Election Day? Or at the meetings for public input? I'm not picking on Denison. That is America. People are used to complaining. I have to put on a thick skin. Every town I've worked in has had a Dick Knowles. One difference is that in other places, they're not as smart as he is. He knows what he's doing. That's what bothers me. It seems to be pure maliciousness."

If a popularity contest were held, Dick would not win among a broad spectrum of people, largely from his days running the paper. He had raked a lot of muck. Yet he had a loyal base of followers. One city official called these fans the "Dickheads."

But Dick was a positive by one definition: he ran monthly meetings of the city's Cultural Diversity Committee, where he often announced, "I'm impatient," with regard to the Latinos' being integrated: he wanted the evolution to happen faster. For example, to encourage home buying, Dick had set up a meeting at a church to explain a program of low-interest loans. Dick walked a trailer court where many Latinos lived, handing out fliers. But only two people came to the meeting.

Dick opposed Streetscape. He maintained it didn't cost out and that it was sending the city toward financial ruin. Some building owners were upset with an estimated average $38 per linear frontage foot assessment for sidewalks. The *Denison Bulletin & Review* had published a straw poll ballot for citizens to give their opinions; on January 27, the newspaper ran the results, saying 91 percent of the 144 respondents were against the project. (Left unmentioned was that the poll was anything but scientific; one person could have submitted thirty replies.)

Two days later, the city held a public forum to discuss Streetscape. The stated purpose was to listen to residents, but in reality the mayor and his staff wanted to stem the tide of opposition. Dick showed up first. He signed the registry for those who wished to speak. It was a bitterly cold afternoon, but citizens poured in, forty, then fifty—at the end, some seventy people. The meeting opened at 5:15 P.M.

"Our position here is to listen and keep an open mind," Ken said. He called on the first of the public to speak.

Dick was in the front row, to the left of the officials seated at a long desk. He stood, his posture directed more at the citizens—his real audience—than the council.

Dick shot questions in rapid succession. Could the council explain the benefits of the project? Did members know that beleaguered businesses could not pay for the sidewalk assessments via sales? Why was the city narrowing the streets? What about trucks making deliveries? Where would they park?

"The city of Denison has failed to show that widening sidewalks and narrowing the streets will have any effect."

Dick talked more than the five minutes allotted. He ended by saying the process had been essentially a sham, with no public input, no public meetings, until this month.

"Does council have any comment to make to Mr. Knowles?" Ken asked.

Stony faces. No one was touching this one.

Ken announced that he had a few things to say.

"There have been numerous public meetings. There were meetings beginning in January of 2002."

Ken, whose eyes were locked on those of Dick, still standing, added that there were many 2020 committee meetings and a lot of public input.

"And I went and passed out fliers. And when they weren't there, I put them under doors. There was discussion in heavily advertised meetings that were woefully underattended. It just *interests* me to no end that you say we didn't put anything out about this 'til this January."

"Your honor!" Dick loudly interjected, violating the rules of order. Dick disputed Ken's account and said he was not at any of the public meetings. Ken countered that Dick had been at one of the meetings.

"I looked at you!"

"You'll have to prove that to me!"

"I made the statement at that meeting that we are a pretty conservative community, and we're going to have to pay as we go."

Dick again repeated he was not at the meeting.

"Sir, you were in the planning meeting."

"Not true! I want to see the minutes!"

Ken now ruled Dick out of order, saying others had signed the list to speak.

"The taxpayers want to be heard!" a woman shouted, also out of order. The meeting was growing to feel more like a western film, with the crowd playing the role of lynch mob.

Councilman Earl McCollough spoke.

"I've been here since 1947," McCollough said. "Our Uptown is fading fast! Oh, I remember what it used to be like. Things have changed. We aren't the same. On Saturday nights, this town was full! You couldn't walk down the sidewalk. It's been a long time since it's been that way."

He thought the community was behind the 2020 Plan, given the results of the long effort of study. The octogenarian councilman's words seemed to calm the crowd. There followed an hour and a half of citizens talking. The sentiments were mixed.

On Dick's side, there were impassioned statements.

"I'm taxed out. I don't know if I can afford it!" said one building owner.

"Hey, my pockets are empty, and I'm bleedin'!" said an older man.

Another man said taxes on his building went up $1,200.

"That's hard to push off on my renters. They're having a hard time, barely getting by now." The assessments, he asserted, would cause him to raise his rent.

On the mayor's side, several building owners made ardent comments. Attorney Michael Mundt, who owned the century-old former Montgomery Ward building, said his assessments would cost $23,000, and he would gladly pay it.

"If we don't do this, ladies and gentlemen, we might as well turn out the lights on Uptown Denison. Is there a guarantee? No. But if we don't do it, it's going down the chute. I don't like paying taxes. But what about community pride? The Uptown, in my opinion, looks ugly. If we do things, people will want to come. Otherwise it's a slow slide to oblivion."

The entire time, Dick glared at Ken, and when Ken spoke to someone else's question, he often glared back at Dick. When the meeting ended, the two men were still staring each other down.

LIFE IN A SMALL TOWN

THE MAYOR

A cheap description after studying a photograph of the mayor would be "grandfatherly." Ken Livingston, with his sparse white hair and balding dome, seemed older than sixty-four, his age; his was a fragile appearance. But this was merely a shell.

He was retired, and society's norms dictated that he be winding down. But Ken defied this. He put in sixty-hour weeks for the part-time job that paid $111 pretax dollars per week. During meetings, he had to restrain himself and twitched while waiting for others to finish speaking. He came at the job with a big-city sense of humor and a big-city sense of business. He had big ideas. He intended to accomplish big things.

In other words, he was the very un-Iowa mayor of a small Iowa city.

Ken was without peer as the most controversial and talked-about man in Denison, even with Dick Knowles in town. He prompted utterances from the mouths of religious Iowans not otherwise prone to fouling their language.

"That son of a bitch."

"I hope he has a heart attack."

"He'll mess things up and then leave town."

Most, however, harrumphed and acted like typical Iowans when asked about Ken. All they'd reveal was a grimace or a throaty exhalation that came out sounding like a sizzle.

At least one negative went beyond invective and grimace and sizzle. On three occasions, someone had salted the mayor's driveway with razor-edged chunks of metal intended to puncture his car's tires. There was never a note. Ken told the chief of police, but didn't go public for fear of encouraging the culprit, or others. Ken was undaunted, save for worrying about his nephew who mowed the lawn being hurt by flying metal.

The positives felt warmly toward Ken. But how many were there? One measure came in the 2003 election, when 332 out of 3,995 registered voters—or 8 percent—went to the polls, and 273 of them cast a ballot for the mayor who was unopposed, as were two council candidates. How many negatives remained home rather than partake in this coronation? Whatever the size of either camp—amid a majority of citizens who were apathetic—in a town of 7,339 persons it was difficult not to be overwhelmed by the sentiment of the anti-Ken crowd.

Why did a man who generated so much enmity remain unchallenged? The only people with any desire to seek the office were business owners. If they ran and won—even if they did absolutely nothing, as had a string of mayors—it wouldn't matter. They'd still make enemies by default, and thus lose sales. This had happened to the others. No one could afford to be mayor in an economic climate where customers were scarce, overhead high, and the profit margin as narrow as a blade of young prairie grass.

The hatred toward Ken was a story larger than the man himself, and it was at the root of why Denison was in trouble as the second millennium began. The town had been on a long downward drift because no one had taken charge to halt the decline. It was now a monumental task to do anything, and anyone who attempted was guaranteed to upset a lot of people.

At the root of the anger were the tax dollars required to change Denison. While national economic statistics told of a country doing well, Denison was like everywhere else: only a tiny percentage in the top tier flourished. The majority in the middle and upper-middle classes were doing worse and had less real income. I discovered that many of the town's white elite were struggling. Business was down. And the packing plant workers were just surviving. Health care and other costs were going up. This occurred amid a top-down starvation from the federal government. For the first time in modern history, the feds didn't help states during the recession that had allegedly just ended. The states in turn put the screws to the counties and cities.

Just when Denison needed the most help, it was the worst climate in which to attempt resurrection.

Along came Ken, who wanted to try. On his office wall were words, on parchment in a frame, that advised him daily:

IS THIS IN THE BEST INTERESTS
OF THE CITIZENS OF DENISON?

I wondered what motivated him. I had a glimpse one night early that winter. Ken had spent the day fund-raising for the child care center, among other work. That evening there was a meeting at the Donna Reed Theater for Streetscape. But the most important part of his twelve-hour day was yet to come. At seven o'clock, when the meeting wrapped, the mayor hurried from the theater. He was starving.

"I didn't have time to eat lunch."

Ken piled into a huge SUV driven by city manager Al Roder, along with a banker, Joel Franken, me, and another person. The destination was a nearby town where a nascent design business with nationwide accounts was located. The owner was thinking of relocating in Uptown, and Ken wanted to convince him to buy the building that once was *Der Denison Herold* when it was fixed up.

I made an offhand comment about the meaning for the town if the businessman chose to relocate.

"This would be huge . . ."

Ken swung around in his seat, eyes intense.

"What do you mean!?"

Ken leaned toward me.

"It sends a message. It would be the first hip business. You get him and a few others, you get the hip coffeehouse. Then other things happen. It changes the atmosphere."

Ken absorbed this answer as the van stopped at the Hy-Vee where he had to pick up a child care center donation from Todd Tetmyer, the store manager. As Ken hurriedly exited, I suggested he at least get a granola bar. Minutes later he came back to the SUV, hands empty of food. There was no time. He'd go hungry.

The vehicle sped through the night. En route, talk was about state budget cuts that were strapping Crawford County and in turn were affecting Denison. Ken said they had to run the city smarter. The SUV pulled up in front of a century-old former bank building in the heart of a dead little town. Inside was a studio designed like a Manhattan or San Francisco loft/workspace, with a "creative tension" room that had free weights and a foosball table. The owner was working late.

Ken went into sales mode—it was down-home and yet slick. He was passionate as he explained that he wanted Denison to move forward and that the relocation of this man's business would be part of the dynamic.

"Some people think we're doing things too fast, costing them money."

They were wrong and Denison was a city on the move, Ken assured the businessman. He all but said the city would roll out a red carpet. Ken explained how he could buy *Der Denison Herold* at cost, that it was in a prime location, and the banker who had come with them would talk about financing. After an hour, Ken and the others drove back satisfied that they had made a good pitch. He didn't appear tired.

The previous night Ken had also worked, speaking at a sparsely attended candidates' forum. One resident focused on another popular-to-despise project, the child day care facility, calling it a "Taj Mahal," a waste of money.

Ken noted that the city was not losing money. It owned the building and took rent from the county, which ran the center. The building was break-even for the city, but the county was in the red. That missed the real point, Ken said, noting that the county loses between seven and eight dollars on services to the elderly compared with every dollar it loses serving children. Could it be no one complained about the money being spent on seniors because kids didn't vote?

Ken told a story of long ago, when he was first married, of how he went with his wife to work their farm south of town. The men labored in the fields while the women stayed home and cooked. Nowadays they go to a restaurant. Why? Both the men and women have day jobs off the farm. In contemporary society, he said, the day care center is vital.

"For some reason, they've singled out the care of children. Maybe they feel child care is a personal responsibility. We need to give kids care; it will save in the long run. My attitude is, how can we afford not to?"

Ken sounded liberal. But he was a Republican. For years he'd been a Democrat. His switch came down to one issue: abortion. He was vehemently against it, and so was the Republican Party.

One day we had lunch at the Candy Kitchen where Donna Reed used to sip phosphates, and he told me his life's story.

Ken had been born in Salt Lake City, where his father worked for the Union Pacific Railroad. His mother was a nurse who quit her job to have a family. His parents missed Omaha, and they returned. His father became a salesman at Montgomery Ward. While in school, Ken worked for his father, setting up window displays.

"I usually did that at night because I didn't want my friends to see me dressing mannequins."

In high school there was one weird red-haired teen whom he often ran into—a kid named Charlie—who became a garbageman in Lincoln. In January 1958, with his fourteen-year-old girlfriend, Caril Ann Fugate, Charles Starkweather went on an eight-day killing spree across Nebraska. Eleven people were slain. The rampage by the vacant-eyed Starkweather seemed to signify that something was wrong in the heartland to a nation wrapped up in the 1950s. What produced the blank-eyed monster? Ken had no answers.

Ken went into the army. He was stationed in Germany, and his job as a courier took him all over the continent. Upon discharge in 1962, he returned to Omaha. The city was an insurance business center, and he gravitated to a job in this industry. He was hired by Equifax as an investigator.

"In those days, every life, car, and homeowner's policy, they were all investigated. I had to interview people, and talk to at least one outside source. I then typed up a report. I'd do twelve to fifteen a day."

He went to college at night as he moved up in the company and was transferred around: Oklahoma City, Louisville, Atlanta, Chicago. He became a salesman and had a reputation as a problem solver. There were fifteen moves for his family—his wife, Shary, and their five children. In the end, he held the top sales position in Equifax, handling the Allstate and Sears accounts.

He was obliquely like the character Jack Nicholson played in *About Schmidt*, an actuary for an Omaha insurance company whose life crumbles when his wife dies and other things go wrong. Ken's personal life was wonderful, but, akin to the Nicholson character, work grew less satisfying. At Equifax, young upstarts came in and they didn't know the business; they ignored Ken. So after more than thirty-two years, he retired at age fifty-five in 1994. He wife was raised in the nearby town of Dunlap, one of eleven children. Many of her siblings farmed here.

"I told her, 'After fifteen moves, you have the choice for the last one.'"

So Denison it was. For seven years, he worked as a consultant, traveling about ten days each month. Then one day he was sitting in a pew at St. Rose of Lima Catholic Church, when a parishioner asked him to help with fund-raising for a childhood development center. They had to raise $1 million, and Ken threw himself into the work. They more than met the goal. Through this drive, he met Superintendent Bill Wright.

"He started talking to me about serving on the city council. Had I thought of something like that? I hadn't."

A councilman's term was four years. The mayor's, two. He chose the latter because he wanted to test the water and not commit to four years. So he ran for mayor and won in 2002. It was an amazing confluence—the 2020 Plan was being finalized. He was unencumbered by owning a business and there was no way being mayor could harm him financially. And he felt he owed service to his community that could be realized through the 2020 Plan. For months, I mistakenly thought the plan had been the mayor's, not realizing he had nothing to do with its conception. Many Denisonites thought the same: the name of the mayor and the 2020 Plan were synonymous.

But was the plan being played out in the best manner possible? Initial talk had been about putting the community center in Uptown. I recalled a night months earlier when Ken told the story about how he and Al Roder were walking in the alley next to Kehl Drug on Broadway and how he had a vision when he looked at the desolate area of a parking lot: he saw a broad plaza with fountains, ringed by shops, and a community center. This vision harkened to a Mexican town center. It would appeal to the Spanish speakers. It would signify a new Denison.

Ken had talked dreamily of this plan, but it was abandoned in favor of the community and conference center across the river. The town could not have both.

By the time the mayor and I had lunch, there was increasing uncertainty about the golf course project. The men trying to put it together were desperately raising funds. They had obtained many pledges that ranged from a few hundred dollars to $5,000 but were still short. They tried to talk the American Legion into selling its Uptown building, giving the money to the center in which the legion could hold its meetings. That failed.

The latest plan was to have companies donate materials and labor free to construct the parking lot. With this in-kind contribution, they were still $140,000 short of $1.5 million. Critics said that many promised pledges were no longer good. Even if the center were built, it was a dicey economic project.

I reminded Ken that I saw excitement in his eyes when he talked about the Spanish plaza. Now, when he talked about the golf course conference center, he seemed dispassionate.

This observation was wrong, Ken insisted. He was strongly behind the golf course plan. The plaza was a dead idea. Ken had suddenly turned into a politician. Or was it a middle management corporate executive? It was probably the latter. I recalled seeing the inside cover of a brown hardback file Ken carried to meetings: on it was the top 2020 Plan goals, among them the conference center, in large handwritten print. Ken was managing by objective. He would live or die by the conference center.

"It's my baby," he insisted.

Ken turned the conversation without prompt to how some Denison citizens viewed him. He was trying to be patient, and he volunteered that running a business is unlike moving a city in a new direction. It required a different skill set. But he was proud of his ability to hire or appoint the right people.

"I'm a perfectionist. I'm not a patient person. This is not the kind of place for that person."

Yet that person was here and was mayor. How that came to pass dated to 1976, when Ken was stationed in Atlanta. There was a co-equal in the company who was making his life miserable. Ken began spending weekends at a Trappist monastery. A monk said it was vital that he look back on his life and assess what was important—what worked and what did not. By summer's end, he realized he had to quit his job in order to move on, even though he had children to feed. On the Monday after this realization, he went into the boss's office, but before he opened his mouth, the boss said the co-equal had been fired.

Ken told the boss he'd come in to quit, and said he was thankful for the co-equal, for the man had made him see his own life more clearly. This zen outlook matured as he aged, along with a growing sense that he had to give to the community in which he lived. A critical moment occurred one afternoon when he was bedridden with terrible back pain. He couldn't move.

"I said to God if the pain would go away, I will volunteer. I will do something."

At that instant, the pain vanished. And simultaneously the phone rang. His wife came into the room and said it was someone from the church asking if he'd volunteer as a reader.

"I had to do it."

He became a reader. Now, years later, he was still answering that long-ago promise to volunteer.

Lunch was finished. Work at city hall remained. As we got up to leave the Candy Kitchen after talking so much about how so many in town felt toward him, Ken now appeared to be the one-dimensional image of the man in a photograph—fragile.

"I'm a human being. I have feelings. I'm probably regarded by some as arrogant and not willing to listen. I'm not that way at all."

THE BUSINESSMAN

"I'm glad Ken Livingston is mayor. After twenty-five years of inbreds running this place and doing nothing, he's doing something. He's shaking them up! I love watching it. I may not agree with all that he's doing, but at least he's doing something!"

This Denison merchant sat talking with me and another man in the late afternoon. Business had been as slow as the Wisconsin glaciation that last covered Iowa. The merchant was gleeful for the company and a willing set of ears to listen to his frustrations that were many years in building. He grew increasingly animated as the sun set on another lousy business day.

"If they stop him, the inbreds will have won!"

The merchant made a goofy face rubbery as a mask, stuck out his teeth to mock the negatives, and he spoke in an affected hick voice.

"A dentist, what's that?"

His face returned to normal.

"Inbreds! We'd still have gravel streets in town if it were for them. It's being German. It's an automatic NO to anything, especially if it's going to cost. Inbred rotten-teeth know-nothings. That horrible wretched paper—for half of them, it's the only news they get at all. They don't want to koow anything. It's just NO. Hispanics? If it weren't for them, there'd be eleven thousand people in this county. Germans are like that [against Latinos] because they're Germans, I tell you. I talk to them, and they say they should speak English and I ask, What did your grandparents speak? German. What did your parents speak? English and German. The Hispanics, it's the same. Their kids speak English. You tell them this, and they look at you."

Again came the distorted rubber face with teeth sticking out, a pantomimed drool, but now the merchant flailed his arms as if having a spastic attack.

"German Lutherans! Anything to do with Denison or the county, it's a NO! Anything to do with the schools, no matter how much money for their wretched precious little ones, it's an automatic YES! Where can I sign the check? Over in Carroll, it's the opposite. They're 90 percent Catholic, German Catholics. Them, anything with the city, they'll spend for it. But for the schools, nothing. This town. I don't think it's any different than anywhere else. People are fat, apathetic. They stuff their faces and sit on their behinds. The fat women and their fat precious ones sitting at their Nintendo. At the Hy-Vee they look in my shopping cart to see what I'm buying. I've had them come and pull things right out of my cart! And you have to go through all that phony friendliness, or they'll think you're being rude. It's always blah-blah-blah-blah. You wound people here without ever realizing it. If it's food, it has to cost under five dollars. Or be a buffet. Or as they say, 'buFFiTT.' Why can't there be a good restaurant here? They won't spend twelve dollars for a meal; the place wouldn't last. It's pathetic. If it's free, they'll come. You can wipe a dog's ass with a bread roll, and even if they see you do it, they'll eat it anyway— if it's free. Germans. They hate Donna Reed. *Who does she think she was, anyway? She was nothing. Dead Donna. Dead Donna.* They don't understand it's a hook for this town. Or even what she was about. They won't spend ten dollars during the festival for some good food. NO! I won't do anything to support HER. I like Ken Livingston. Anyone else, they were all afraid. He's got nothing to lose. He isn't from here. He has no baggage. I'm cheering Ken Livingston on. For once, for ONCE, someone is doing something! IhatethistownwhyIamIhere? Germaninbredcrazyrottingteeth-fatjustsayNOOOOOtoeverything!"

The merchant was indefatigable in his frustration. But he now took a breath, sighed.

"It's crazy. Why do I live here? They're going to win, and nothing will get done."

THE ADVERSARY

Dick Knowles arrived in 1954, hired by two men who owned the Denison newspapers. They promised the twenty-six year old he'd have his own newspaper to run. Two and a half months later, both men were killed in an airplane crash at the Denison Airport.

The widows hired Dick to run the papers. Later he bought a third of the operation, then half. And then he took control from his partner by forming an employee ownership plan: Dick owned half and the employees the other half.

It was a small town whose fortunes were tied up with that of the newspaper. Things were bleak.

"We were going down. Farmers were leaving. Hundreds left every year in the Fifties. In '55, we had a drought. To top that off, the price of hogs went down to ten dollars a hundredweight. The chamber of commerce said, 'We've got to do something . . . hogs were cheap. Let's make them worth more.'"

The idea was to bring the packing plants out of the big cities, to the country. It would give farmers a better price and keep more money in town. It was also thought the farmers could work part time in the plant and thus keep their farms.

Dick went to the chamber president and pointed out an empty egg plant. It was cheap, and they could process the hogs there. They found two men, one of them, Andy Anderson, who said they could run the operation—$385,000 was raised, a quarter from Anderson and the rest by the community. The operation was called Crawford County Packing Company, later to become Farmland Foods. It opened in 1958 and grossed over $15 million the first year.

In 1965 Dick also became involved with starting up Midwestern College, traveling east to promote it.

"We had a crazy idea, and we sold it in New York City."

When the college failed in 1970, he also worked on getting something on the site—a prison, then a cult. When those did not come, he worked on luring the U.S. Department of Labor to locate Job Corps there. Dick had spent most of his adult life promoting the business interests of Denison. In his view, he was anything but a "negative," though when I mentioned that city hall used this word to describe him, he paused for a long time.

"They don't say that to me."

Regarding his view of the mayor, he added, "We agree something has to be done. Only we disagree on what that something is. I'm not afraid to put my money where my mouth is. I have built buildings. You want to complain? Do something about it. I don't want to fight with them. I think in their heart they want to do the right thing."

The problem, as he sees it, is they bulldoze through what they want.

"They have to be willing to ask the people's support."

Dick explained why he appeared to be so crazy at the Streetscape hearing, when he demanded the mayor show him the minutes of the meeting Ken claimed he'd attended. That meeting was, he felt, not officially announced and thus illegal, because the agenda had not been publicly posted. That's why he'd badgered the mayor to show him the minutes. He was there, but there were no minutes in existence, Dick said.

Dick said something had to be done with Uptown. He cited one study that said it was more important to fix up the interior and exterior of businesses than redoing sidewalks and streets. The city was putting its money in the wrong place, Dick felt.

"It's a piecemeal deal. It's the cart before the horse."

Ken and Al Roder kept changing things as they went along, according to whim, Dick maintained, and this angered people. With the golf course community center project, Dick added, "It's the same story. You have people asking for support but not being willing to tell the whole story up front and changing the way they're going about it."

The depth of resentment toward Dick on the part of Ken was such that he once said, "I'm not so sure he is the man to be heading cultural diversity." Ken said Dick owned rentals and sold houses to Latinos, that he was making money off them, and this was his motive for helping.

"When he says stuff like that, the first thing I would say to him, 'If you really believe that, you should sit down with me and let me show you,'" Dick responded. "Because it's not true. Yeah, I could make money. But I'm not in it to make money."

He asked that at his age, how much money did he need? In fact, he has lost money at times. "It's partly because I'm not as careful as I should be." He said he is motivated by seeing the newcomers enter his office afraid, and then as time passes becoming Americans, owning homes.

"They overcome their shyness, their fear of the white guy. They hug me. They come in here with a great big grin on their faces. I never felt that way, except with my own family. They hug me. Yeah, I'm getting rich. But it's not like the mayor says. You can't get any richer than that."

THE ARTIST

Uptown and its environs were an immediate draw when I first set foot in Denison, the Victorian mansions in states of decay, buildings made from brick fired from local clay. Among the most compelling was the first courthouse, built in 1859; cracks now ran down the exterior, which had some unreadable 1920s' vintage advertisement on its west side. A bastardization of Henry David Thoreau came to mind: the greatest shapers of stately buildings come from the gentle effects of wind and water, with a liberal allowance of time.

Inside the "new" courthouse, a century old, the stone steps were worn into saddles from the eroding impact of generations of feet belonging to train robbers, petty thieves, public inebriates at the reins of horse-drawn carts or the wheels of motor vehicles, men registering for service in two world wars and Vietnam, young couples filing marriage licenses or recording births, schoolchildren trekking to the exhibit on the second floor: formaldehyde-filled jars of corn snakes, a worm snake, a yellow rat snake, and what they really came for—the two-headed pig, the three-nosed pig, and the four-legged chicken.

The town was a poem, a ballad in brick and mortar and slate and concrete and faded paint. But it was an anonymous poem to me, no different from a hundred other Midwest burgs I'd passed through that were monuments to a time gone, the cinematic reel stopped and held freeze-frame at the moment of my visit, then released in a march of continuing rot and crumble and failed aspirations.

Not so to Joel Franken, who was born over a half-century ago, before the paint had dulled and the storefronts emptied, before the grand Lincoln Highway–era Denison Hotel was razed for the Topko Drug store. Every weathered building presented a personal journey to Joel. I began to understand the way he saw the town one night when I was a passenger in his pickup truck.

We toured all that was gone, streets now closed, Victorians vanished. We passed the vacant storefront that had been Nigger John's, where you could purchase great ribs and chicken, or a woman if you were a different kind of guy than was Joel, who never sought any of that head cheese. He had plenty of free action. It was a city with a few dozen women in each generation as beautiful and blonde as Donna Reed, a benefit of the German heritage. Joel knew where to take them at night when the corn was high, deep in Fuller's Woods across the Boyer River, or that narrow lane that ran between the Shaw Mausoleum and the Denison family stones to the back of Oakland Cemetery.

Every street, building, and house held a memory. As we passed the Bank of Iowa on Broadway, Joel pointed.

"My father ran a grocery store there. I carried a lot of groceries out of that front door."

Between bagging groceries and schoolwork, Joel dreamed. He had tremendous artistic talent, and it seemed he could take it anywhere. He painted and impressed his teachers. Perhaps the big city and the East Coast lay in his future.

The Beatles landed in America, but that didn't register in Denison. Joel was a jock and had letters in football, basketball, track, baseball. The

Fab Four had grown hairier by the time Joel was a senior at the University of Northern Iowa in Cedar Falls, but the 1960s' cultural revolution didn't wash inland. It was still the 1950s for him: Joel has pictures in which he wears geeky thick-rimmed glasses and has farmboy-short hair. No matter his artistic aspirations, if there was a musical soundtrack for his life's choices, it was set to a Lawrence Welk tune rather than Sgt. Pepper.

"I ran into the artistic dilemma. Do I want to do art? Or play it safe?"

He didn't become a potential young New York talent. He became the Denison High School art teacher. Joel married. The young couple, who did not have children, purchased an English cottage–style home that Joel had admired since he was a boy. Before Joel knew it, thirty-four years had rolled past, and he retired. This isn't to say Joel didn't enjoy a different kind of celebration, for he had an impact on generations of kids. I met his former students and saw the depth of this influence. But I also saw that much of Joel's dream had been repressed.

"I never reached my potential."

It wasn't as if he were a small-town talent grateful to sell a few pieces at the local crafts store. I'd just spent the weekend at the new home of Bill Wright, the school superintendent who was about to retire to a distant lakefront residence. I'd admired the artwork decorating the house—fired clay pieces, watercolors, oil paintings—and assumed Bill had purchased them from galleries. I learned they all were Joel's work.

At Joel's home, I studied oils on walls and watercolors stored in boxes. Joel was a literalist as well as an abstractionist. His chromatography works were done on paper towels. This is art that combines with science. Only black ink is used. One outlines the image, paints water on one side of the line, applies ink on the other. Through capillary action, the water actually repels the ink, which breaks down so that different colors emerge—rusts and pinks and browns. The effect is weird and wild, and a series of faces made by Joel using this method are a punk-hippie-Picasso fusion.

A few months earlier in New York City, I'd been at a warehouse art show in Chelsea, an exhibit of exquisite mediocrity, and I now thought how the unknown artist from Denison would have shamed their work. On the plains of Iowa, I saw a man who had begun life with a dream rooted in his art. He'd lived most of his entire life here with the dream contained. One question remained. Would he die here, along with the dream? When we first met, the answer was clearly affirmative.

Joel then lived in the cottage with his wife of twenty-nine years and eleven months. He was fifty-six and had just retired. He'd served three consecutive terms on the city council between 1985 and 1997. And he'd spent the previous year painting the storefronts as they would look after the Streetscape renovation. He was motivated by civic desire, yet there was more: if he'd missed out on living in New York City, now he could create a piece of Manhattan on the prairie on the second floor of a nearly century-old building, over Bill Norelius's law practice. As he painted, he was designing his own future. He had in mind a Soho-like loft with a long bank of windows exposed to the south, a work space of light.

By that summer after our first winter meeting, as Joel told it, his wife dumped him for her grade school sweetheart. I never heard her side; I only knew that Joel was crushed. Everything had been mapped out for retirement. Now everything was different.

This was hot oil for gossip, and it lubricated numerous jaws in town. Joel fled on a road trip to avoid hearing the bulk of this talk and to allow it to spread and then die down. On this trip, he reflected on his life.

Upon returning, he busied himself with civic responsibilities. Joel was now head of the new Donna Reed Museum: after some two decades of talking, the museum was finally going to open in June. Contractors were doing the major work, and Nathan Mahrt was doing other construction after his day job. Streetscape was coming up for a vote with the city council. There were now thirty-five owners signed on who wanted to remake their building fronts in Uptown and on the Lincoln Highway. Joel would get to vote on this vision, for he'd been talked into once again running. No one else came forward to seek the at-large seat, and he sat in his council chair at the start of 2004.

If one wanted to create a near-perfect scenario about life in small-town America, Joel was in a public sense at a pinnacle. He was a town elder, part of the power structure, a retired teacher who garnered respect, a man leaving a legacy of a revitalized Uptown for the next generation.

With the exception of the looming divorce, it should have been a happy time. Yet something deeper was amiss. Joel was trying to right himself. At first, friends set him up. He went on a few dates. He was philosophical.

"When one door closes, three open."

But these local women were just not that interesting. He wanted a person to match the kind of life he'd imagined in the New York–style loft over Bill Norelius's law office.

Amid these dates, he got around to emailing distant friends about his situation. He had been on the National Board for Professional Teaching Standards, one of several dozen directors of this nonprofit group that developed assessment programs for teachers. He'd traveled to conventions, and there was one fellow director whom he'd always gotten along with especially well. She replied to his email that she too was in a marriage that was ending. A correspondence developed. The woman, who lived in New Jersey, was going to briefly visit eastern Iowa, and they planned a first date.

Joel talked excitedly about the coming date. He was like a teenager. The date went well. Joel soon flew to New Jersey. Then late that fall the couple went on a Caribbean cruise.

During this budding romance, tensions were mounting among the citizenry over the 2020 Plan. There was opposition to Streetscape. There were angst-filled sessions when the 2020 Executive Committee held meetings at Cronk's Cafe. How should they deal with the negatives? And how could they move to the next step? In the end, Denison was still left with an image problem: it was a blue-collar town, and no one was working to attract new business. They were making cosmetic changes. They could change the streets and make things look pretty, but if there was no promotion, it would all be a waste.

In one meeting, Joel gave a presentation. He invoked the film *Field of Dreams*, set in Dyersville, Iowa, to the east. The movie's message had become a cliché across the nation, but to Denison, it was stark and real.

"I'm not so sure that we can look over at Dyersville and say if we build it, they will come."

Should they create a new entity beyond the chamber of commerce or the county development agency (the latter a failure to most in the room) to promote the town? This would be a job for a marketing person. Joel noted it was a critical time. Things were happening now, and they had to act now. When he was finished, a serious discussion ensued. Joel's cellular phone vibrated, and he pulled it from his pocket. He winked at me and hurried from the meeting.

As the discussion progressed, members had questions about the presentation.

"Where'd he go?" someone asked.

No one understood what call could have been so important to pull Joel from the room. The woman back East was still married and could talk only from her office on Mondays and Fridays. It was Monday.

Joel couldn't see the woman again until April, so he immersed himself in the museum project, scheduled to open in five months. Joel and Nathan had discovered a set of heavy oak doors from the original lobby in the basement. It was decided to hook them together to use as partitions in the museum now being sheetrocked on the first floor. Joel and volunteers began working in an empty space on the second floor above the museum, stripping heavy layers of paint covering the beautiful oak.

I showed up to help those days. As many as five people worked, scraping between applications of chemical stripper. Some doors contained glass that had been painted over. There were three coats. When the remover ate down to the bottom coat, which was white, it revealed graffiti: it was a time capsule to kids standing in the dark at the back of the theater during the era of James Dean films, who had pulled pen knives to etch their existence in the shadows. "Kathy Holland '56'" stood out. Joel was a boy back then, and he knew some of these older kids.

One day Joel and I were alone in the loft above the museum, working on the final two doors. Joel's woman friend had recently visited Denison for the first time. She'd met some of Joel's friends; one woman said his new girlfriend was stuck up.

"Her fear is she is going to pull me away. She isn't going to pull me away. If I want to go, it's me who wants to go."

This was new talk. Very new.

"I think I'm going to have to move."

I let this comment ride as we scraped without using solvent. We were on the reddish layer, the thickest, and paint chips flew in all directions. The sound of two scrapers echoed in the bare-studded chamber looking down on Broadway. It was sunny, but the bank time/temperature sign up the street announced: 1:16/23 degrees.

Joel worked his way up to the glass, now using remover, which ate paint down to 1957-era graffiti; he knew some of these people too. He studied the names, then applied solvent, and scraped them away. Now there was clear glass, released to the light for the first time in fifty years.

"Do you think you can do it, move away?"

"She wants to live in Hoboken, right across from New York City."

I gave the opinion that this might be good, no?

"I'll have to confront creation."

There would be no more excuses. Here, Joel said, he's pulled by small-town responsibilities. He goes home tired and falls in bed; he had recently fantasized that he had a button he could push before nodding off so that a printout of his artistic visualization would be there come morning.

"If you lived in Hoboken, you could be over in the city in minutes. You'd run in a different circle. You might hang out with an artists' community. It would inspire you."

Joel agreed and asked himself aloud about how much time he had left. Our scrapers worked on as the bank clock approached two o'clock.

"When might this move happen?"

"As soon as this summer. July."

"Would you keep the house?"

"I was thinking of renting it."

"Or you maybe should just sell it. Don't give yourself that out."

"Absolutely. I've been thinking about that too."

The paint was nearly all off the last two doors. We quit and cleaned up.

"I know what's out there. But . . ."

Joel was nervous. He knew about the larger world. But visiting it and living in it were different matters. He was talking about cutting all ties to the town in which he was born, booming out for the big city. His eyes were wide, and he marveled at the words coming out of his mouth.

Was it possible? Could he do what most men and women do in their twenties?

THE IDEALIST

Nathan Mahrt watched as the plan hatched for revitalizing Denison. He sat in on meetings as city leaders and townspeople talked in 2000 and

2001. He was usually quiet, as was normal, but he spoke up at key points. He was mostly ignored.

The plans bothered him. Nathan agreed that Uptown's streets and buildings needed attention and some love, but to him, the execution of the redesign was flawed.

"Let's make it retro. But in twenty-first-century terms. Why build something new that looks old when you already have it?"

He showed pictures of contemporary Uptown buildings, plain and ugly, but which were once venerable. One was Denison City Hall, not long after it was constructed by Henry Laub, with a bell tower and stunning character. It was hard to believe that they were the same structure.

"What happened to it?"

"The 1960s. They modernized it."

Nathan said the old town was beneath the modern facades. His desire was that it be put back just the way it was. It would be a lot cheaper and a lot more dramatic.

A much bigger problem was the golf course conference center and hotel planned across the Boyer River. Nathan said city officials used a flawed cost-benefit ratio. They went to the courthouse and saw how many weddings happened in one year, but the receptions had all been held out of town because Denison did not have a community center to rent for such events. The assumption was that many of these events would end up in the center. A marketing study by TR Mandigo & Co. used income projections based on fifty large weddings and social functions per year renting the hall for $500; another fifty, smaller parties, would rent for between $100 and $250.

The problem as Nathan saw it was that Denison is a blue-collar town. People won't pay $500 to rent a hall, Latinos in particular. "If they catered more to Hispanics, they'd make a hell of a lot more money."

Nathan practically sputtered when talking about the city's $1 million commitment to the golf course project. "I call it the 2020 Bullshit Plan," Nathan said. Then why wasn't he more vocal?

"Oh, I hate confrontation!"

Nathan stewed quietly. Some officials had doubts about the golf course project too. Then why were they behind it? As one official explained it, volunteerism and energy are rare commodities in a small town. One or two men with drive can swing plans so that the rest of the aristocracy goes along. The two men pushing the golf course project were in their thirties. All the others involved in executing the 2020 Plan were, on average, in their fifties. The younger men were seen as the next generation of leaders, and if they wanted to put their energy into the center, they had to be given their shot. But Nathan was young too, and he saw this support by default as supreme idiocy.

Nathan had a secret plan.

He told me to meet him one afternoon on First Avenue North, mid-block down from the old German newspaper office.

I showed up in front of a white stucco building with an Art Deco front: it was otherwise plain, a big boxy structure with a slate roof. Up near the roof line was the symbol for the Masonic order—a compass and square. On the front door was a sign advertising Tae Kwan Do classes. It was a rainy day, and I stood beneath an umbrella. Minutes later Nathan arrived with another man, a Mason, who opened the front door. We stepped into the past.

It was the original Germania Opera House that once was on the corner where the U.S. Post Office now stands. Built in 1886, it had been the focus of not just Germans but the entire Denison community. In its heyday, an untold number of performances were held on its stage. For years it hosted high school graduation. In the basement were a billiard room and social club. Speeches occurred on its stage, including the one that launched Leslie Shaw's political career. It was used until 1913, when it was moved to make way for the postal building, and it was usurped by the larger Deutsche Opernhaus Gesellschaft that later became the Ritz Movie Theater and then the Donna Reed Center.

When the building was moved, the back fifty feet of the stage area was cut off so that the hall could not compete with the new opera house. On April 27, 1928, it was sold to the Masonic order, Sylvan Lodge #507 A.F. & A.M. The Italianate front was then "modernized." It was then the Art Deco period, and so it was Decoized.

We faced the stage and pried open a long-sealed door. I had a flashlight, and we climbed up on what remained of the stage. As the beam shined around, we discovered the names of stagehands or actors carved in the woodwork facing the audience. Fifteen feet up, the beam caught posters for pre-1913 plays. We did not have a ladder to reach them.

At some unknown point in time, the second-floor balcony area was floored in. A ceiling now existed where there had been open air. Upstairs, the balcony area was an 1886 time capsule: there were still seats, the original columns, and cool alcoves and fine woodwork. It was a room from horse-and-buggy times.

Nathan explained his dream: take the floor out, restoring the interior to its original appearance; then rebuild the backstage area by adding fifty feet to the building. For a lot less than $1 million, Denison would have its community center while at the same time honoring the town's past. Nathan saw music being performed on the stage and an activity room in the vast basement, perhaps even a coffeehouse.

"And it would rent at an affordable rate, probably $150 for events."

It would be a community center in the heart of the community. Nathan spoke excitedly of restoring the front to its pre-Deco majesty. He figured the golf course idea would perish, and he'd spring forth with this plan. And he'd do it with no city monies, by seeking grants and using volunteer labor—most of it his. He said the only salvation for Denison would be to restore everything possible, with the opera house as the Rosetta Stone. People would see a dramatic result, and they would have no cause for complaint.

There were political and other hurdles. Nathan had to get the Masons to sign on to the deal. He had to wait out the golf course plan. And he had to raise money.

Days later, Nathan talked to the Masons. The order was much reduced, and only a handful came to meetings. The core members agreed that it was a good plan, for they had trouble maintaining the building, and it would allow them to continue using it. That settled, Nathan sat back to bide his time. The biggest remaining problem was that he had no money.

Then one afternoon, I was walking down Broadway to go dine at one of the four Mexican restaurants in town that I had not yet tried. As I passed the Donna Reed Museum, Nathan was working inside. Nathan was troubled. Word of his not-so-secret plan had reached a man of means who opposed the golf course project. This man dangled an offer: he had some $100,000 and knew another man who had as much. They wanted to "get" the city and were ready to pour their money into restoring the old opera house. This would kill the golf course project, for a big part of the economics of that project was wedding rentals.

Nathan fretted.

"They want to use me to get at the mayor."

Nathan had explained that he was grateful. He noted, however, that if he took the money, things would blow up politically. He'd promised he'd wait until the golf course project died of its own accord. The man with the money chided Nathan for doing what others told him to do. Two hundred thousand dollars was a chance to save a piece of Denison's history, and to do it right.

"I feel like a big rubber band is pulled tight. It's a slingshot and I'm in the center, aimed straight at the Masons' Lodge."

I nodded.

"And no matter what you do, you will splatter."

"Exactly."

"You could have said, 'Yes, Mr. Faust.'"

Nathan looked around the empty chamber that would soon be filled with Donna Reed's pictures and memorabilia about the film *It's a Wonderful Life*.

"In this setting, it would be more appropriate to say, 'Yes Mr. Potter.'"

THE BUILDER

The Mexican novelist Carlos Fuentes talks about Latinos having feet in two worlds—one of Europe and the other of his or her indigenous roots.

Luis Navar had his feet in four worlds.

There were the two noted by Fuentes, and Luis felt them. He thinks about his native side all the time.

"It is smaller in me than some people who live here, but it is in here."

Luis thumped his chest. He talked about Mexican folklore with its indigenous beliefs: one should not cut one's hair unless the moon is a one-quarter crescent or less, or one's hair will grow back too fast; don't approach people with business propositions or anything on which a decision must be made during the full moon. And there were others.

The third world for Luis had been that of Los Angeles, and the fourth was Iowa.

"I saw discrimination in Los Angeles," Luis said, but it was different. "There it's about money. This is hard to explain. If you have the money, you have the power. In Los Angeles, it is about groups, not people."

I did not fully understand what he was getting at.

"Here it is personal. In Los Angeles, all the people doing lawns, yard work, they are Latino. Here you see the whites doing the garden work. You work with the white people. You make the same wages. You live in the same kind of houses. You have two different colors in the same position."

He felt the racism was more intense here. You could not escape it by having money, or hiding in your group if you did not have money. In California, race did not matter for those who had money. They could move into a gated community and live behind walls.

"It's bigger in California."

There was one man in town who made him feel better: Nathan.

"He cures me. He cures me about my feelings about white people. He helps me so much. I don't know why. There is so much bad feelings here, and then there are people like Nathan. We all do the same thing. We find the good place for the family."

THE WEST COAST GIRL

Liliana Gonzalez was born in Mexico but grew up in Pomona, in the Los Angeles basin. She was now seventeen and a junior at Denison High School. She'd arrived six months earlier after her parents sold the Pomona house and purchased a much better one here. In California, her school and neighborhood had been Latino, with some blacks and Asians. Whites were few in number. All she knew was that the United States seemed brown.

"It's weird," she said of her move to Iowa. "I never thought there were so many white people."

She and her three siblings were in for other surprises.

"When we got here, we said, 'Where's the mall? Where's everything?' My dad said, 'It's all an hour away.'"

There were bigger culture shocks.

"When I first came here, during lunch, I hung out with white people," she said, just as she had done in Pomona. "There was a lot of mixing there. People weren't afraid. My friends called me a racist," she said of the Latinas in Denison. She was befuddled. They meant she was acting too white, spurning them. They were not really her friends, and she added they thought of her as being "stuck up." That's because her English was impeccable, and she had good grades. Her detractors were not doing so well in both areas.

"I don't like it," she says of the gossip. In a mirror of the adult world, kids made up stories, usually of a perverse sexual nature, about others. "There's no privacy here. It's too close. Everyone knows your life."

Liliana laughed when asked about Denison's leaders trying to build bridges across cultural divides. She blamed both sides.

"Either white or Latino, it's the same. No one really tries. I see all talk and no action."

I'd heard of a curious development that began just before Liliana arrived in town: an inter-Mexican rivalry that was surpassing that of white-Latino tensions. (The last white-Latino fight had been a big rumble outside the school the previous year; by Christmas this year, those tensions seemed quiet.) The two largest groups of Mexicans in Denison were either from the state of Campeche, on the Yucatán peninsula, or Jalisco in central Mexico. I had just interviewed a Jaliscan boy in Liliana's class with a black eye, from a fight with a group of *Campechano* teens.

"You have to be on one side or the other," Liliana said. "Why should you be on one side? Both groups are Hispanic."

Liliana said kids will lie and say they are *Campechano* to be part of the group.

"They want to fit in."

Her family is from Guanajuato, and she won't play such games. Liliana can't claim a group and feels caught between worlds. She can't hang out with the whites, and Latinas reject her.

"I can't talk about this stuff the way I am talking with you, with anyone else here. Here I truly don't have a friend."

THE ENGINEER

One afternoon, Crawford County engineer Paul Assman drove me to his big house just north of town, on a gravel road, talking about Denison being the new frontier for people from the coasts. The home sits on a hill overlooking the East Boyer River on one hundred acres, a third of it wooded in shagbark hickory, burr oak, and black walnut. It has a pond. The view is stunning.

He reenacted his drive to work that morning as we left his long driveway.

"Note the time. It is 2:48. I'm driving to work. I'm watching deer over there. A beautiful sunrise." We move along and the road turns to pavement. "I am one minute and thirty seconds into my drive. Up that road, it's a minute and a half to the high school for my kids. If I were in a big city, I wouldn't even be out of my subdivision yet. With today's society, I can leave here, go to Omaha and get on a jet, and be in San Juan, Puerto Rico, in half a day. There's so much opportunity out here."

We arrived at the courthouse.

"And now I'm at work. Look at the time."

It was 2:52 P.M.

"Four minutes. How many cars did we see? Two or three? I didn't count. You know what my monthly parking bill is? Zero."

THE GHOST AND WAL-MART PRESENT

It was the snowiest winter in years. Subzero temperatures were the rule—actual air temperature, not wind chill. It was a good time to be at home.

Even if not for the snow and cold, there wasn't much to do on a weekend night in Denison. I'm not a big drinking man. My first Denison bar visit occurred that winter when a friend visited. We went to U.S.-flag-festooned Mike's: An American Bar—owned by a Latino. We were the sole customers. The Friday evening happy hour hors d'oeuvres of mini tacos were crisping for want of patrons, happy or otherwise. The white bartender lamented that business was down for everyone.

"No one's buying anything—at the clothing stores, the car dealerships, anywhere in town."

High school sporting events (go Monarchs!) were another activity—not exactly a magnetic draw for a nonparent. Another social pastime was pancake suppers, put on by various groups at different locations, that cost four or five bucks for 'cakes and sausage to raise funds for assorted causes. For teens, a lure was the "Safety Zone," the name for an Uptown parking lot behind the Broadway stores. Police enforce a no-loitering policy everywhere else but tolerate the zone as a means of containment. Kids mill and talk during the summer; in the winter they park their vehicles open-driver-window-to-open-driver-window, heaters blasting.

I was neither a parent nor a teen, and one can eat only so many pancakes. I didn't get out much. I spent nights in the Shaw Mansion—writing, reading, occasionally cursing my cheap boom box and Wal-Mart chair whose back continued flopping off when I got up to make coffee or visit the bathroom. I paced the cold halls. For diversion I shoveled the perpetually falling snow.

The friend who had visited sent an email asking about my "exciting" Iowa nights. Did I have any more ghost experiences? Was I getting any action? I wrote, "If only the ghost were a woman and would go down on me, I'd be in great shape."

After the email, the house grew cold. I waited for the central heating system to kick on. It did not. I went down the grand staircase, then descended into the dark basement. My furnace pilot had gone out. Yet the pilot for the separate furnace that heated the old woman's former quarters was lit. I went through a dozen matches as I figured out how to reignite it.

I worked late. I fell into the deepest of sleeps, then had this sensation: a 400-pound person was seated atop my chest and arms. I awakened enough to think, *the ghost!* I absolutely could not breathe, and my arms would not move. It seemed like forever that I pushed and struggled. Finally I shot up with great effort, sputtering a shout. Subsequent sleep was wretched.

A week later, I was fast at work at one o'clock in the morning. It was 8 degrees below zero outside. Another New York friend rang and also inquired about my social life. I told the story of the earlier email, about how the ghost could sexually help me out. She laughed. As we talked, I felt a maturing chill: the furnace was not kicking on. After hanging up, I went to the thermostat and turned it up to 80 degrees. Nothing.

At that hour, I didn't want to venture into the bowels of the house. I had a small electric heater that I cranked up, but it did not help. It was a windy night, and a subzero draft leaked through the ancient windows.

I grabbed a flashlight and opened the door to the grand oak staircase. The beam shot around as I descended, striking the Victorian fretwork, casting shadows as intense as giant spider webs. I moved slowly for fear of tripping and breaking my neck. I thought that if this were a movie, it's the point where the audience thinks: *Why is that idiot going down there!?* It was a basic Horror 101 cliché. *Who would be so stupid? And what moron would have insulted the ghost a second time?*

I stopped at the bottom. The loose downspout clanged against the side of the mansion. I thought: *I can go to bed now in my sleeping bag and deal with the furnace come daylight.* I turned to go back upstairs. And then: *This is stupid. The furnace going off was merely a coincidence.*

I repeated this mantra as I went down the basement steps. I passed through rooms cluttered with a refrigerator, old light fixtures, doors, and tools. I peered into the furnace that heated the old woman's rooms. The pilot was on. Mine was dead cold. The first lighting attempt, by inserting a match hooked to a wire into the innards, failed. The second took. I had to hold the starter down for a full minute to make it remain lit; I had the cold sensation of now being watched. This feeling intensified as the minute progressed. I forgot the mantra. I let go of the button. The pilot remained on. And something remained fixated on me, burning and fierce. I raced up the stairs.

I worked for a few more hours, retiring at four o'clock. Five o'clock came, and still I was awake. What happened after the previous pilot outage occupied my thoughts. Somehow I drifted off. I awakened at noon the next day. Nothing disturbed my sleep.

Never again did I offer sexual insult to the ghost. The pilot never again went out.

* * *

There were others who had incidents with ghosts.

A librarian in the children's reading room at the Norelius Community Library kept experiencing weird happenings. Once a book and a video simultaneously jumped from their slots on shelves, flying three feet out into the room. Other times the photocopier turned itself on and made a copy of nothing. Librarians point to a century-old photograph from when the building opened. In the window glass of a door in that photo is a ghostly image of a man's face.

Amber Mahrt had seen the "pea coat man." This little old ghost man wears a distinctive coat and wanders the alleys at night; others had seen him too. Many Latinos also believed in ghosts. One day Luis Navar said, "If you ever don't want to rent a house to a Mexican, tell them it's haunted."

Denison as a city inhabited by ghosts is not, however, a universal view. After the furnace outages, I felt compelled to find the woman who had rented the ballroom and seen the man walk through the wall. I went to Topko Drug where she'd once worked. Two suspicious middle-aged women clerks wanted to know why I sought the former employee. I was compelled to explain about the old house down the street.

"So," one clerk said with a smirk. "Are you a ghostbuster?"

I shrugged and left.

One afternoon Nathan was home watching his daughter while Amber pulled a weekend nursing shift. We sat at his kitchen table discussing the application for placing the old opera house on the National Register of Historic Buildings. The building was sound, with the original slate roof. The repairs would go in phases, the front first, opening up the balcony, and finally restoring the 50 feet of stage. The money man, to Nathan's relief, had mysteriously withdrawn his offer. Nathan was waiting out the golf course project.

Nathan was industrious on many fronts. He'd just bought a 1930s Uptown brick building that had been a garage; he wanted to fix it up and rent it to a restaurant or other business.

Talk turned to the Shaw Mansion. My landlord continued to ignore Nathan's pleas to bring in a real estate appraiser. He worried that the Des Moines man who wanted to gut the fine woodwork was scheming to get it without letting my landlord give Nathan a shot at bidding.

I related the furnace incidents. Nathan said that five years earlier, the late wife of my landlord had given him the key so he could do some work in the basement. When he was done, he spied a sink once used upstairs, set against a wall. It was carved from solid marble and he feared either someone throwing it out not knowing its value, or stealing it. He thought: *I'm going to hide it.* That way the sink would be there for the day when someone would restore the house. Nathan picked it up—and the moment he did so, a cold rush overcame him.

"I was being watched. It didn't want me touching it. I took another step, and it was really bad. Something bad was going to happen if I didn't put it down. I set it down and ran the hell out of there. It followed me to the door."

What was in the Shaw Mansion? I wondered if it had anything to do with Leslie Shaw. Nathan didn't think so. Perhaps it was the opera singer and his wife who had gone senile in the house, Nathan said. I wasn't so sure.

That afternoon we ended up in Nathan's attic, sitting on the floor surrounded by boxes filled with his collection of Denison-related historical documents. He turned on a computer to show me a painting he'd downloaded of Shaw, one that hangs in the U.S. Treasury Department. As the image came up, Shaw glared at us. He'd aged a lot as treasury secretary, and his eyes showed an intensity that did not exist in Iowa photographs and paintings. They were eyes of wild fury.

To understand what was going on in the Shaw Mansion, I felt compelled to learn all I could about its original owner. I stopped all other work and concentrated on the man in whose bedroom I spent my nights tapping away at a computer.

Before I dug into my research, I thought Shaw was an unlikely character to be plucked off the Great Plains into the administration of the man who forged the birth of Pax Americana. To a casual observer, Shaw didn't seem worldly. Wasn't he just a small-town lawyer and banker who got lucky? After all, he hadn't even dreamed of politics until 1896. Yet just over five years later he was the money mind behind Theodore Roosevelt.

As those of us who teach journalism tell our students as they work to uncover truths, "Follow the money." In this case, I set out to follow the money man. At the start of this research, I imagined Leslie Shaw might not appreciate me in his house and that if he were able to appear as a spirit, it's likely he would delight in sitting on my chest as I slept, or doing far worse.

* * *

Leslie Mortier Shaw was born in 1848 in a log cabin in Morristown, Vermont. His parents, Lovisa and Spaulding, were farmers whose children worked the fields from five o'clock in the morning to dinner, when they hurriedly ate, and then returned to the fields. Shaw somehow found time for books and newspapers, and he'd read Horace Greeley's advice. In 1869 he headed west, lured by tales of the frontier and money. He dreamed of staking a spread so vast that it would have its own private railroad.

Shaw made it to eastern Iowa and learned that he was fifteen years too late for easy land and fast money. His first work was shucking corn. He then got a teaching job. When school ended, to save railroad fare, he walked forty miles seeking new opportunity in Mount Vernon, Iowa, where Cornell College was located. Shaw desired a higher education, but he lacked tuition. A nurseryman offered him a job peddling fruit trees.

"In the spring of 1870, I tramped the country over from farm to farm," Shaw said in an account by historian F. G. Moorhead. "It was a cold, wet spring and every night my limbs were wet clear to my body. Often I have been compelled to take off my shoes and ford streams barefooted, while there was snow on the banks."

He enrolled at Cornell in 1871 and, during breaks, continued selling trees; when he couldn't sell those, he hawked books.

"They called him 'Apple-Tree Shaw,'" Moorhead wrote. "As one of the old farmers to whom Shaw repeatedly sold stock once remarked: 'When Apple-Tree Shaw began to talk about plantin' an orchard you might as well consider it a-growin.'"

He graduated from Cornell College in 1874. He next went to the Iowa College of Law in Des Moines, earning a degree in 1876.

The young lawyer headed to Denison—he'd shipped $4,000 worth of trees to town in two seasons. He showed up at the law firm of James Perry Conner, whose practice was three years old. Conner agreed to take him on as a partner if Shaw would buy $600 worth of books that were in his office. Shaw agreed, sold the books to farmers at a profit, and the name plate then read Conner & Shaw. Shaw worked hard. He had to. In 1877 he married Alice Crawshaw, and they quickly had three children. Shaw had to support a family in a town overstocked with twenty-five lawyers, some barely eking out a living. According to Moorhead, "Shaw says he sometimes drove ninety miles in one day to try a case. 'I would get up at 2 o'clock in the morning and would get back late at night, changing teams on the way.'" Shaw later wrote, "I am on record as offering to travel a thousand miles to see the grave of a man who has died from overwork, but the cemeteries contain both men and women who have died for want of work."

In advice to young people Shaw later said that no matter the era, there are always opportunities for those with ambition:

It was not so very long ago that I looked out on the world and came to the deliberate conclusion that I had reached man's estate at a very unfortunate time.... In this frame of mind I left the home of my childhood, and put 1,200 miles and the Big River between me and the roof that had been my protection.... I soon found myself in a settlement of homesteaders. Even there the land had all been entered, and there was not a vacant forty. I soon learned from observation, however, that some of those who made entries did not properly "work their claims. . . ." I also learned that the same principle prevailed in every other walk of life. The man who did not properly "work his claim," whether it was the practice of law or of medicine or business of any kind, would be very soon looking for something else to do.

Shaw was motivated to work multiple claims.

"Shaw found the returns coming in too slowly," wrote Moorhead. "In the neighborhood were scores of farmers striving to pay for their homesteads. The country was new, the interest rates high and money scarce."

Shaw returned to Vermont seeking funds from eastern money people to open a bank. Moorhead said a skeptical financier accompanied Shaw to Iowa, and the two visited farms across Crawford County. They went to farms with mature orchards sold by Shaw. The financier saw books sold by Shaw in the parlors, the wills in safes drawn up by him, and how he told stories and laughed at the farmers' jokes. He backed Shaw, who founded the Bank of Denison in 1890.

"So successful was Shaw in judging men that not a single dollar was ever lost or mortgage foreclosed, even in the panic of 1893," Moorhead wrote.

Shaw invested in rice-growing lands in Louisiana; a decade later, oil was found there, and Shaw pocketed $800,000. In 1892 Shaw and two partners were granted the right by the Denison City Council to provide electric light and steam heat. The charge "for each 16-candlepower incandescent lamp" could not exceed $1 per month, according to Ordinance Number 86. That same year Shaw began organizing the Denison Normal School Association, a teachers' college; he was its biggest patron, contributing $5,000.

Also in 1892 Leslie and Alice and their three children moved into the freshly completed mansion built on a lot Shaw had purchased in 1886. It had frescoed ceilings and was decorated in superb Victorian fashion: a bust of Beethoven on a pedestal, a Ming vase, Oriental rugs, elaborately carved sitting chairs, an upright grand piano. The Shaws enjoyed entertaining. The *Denison Review* on November 29, 1893, reported two back-to-back receptions on a Friday and Saturday for 450 people. In an account of the first, the paper wrote,

A GRAND RECEPTION

Mr. L. M. Shaw and lady sent out about three hundred invitations to their reception last Friday. Their capacious mansion was well filled between the hours of seven and eleven. The interior of the house is well arranged for the entertainment of a large company. A string band played in the ball[room] upstairs. . . . Refreshments consisting of chicken salad, ice cream and confectionery, were served to as many as the dining room could seat, continuously.

It is the highest merit of the American Republic, and our common school system, that nine-tenths of the inhabitants of any Western community have manners, dress and appearance of gentlemen and ladies who can pass muster in any drawing room. . . . Mr. Shaw's reception was a new departure and we only regret that comparatively few homes are large enough to hold a similar assemblage.

Shaw was a big man in a small place, manufacturing a version of an East Coast socialite scene. He was happy working long hours. If he had any vision for a larger station in life, it was not apparent. His main interest was being the head Sunday school teacher at the Denison Methodist Church, a position he held for twenty years. Sunday was sacred. He once ended one of his famously long but compelling speeches on a Saturday at the stroke of midnight, for he said he never talked politics on Sunday. He opposed dancing.

As Shaw's wealth grew in the 1890s, Denison was in its heyday. It was a rich agricultural county seat, in a country that was going through profound changes in industry and commerce.

* * *

In its first full century as a nation, America was a classic developing country. Foreign money financed factories and railroads, and labor was cheap. America exported little beyond raw materials such as cotton. For the nation's nascent industries, there was a policy of protectionism, championed by the Republican Party and its antecedents. At first the policy was to nurture manufacturing; later, as wealth accumulated, it protected industrialists and, by default, their workers.

A handful of men were titans. In 1882 Andrew Carnegie built his first blast furnace on the banks of the Monongahela River in Pennsylvania, beginning his steel empire. There was railroad baron E. H. Harriman, who dominated the West with the Union Pacific and Southern Pacific. In the South, James Buchanan Duke had control of four-fifths of all tobacco production. John D. Rockefeller amassed the Standard Oil Company, crushing all competitors. As the nineteenth century drew to a close, these men were heralded in some quarters as the Jack Welches and Bill Gateses of their day. Others saw ruthless men who skirted the law and morality on the path to their millions. There was a movement to share the wealth by workers who often put in twelve-hour days, seven days per week. In 1886, the Haymarket Riot happened in Chicago at a rally for the eight-hour workday; four anarchists were found guilty and hanged.

It was a vastly different nation from the one that existed in 1801 when Thomas Jefferson was elected president. He envisioned a nation of small farmers; 95 percent of Americans then lived on farms. The industrial age put citizens in factories by the century's end, when fewer than half of Americans worked the soil. (Nearly two hundred years after Jefferson, in 1993, there were so few farmers that the U.S. Census stopped counting them.)

If any year marks a turning point in this two-century arc of change, it was 1890. Following that year's census, historian Frederick Jackson Turner declared the wilderness frontier closed. That same year the last "battle" against the Indians resulted in the massacre at Wounded Knee. It was clearly the end of the frontiersman and the Indian. The nation was settled. But there was no interim period of agrarian stability. America had gone from cowboys and Indians straight into capitalists and industrial workers. Farmers would hang on, but their political power was on the wane.

Yet the farmers were not going down without a fight.

* * *

In this critical period, while Shaw was building his successful bank and other interests, two men who would soon intersect with his life had moved into the region: Theodore Roosevelt and William Jennings Bryan.

Both had ties to Denison. Both would become players in the struggle between farmers, factory workers, and business moguls.

Roosevelt was the son of privilege—his father was a New York merchant—who was born sickly and asthmatic. His father once told the young Theodore his body would prevent him doing anything useful. "I'll make my body," the boy replied. He went to Harvard and embarked on a life of proving himself through boxing and hunting and other masculine feats. He entered politics and was elected to the New York State Assembly. But when his wife died during childbirth, he quit and came west in the 1880s to escape his depression. Roosevelt owned a ranch in North Dakota and by many accounts was a poseur: he wore ornate cowboy costumes and buckskins that no real rancher would ever be caught dead in. It seemed to be a continuation of the once-sickly boy trying to prove himself.

The not-yet-famous Roosevelt spent time in Denison, according to Nathan Mahrt. He became friends with several Denison businessmen, including the Ben Broderson who built the house Nathan grew up in. (Broderson owned a ranch adjacent to Roosevelt's North Dakota spread.) Roosevelt was envious of his newfound prairie pals, as Nathan saw it, for they were self-made men who came west with nothing but proverbial spit and song and ended up owning mansions, banks, tracts of land. They were the opposite of how he was reared, and some historians believe the Harvard graduate would have gladly changed lives with any of them.

Did Roosevelt and Shaw run into each other in the 1880s? No record exists. The first documentable meeting didn't occur until over a decade later. But a die had been cast for Roosevelt: he liked Shaw's type.

At the other end of the spectrum was William Jennings Bryan. He was born in Illinois and became a lawyer at the age of twenty-three in 1883. He moved to Nebraska four years later. He was a Democrat and harbored the opposite of worship for men of means. He quickly garnered the nickname the "Great Commoner" for his championing of the "little man"—farmers and industrial workers. In 1890 Bryan became only the second Democrat ever elected to Congress from Nebraska, a Republican bastion.

There were vast differences between the parties. Democrats despised the Republican policy of protectionism. Many Democrats agitated for free world trade, maintaining that cheaper goods would help American workers; they saw tariffs on foreign goods as a tax. Democrats also pushed for economic policies that would help struggling farmers.

The Nebraska Democrat was good friends with J. B. Romans, a Denison businessman who owned a mansion one block north of Shaw's. Bryan visited when he was in Congress in his first two terms and was gearing up to run for president.

Bryan chose free silver as an issue. In those days, the United States was on the gold standard, that is, each greenback was backed in value with gold. (The gold standard was abolished in the first term of Franklin D. Roosevelt.) "Bimetallists" desired to include silver as a measure of value proportional to gold to expand the money supply. In other words, if it took 9 pounds of silver to equal that of 1 pound of gold, that 9 pounds of silver would be counted on as backing up the paper money supply. It's a complicated issue foreign to modern Americans; a good explanation was written by Paolo E. Coletta, a U.S. Naval Academy history professor:

> The election of 1896 remains "critical" because of its lasting import as a milestone in the conflict between agrarian and industrial America. Conservative Northeastern creditor interests viewed Bryan's advocacy of free silver as a sectional and agrarian demand for dishonorable repudiation of debt. To Western and Southern debtors, however, the free-silver issue represented the determination of "productive workers" to use the ballot to seek economic justice in a government-directed redistribution of the national wealth.

This debate took on increased seriousness after the economic crash of 1893 that led to a four-year-long depression. Armies of hobos in search of work swarmed on the trains going through Denison, including members of "Coxey's Army," followers of Jacob S. Coxey who marched on Washington to demand job creation; they were clubbed upon arrival in the capital. And there were calls for socialism, alarming the monied class.

Amid this nineteenth-century depression, a friend of Shaw wanted to bring Bryan to Denison in early February 1896 to hear the Nebraskan's monetary policy.

"I contributed toward the expense of the lecture," Shaw said in a 1906 interview with a newspaperman while sitting in the office of his Denison mansion. "Bryan spoke at the opera house on Saturday night and turned the town upside down."

Shaw saw expanding the money supply as leading to economic ruin. Shaw, the banker, was horrified by the results of Bryan's talk: there were many sudden free silver converts in Denison.

"On Monday I said that Bryan ought to be answered. Three or four of us met to discuss the matter. It was agreed that the speaker who came should be so much the superior of Bryan . . . but we couldn't find the man. Finally the others promised to rent the hall if I would make the speech."

Shaw knew a bad speech would either flop or simply make matters worse, wrote Shaw's friend, William R. Boyd in the *Annals of Iowa*, published by the Iowa State Department of History.

"So I studied, as I had never studied before," Shaw told Boyd. "I made a large easel and got some large sheets of manilla paper. I drew graphs and made charts to illustrate my speech."

In one account, the first speech tanked. Shaw went back and refined it. According to Boyd, Shaw discarded the boilerplate lecture sent by the national Republican Party. "Instead, he drew on his experiences as a farmhand, land owner, banker and lawyer."

Shaw's reply at the Germania Opera House went well.

"When Bryan appeared in the next county I was asked to repeat my Denison speech," Shaw said. "Then he was billed at some other town and I got there ahead of him, told what he would say and made my answer."

The pace increased after Bryan, the "boy orator of the Platte," won the Democratic nomination in Chicago on July 10, 1896. Bryan delivered his famous "cross of gold" speech at the convention.

"You shall not press down upon the brow of labor this crown of thorns, you shall not crucify mankind upon a cross of gold," Bryan thundered.

Passions ran deep. People started fistfights over gold versus silver. Shaw gave more than fifty anti–free silver speeches in Iowa and the region.

"I frequently spoke seven hours a day," Shaw said.

In each county where Shaw appeared, there was an increased number of votes for Republican candidate William McKinley. After Bryan was defeated, Shaw returned to his neglected business affairs, until the Iowa Republican convention in Cedar Rapids the following summer, and "that man Shaw" kept coming up, according to Boyd. Shaw was drafted to run for governor and wore out committeemen and reporters who followed the campaign. He won by a handsome margin.

Shaw was a popular governor. In 1898 he supported the war against Spain, championed by Theodore Roosevelt, the naval secretary in the McKinley White House and the prime mover to get the reluctant president to declare war. Governor Shaw mustered three regiments of infantry and two artillery batteries from Iowa citizens. After the war, he secured for Denison a captured Spanish cannon, manufactured in 1793 in Seville. (It remains mounted in front of the courthouse.)

Shaw easily won reelection in 1900 and that fall campaigned for McKinley's reelection. In South Dakota, probably in the town of Yankton by accounts, Shaw met up with Roosevelt, McKinley's vice-presidential pick. Roosevelt had gained fame because after he had a custom uniform made (as prissy as his western outfits), he led the charge up San Juan Hill in Cuba, and he later marketed his exploits to the press.

Roosevelt was to be the main speaker, but his voice gave out. He decided to make a "curtain raiser" and turn things over to the governor of Iowa. Roosevelt later said,

I was weary and my voice was frayed. It was arranged that I should speak for a few minutes and then return to my [rail] car to rest, and that governor Shaw should make the main address. When he was introduced, I thought I would stop for a few minutes to see how he started in that populistic hell-hole. I didn't go to my car at all. I stood there for two hours, wedged in between a lot of people. And I listened to the most masterly speech on the tariff and finance that I had ever listened to. I made up my mind that if I ever became president, I wanted that man as secretary of the treasury.

On December 12, 1900, Shaw was in Washington for the one hundredth anniversary of the District of Columbia being chosen for the seat of government. His speech, "The Development of the States During the Century," was given to a joint session of Congress, justices of the Supreme Court, and the president.

"This address drew from President McKinley the remark that he had never before found a man who could crystallize statistics into poetry," wrote Johnson Brigham in *Iowa: Its History and Its Foremost Citizens*.

Vice President Roosevelt, fresh off the war with Spain, was hawkish about building the young nation into a dominant world power. Shaw played to this tune in the speech, talking excitedly about the Panama Canal, then in the planning stage, "through which in coming years shall pass the commerce of the world, a moiety of which, let us hope, shall be in American bottoms. Events, unplanned and by some unwelcomed, have made the United States the mistress of the Pacific."

Shaw returned from this heady audience to fill out his last year as governor. He chose not to seek reelection and spurned calls to run for Congress. He was eager to return to Denison and the mansion that he'd barely lived in.

On September 6, 1901, President McKinley was assassinated in Buffalo, New York, at the Pan-American Exposition. Roosevelt was now president, but he didn't change the cabinet. Then in December, Treasury Secretary Lyman J. Gage stepped down.

Roosevelt appointed Shaw—to the surprise of many. Why did the president pick him? Shaw had been making waves about running for president in 1902, despite his pronouncements about wanting to return to Denison. A December 26, 1901, *New York Times* article speculated that Roosevelt chose Shaw as a means of neutralizing the threat of not picking up Iowa at the Republican convention. But Roosevelt was a strong candidate, and the *Times's* conjecture seems off base. There were many things working against the pick—for instance, no treasury secretary had ever come from an agricultural state, and Roosevelt stretched the credulity of Wall Street with an unknown. There were other high-profile men he could have chosen.

* * *

On January 26, 1902, Leslie and Alice Shaw were packing trunks in their mansion; in a few days, they were to leave for Washington. On this date

102 years later, I was at a lunch meeting of the 2020 Plan Executive Committee at Cronk's Cafe.

I was underslept and arrived late. The meeting occurred the morning after the first furnace pilot outage in the Shaw Mansion, and I had sputtered awake with the great weight on my chest. When I finally fell asleep, I didn't reawaken 'til nearly noon. I had hurriedly dressed and raced to the meeting.

Things were testy. Emotions ran high, for rumors abounded of more family businesses closing. And the Wal-Mart supercenter had come up, which would mean the death of even more Denison businesses.

Something had to be done, and it had to occur yesterday. This was the tone set by Mayor Ken Livingston and city manager Al Roder, and it was echoed by other members of the committee. Two entities were on the hot seat: the Crawford County Development Corporation (CCDC) and the Denison Chamber of Commerce. Were they doing enough not only to attract new business but to retain and help those already here? The CCDC was especially seen as ineffective. The chamber was in a bind, for it survived by the dues of current members. Many members feared new merchants who would be their competitors. If the chamber leadership angered members, they would quit, effectively killing the chamber. It was not the agency to lead.

Susan Pitts, the chamber executive vice president, was talking about why Denison residents did not shop in town. She noted that some residents want a wider range of baby clothes, but there wasn't enough of a population base to support this kind of a specialty store. Pitts suggested doing a survey among business leaders to determine what should be done, what kind of new business the town should attract.

"Shouldn't we ask what people want?" Doug Skarin, the past chamber president, asked. He noted they should be listening to residents rather than telling them what they need.

"When you ask people, they say they want a Target or an Applebee's," said Pitts. "Those companies look at communities with populations of 30,000 and higher. We're not ever going to get that." She paused. "I won't say never, but it's unlikely."

Al Roder turned the conversation in a new direction, noting that local businesses via the chamber of commerce may be their own worst enemy when it comes to recruiting new merchants.

"The first thing you hear is, 'Are they our competitor?'" Roder said. "But the worst thing in Uptown is empty storefronts, not a competitor."

One participant noted that there are many competitors in the huge Mall of America in Minnesota, and all thrive: more stores create a critical mass of traffic, begetting more business. Perhaps the chamber had to educate its members to this fact.

Pitts took the conversation back to the imminent danger.

"If a Super Wal-Mart comes in," Pitts said, "we have three grocery stores now. They say there will be just one left." Not only would supermarkets shutter; other businesses certainly would close.

"Won't the competition make them better?" asked Eric Skoog, who owns Cronk's.

Fred Dietze, the current chamber president, now grew excited.

"If a Super Wal-Mart comes in and we lose grocery stores, something is wrong with those stores. America is built on competition!"

A debate over Wal-Mart ensued. Skarin smirked through the conversation.

"McDonald's and Burger King didn't get recruited to come to Denison," Skarin said. "They came to us. I know, because I sold them the land. Wal-Mart won't build a superstore here or not because of anything we do or say."

Ken Livingston weighed in. Denison was drifting. He vented anger over those who were vocally opposing Streetscape and other aspects of the 2020 Plan.

"It's a bunch of crap!" he said about the opponents. "Somehow a public relations job is not being done!" The creation of a new entity to promote the town through marketing was absolutely vital, he expounded.

If they could combine the chamber of commerce, the county development agency, and the Donna Reed Foundation, perhaps they could fund a marketing person.

"We have to find a way to come up with $50,000 to enable the hiring of this person," Al said. "I did research for a person for a community our size. A strong person is $55,000 to $65,000. If you want a superstar, you're talking $80,000."

Ken sighed. "Everyone seems reactive. We're not proactive. We need some focus and conviction that is not taking place today."

* * *

After this meeting I ran into Betty Hawn, who, with her husband, Warren, owns V & H Tire on Highway 30. Betty visibly shuddered at the mention of a Wal-Mart supercenter.

"It's killing everyone!"

Theirs is a family-owned tire store, and they were hanging on.

"Business has been down since 9/11," Betty said. It fell after that date and never picked up. Why 9/11 saw the falloff for their business in Denison remained a mystery to Betty. They'd opened the store in 1968. Warren had been in the U.S. Air Force. When he came home, he went to college, then went to work for Firestone Tire.

"We started with . . . ," Betty said, and she paused, trying to find the words for nothing, " . . . with nothing. I mean we had nothing. When we started, we had to borrow money. If you tried to do that today, there's no way you could. It's hard for the small businessman."

In those days there were more tire manufacturers, and they granted exclusive sales zones. With consolidation in the industry, the few corporations remaining no longer needed to cater to dealers. Exclusive zones are history. Tires are sold everywhere, even on the Internet. A big problem is that tire makers cater to Wal-Mart.

"They sell to them for one price and to you for another. How can you compete? It's hard for the little person. Our son is about to take over, and I worry if he is going to be able to make it."

Was this just competition squeezing out an inferior competitor?

Things were moving slowly with the plan to consolidate the chamber and county development agency. The agencies were talking, but not much was happening. In this period of angst, there was more bad news to pile on for Denison. A second woman's clothing store was shutting its doors. On the Latino end of things, to my sadness, La Estrella went under as well.

But all these were not as devastating to townspeople as the news that Topko Drug would close. One day the windows were plastered with signs advertising 25 percent off. I walked by as a middle-aged man on a bicycle pulled up, shock visible on his face.

"They're going out of business!" he exclaimed to an older man coming out the door.

"We all are," the man replied.

Inside, owner Craig Whited reflected on the twenty-two years since he opened the drugstore in 15,000 square feet of space; his was the largest independent pharmacy in Iowa at the time. Whited, a rugged-looking pharmacist with a graying mustache who rides a Harley-Davidson motorcycle and pilots a small plane, said that what he did then could not be replicated today. Back then, the stakes were lower and the chances of success higher in a town the size of Denison. What was possible in 1982 was not in 2004.

"I don't want to be negative, but a person who would do it wouldn't do it in a community that has 8,500 people and is one-third Hispanic, people who have no use for any of this stuff," he said of many items he sells, such as home oxygen supply for an aging white population. "Why not go to a bigger community where you can start dancing right away?"

He said that to do what he did in 1982, a prospective drugstore owner would need a population base of 50,000 to 60,000. When I mentioned Wal-Mart, Craig visibly stiffened. He emphasized the giant did not do him in. But it had been a long battle, one of which he was proud.

"I turned fifty," he offered as a reason for closing the store. "That is a threshold. I want to do things."

Craig wants to ride his Harley on long road trips. He's tired of working as the pharmacist from 8:30 A.M. to 6:00 P.M., and then at night when people call him at home to come in and fill prescriptions. He often puts in twelve-hour days.

He once had a second pharmacist, but for the past year and a half he was unable to hire a replacement for the last one, who had quit. There was a shortage of pharmacists because the schooling was raised from five to six years and there was a "missing year" of newly minted graduates. At the same time, chains such as Walgreens were expanding: in fiscal 2004, the company opened one store per day. Many Walgreens were twenty-four-hour operations and were eating up pharmacists.

"A professional won't come to a small town," he said as an additional reason. "There aren't the amenities—the good places to eat, the Starbucks, the things to do."

But wasn't Wal-Mart a factor?

Craig again stiffened. It was clearly personal.

"They're predatory. They don't want to compete. They want to elimi-nate you. They felt I would be gone in six months. I thought, 'No way.' We'll be smarter than that. We prepared for them. We studied them, and we went to different items to compete."

One secret of Wal-Mart is that the chain is low-priced on hundreds of key common items but that it charges higher on many others.

"You have to carry Tylenol head to head with them and lose money on it, but you sell the generic, and that is where you make money. I can com-pete on house brands."

Topko saw a 5 percent drop in sales after Wal-Mart opened in 1992. But then Craig held his own. The store had been in constant evolution. He once had a large custom picture framing department and sold large-sized women's clothing. Then he went into care products for elderly peo-ple, something Wal-Mart does not deal with. I asked how often he'd changed Topko.

"Eighteen times."

I was astonished. He laughed. You have to constantly reinvent yourself, he noted. "What's right today is going to be wrong tomorrow."

Craig marveled at Wal-Mart's savvy. The company began in Denison by raiding his workforce, so there would be familiar local faces in the big box when it opened.

"They took away our employees to give them an immediate warm and cozy feeling for people not used to going to a chain. They do that every-where."

Then they went through his garbage to look at his receipts. I looked in-credulous. But he knew about this because he'd have drinks with his for-mer workers and heard the inside story of what Wal-Mart management was doing.

"They're marketing geniuses. But they're lying dogs," Craig said. He pointed to the plugs paid for by Wal-Mart on the "news" show by radio commentator Paul Harvey, a conservative fossil still popular in rural Iowa.

"They have Paul Harvey telling stories about how their truckers stop and help people." Craig laughed heartily. He doesn't believe it happens.

He said some communities have figured out that Wal-Mart's "warm and fuzzy" is a lie. In upscale areas such as Cape Cod, Craig noted, many citizens have gone back to small pharmacies. But they pay more for what they get.

"This community is not that far along in the curve. This is a dollars-and-cents community. It's a place where the salary is $27,000."

But, I asked, doesn't his service outstrip that of Wal-Mart and buy him loyalty?

He again laughed.

"At this point here, I'll come in at night to fill a prescription for someone, and the next day they'll be back at Wal-Mart."

Craig beamed about his ability to withstand Wal-Mart, and the timing of closing Topko was one last stab at the chain: he sold the name to the Hy-Vee Supermarket across the street, where he would be employed as a pharmacist.

"It will be forty hours. That's no hours to me."

Craig went to store director Todd Tetmyer, who jumped at the opportunity. Hy-Vee saw having an in-store pharmacy as a way to position itself to compete if the Wal-Mart Supercenter came. Within days of the sale, jackhammers were ripping up the sidewalk to add on to the front to make room for the pharmacy.

"With a drug counter, they're not as vulnerable," Craig said. "People will come in to get pharmaceuticals and shop while they wait. It's very important to me that Hy-Vee does well, that downtown does well. I was born here. If Hy-Vee were to go out, Uptown is dead."

Left unspoken after I left Craig at the pharmacy counter in Topko were all the ways Wal-Mart was helped by overarching forces: for example, the fact that the government has made it so much more difficult for workers to organize at such vehemently anti-union companies as Wal-Mart. But there were deeper issues.

When Fred Dietze, the chamber president, thundered, "America is built on competition," he was ignorant of what Wal-Mart really is and does. Wal-Mart long ago went beyond simply being a smart business. It now dictated prices to suppliers and ordered those suppliers to run their businesses in ways advantageous to Wal-Mart.

William Jennings Bryan and the Democrats at the end of the nineteenth century saw their wildest dream come true: cheap imported goods were now the rule of the land. But would the Republicans of a century ago have called Wal-Mart on par with that of the Standard Oil Company trust?

A trust was a monopoly that fixed prices and practiced unfair marketing to the detriment not just of competitors but the American consumer. In the case of Standard Oil, John D. Rockefeller had the idea to crush smaller companies by forming the trust that fixed prices by ending competition; the bigger Standard Oil got, the more power it had to destroy upstarts. In the 1870s, it demanded and got far lower railroad shipping rates than its competitors. Then when pipelines came along, the company bought up controlling interest in those pipelines. Thus, competitors were forced to surrender and sell to the giant. The giant got bigger. At the time, some called this good business, a model of American capitalism at its best.

The first attack on these arrangements was the Sherman Antitrust Act of 1890, but that law was filled with loopholes. It was revived under the administration of Theodore Roosevelt, who broke up forty-five companies in his administration, including the Standard Oil Company.

The myth learned by generations of schoolchildren is that Roosevelt was the trustbuster who hated big business. The reality is more complicated. Roosevelt did not despise business. It was quite the opposite. He was driven by two motives.

One was that he was actually protecting business. Many corporations secretly wanted controls, for regulations would protect their profits from unbridled competition. For example, many companies wanted rate controls on the railroads, and even some railroad companies wanted the restrictions, for they lost profit when large shippers demanded deals.

Two, there was pressure from progressives against the ravages of the worst of the trusts. If the Republicans did nothing, they might lose office. So Roosevelt and Shaw and other members of the administration went after the most flagrant and flamboyant money grubbers. By sacrificing them, it took pressure off the larger business community.

Would Roosevelt and his treasury secretary have seen value in helping V & H Tire in Denison, Iowa, and other small companies in hundreds of American communities? How could one answer the Fred Dietzes of the country, who saw Wal-Mart as the shining pinnacle of American capitalism?

I pondered these questions as I lay in bed in the Shaw Mansion. If there was a ghost, perhaps the ghost was trying to tell me something. In the cold light of day, I laughed this off. But then one evening I sat in my broken Wal-Mart chair and stared at two of Shaw's books that Nathan Mahrt had loaned me, perched unread on the Wal-Mart desk. I'd been saving them to read at some later point. I suddenly felt compelled to immediately open them.

THE GHOST SPEAKS

U.S. Treasury Secretary Leslie M. Shaw traveled to Des Moines in 1904 to speak about the tariff on imported goods, an issue that bitterly split Iowa Republicans in an election year.

"The atmosphere that night was tense," wrote William R. Boyd in the *Annals of Iowa.* "The leaders of the two factions glared at each other from the boxes on opposite sides of the stage. The audience was about evenly divided. Shaw refused to let anybody introduce him. When the hour for the speech arrived, he walked out of the wings and down to the footlights, looked over the audience, and smiled. He was a slender man, slightly stooped, with a keenly intellectual face and kindly eyes":

I am in a very embarrassing position here tonight. I am a Republican. I am a member of a Republican administration. I have to make a Republican speech. I wouldn't want to make any other kind, but I don't want to hurt anybody. The situation reminds me of what took place once upon a time, when a peace-loving Englishman was challenged to a duel by a fiery Frenchman. The Englishman didn't want to fight; neither did he wish to be branded for life as a coward, as he would have been in those days had he refused. Therefore, he accepted, and exercising the prerogative of the challenged party, chose as the place a dark room, and for weapons, pistols.

On the appointed day, the duelers and friends went to the room, in a building near a church with a clock in its steeple. The room contained a huge open fireplace. The men were to fire when the clock struck noon. The friends left, Shaw related, and as they did so, turned off the lights:

Now the Frenchman, who was at heart a coward and fearful that he would get hurt, the moment the room was darkened climbed into the chimney and when the clock struck the first stroke of twelve, the kind-hearted Englishman, not wishing to hurt even his opponent, went and shot the gun off up the chimney. [Pause.] Now I don't want to hurt anybody, but I have to make a Republican speech.

Both sides roared with laughter and the ice was broken.

Shaw used a folksy style to shape policy. His disarming manner belied a hard-core conservatism. In ways he mirrored modern Republicans. Shaw was Ayn Rand before there was Ayn Rand, one discovers on reading his public speeches and official correspondence, published in his 1908 book, *Current Issues*.

"Without stopping to define the recognized distinction between anarchism, nihilism, and communism, I shall proceed to defend individualism against the entire array. . . . Self interest controls the race, and within proper limits, has the stamp of divine approval. It is idle, therefore, to rail against it," he wrote in one of many examples of Rand-like comments. This isn't surprising to a contemporary eye reading *Current Issues* for insight into today's conservative views. But as one turns the pages, there are revelations.

When *Current Issues* was published, nearly a century had passed since Great Britain began following a theory put forth by British economist David Ricardo: that of "comparative advantage." It posited that if each country specialized in what it did best and traded for goods according to its ability to produce them cheaply, the economy of each nation would prosper. Most Democrats at the time of Shaw were ardent free traders and wanted the United States to emulate Great Britain, then the only major industrial country without protective tariffs.

Two centuries have gone by since Great Britain embarked on a policy of free trade, an experiment now wholeheartedly embraced by the United States. Shaw's views in 1908 fall at the midpoint of the evolution of the theory. In a speech in Philadelphia, Shaw summed up the difference between his party and the Democrats based on the election that swept Grover Cleveland into office:

The first complete victory achieved by the Democratic Party in a third of a century was in 1892. That victory was won in a clean-cut, good faith, and honorable issue between the cardinal doctrines of free trade and protection. Our opponents appealed to the American people as consumers, and commiserated them. We appealed to the American people as producers, and congratulated them. They said, "You deserve a better market in which to buy." We said, "You deserve no poorer market in which to sell."

They iterated and reiterated the statement that "the tariff is a tax," and stoutly maintained, from one side of the country to the other, that the abolishment of the protective tariff would afford the people cheap articles of consumption without affecting the price of our products.

After victory in 1892, the Democrats kept tariffs on iron and steel "and a score of other articles," but "put wool and coal and twenty other things on the free list." Shaw blamed the crash of 1893 on this opening of free trade, made worse by the mixed tariff policy. A depression followed and lasted until 1897.

In a 1904 speech to boys in St. Louis, Shaw pointed to the crash and the success of the Roosevelt administration. "Young men," he said, "it is not by accident that this country is prosperous today, nor was it by accident that it was unprosperous in the Nineties.... By giving the American producer an advantage at home over his foreign competitor, we have builded the greatest market in the world."

In his book, Shaw lauded one Democrat, Senator John M. Niles, of Connecticut, who warned that the nation should not open its markets. "Is it to carry out a theory?" Niles asked. "Is it to test the cold, heartless, miserable theory of free trade?"

Neither Niles nor Shaw used language common today, but the end result of the theory is what we would now call a "race to the bottom." Shaw predicted the Chinese would work for nothing, and how could American workers be expected to compete against what was essentially slave labor?

Even in 1908, holes had developed in the theory of comparative advantage. When the United Kingdom bought into free trade, shipping costs were very high. Only the most desirable and hard-to-create goods were imported. The world had gone from sail-powered wooden ships with small holds to steam vessels with massive holds:

> There is one marked difference in conditions prevailing now and fifty years ago. The cost of transportation from Europe to the United States at one time afforded quite a degree of protection to the American producer. Cheap freight rates have very nearly wiped this out. ... The English laborer can pay the transportation charges on a year's supply of food from the United States to England with a single day's work.

A century after Shaw, the era with broadband Internet capacity, even more barriers have fallen to the comparative advantage theory. Indian companies handle telephone calls for American firms, and Indian technicians read X-rays sent in a nanosecond from the United States.

If Americans were expected to compete with workers earning pennies per hour, Shaw predicted great unemployment:

> Eighty million idlers would mean eighty million beggars. Eighty millions of people, with every man employed who is willing to work, means exactly what we now experience—the greatest prosperity ever witnessed on earth. . . . The secret of American prosperity can be couched in four words: "They are working now." And "they" means everybody—farmer and artisan, mechanic and merchant, the man at the forge and the man in the field—and they are all interdependent. Low wages compel poor living, and poor living harms the farmer and manufacturer also, for it restricts the consumptive capacity of the country.

From the 1980s forward, as free trade expanded further, American manufacturing jobs were in steady decline: what now ruled was the "Wal-Mart" economy in which Americans sold cheaply made goods made by overseas workers. It's as if William Jennings Bryan had willed the creation of the behemoth. In a way, he did. Bryan was secretary of state in the administration of Democrat Woodrow Wilson when the president pushed through the Underwood Tariff Act in 1913, which ended tariffs for protection and mandated they be only for revenue, "the first thoroughgoing downward revision of import duties since 1846," wrote novelist and historian John Dos Passos. It began a long series of rollbacks in protections.

One can insert *Wal-Mart* into passages in Shaw's book: the company with its 1 million-plus workers is infamous for wages of seven or eight dollars per hour. Wal-Mart could not exist as it does without free trade. Wal-Mart and its equivalents are synonymous with the working poor who have to visit food banks at the end of the month to feed their children. Wal-Mart now clings to Shaw's party: 85 percent of the campaign donation checks the company writes are to Republicans.

Shaw cast a warning to the future:

> Our Democratic opponents appeal to us from the consumer's side, and say to us that we will be happy and prosperous if we can buy the things we consume sufficiently cheap. They assure us that it is unimportant who produces that which we consume provided the price is low enough. They advocate opening wide the doors of trade so that whoever can produce the thing we eat, or the thing we wear, or the things that unite to form the roof that covers us, the cheapest shall supply our necessities.
>
> The Republican party approaches us from the producer's side, and says to us that we will be contented and prosperous if we can get satisfactory returns for that which we produce, whether it be a day's labor or the resultant of a day's labor. We Republicans say it is relatively unimportant that price we pay, provided we buy of ourselves, so that the proceeds shall remain with us and in turn used to buy other commodities which we also produce. We insist that the foreign competitor shall pay a portion of the proceeds of competing wares which he may sell in this country into the public treasury, thereby contributing to the maintenance of the government, and thereby as well given the American producer an advantage in the American market.
>
> They say, Place us in power and you shall pluck the ripest fruits of the toil of other men's hands without let or hindrance, and you shall be fed from the fields and clothed from the looms of other countries.

We say, Put us in power and you shall be fed from the products of American fields and clothed with the product of the American loom, and the utensils of your trade and the furniture of your home shall bear the imprint of well-paid American labor. They say, Place us in power and we will give you the best market in the world in which to buy. We say, Put us in power and we will give you the best market in the world in which to sell. You cannot have both.

When Shaw published his book in 1908, he wrote about American corporations with American interests. By century's end, many would become multinational corporations with interests beyond the United States. The party of Theodore Roosevelt changed with them. The Republicans became the Democrats, bobble-headed cheerleaders of free trade. Today a majority in both parties support it, and anyone who questions this policy is branded naive.

If Shaw were alive now, would he be a free trader, toeing the party line, as he espoused what then was the party's position in 1908 when it catered to the wish of American business interests?

I strongly suspect he'd buck the party. The passion of his book repeatedly stresses the well-being of the working man and woman. Shaw was familiar with hard work, knew the value of people as individuals. "The best product of the prairie is not corn, but men," he wrote. He also uttered the term *square deal* in his inaugural speech as governor in 1900, a term Teddy Roosevelt used four years later. As late as 1928, four years before his death at age eighty-three, Shaw wrote about how America's workers earned a payroll of some $600 million per week. "Any people with a payroll of $600,000,000 a week would be great, and any country foolish enough to vote itself into competition with all the world in its own markets will gradually drop to the standard of the world."

Shaw anticipated the modern liberal argument that holds that free markets share the world's wealth with developing countries:

I wish all the world well, but if anyone has to be out of employment, if there must be suffering somewhere, then I will use my best efforts that it come not nigh my country. If, to accomplish this, it shall be necessary that I pay more for my clothes, more for my shoes, more for my sewing machine, more for my typewriter, more for the barbed wire used on my Iowa farm, than is paid for the same articles in Europe, then I will not object, so long as the products of American farms feed, and the products of American looms clothe, and the products of American labor generally supply every need of those who produce these things.

LA MAESTRA III

When class resumed in January after Christmas break, there was, at most, just one other volunteer; many nights it was just Georgia and me. There were fewer students—a dozen to twenty—as Georgia had said was normal. There was a new configuration at my table: Mina, Juan Escobar, William Galicia, Martha, a few others. Mina, with her wide eyes and hennaed hair, was now attempting to use English a little bit.

"Hello. How are you?" she asked one night.

"I am fine."

The conversation could go no further in English. But it was advancement. I wondered how far she would proceed by April. She told me in Spanish that she now worked at one of the meat plants.

Latinos continued to arrive in town despite the cold weather. When I went by the Oficina Hispanica de Información, I often saw new families coming in or out. The office ran on pennies derived from *panqueques*, in the manner of the biblical loaves and fishes story. It was the only official welcome Latinos had to Denison. The Lutherans were doing the heavy lifting without proselytizing, while others were merely talking. The packing plants did nothing. One night I was at a social event with Joel Franken, and we ran into a top plant official. I mentioned Georgia's class, and the official looked puzzled.

"Who's Georgia Hollrah?"

"She's teaching your workers English," Joel said.

Yet positive things were happening. The Denison Police Department in February hired its first bilingual officer, Juan Gonzalez, the result of a three-year search by Chief Rod Bradley. Also, the *Denison Bulletin & Review* published a Spanish-language tabloid, *Descubra Denison*, Discover Denison.

Some people were going beyond platitudes. Others had self-interest in mind. *Descubra Denison*, one could argue, was loaded with advertisements. Some who seemed to sincerely desire to reach out didn't have the ability to see what they should do.

At the Denison Chamber of Commerce I talked with Susan Pitts, the executive vice president. She was nervous. I'd heard that a packing plant interpreter had gone to Latino businesses encouraging them to join the chamber. Susan said, "We've done a lot, too!" There were many Latino members. Minutes later, she said no, there were two members out of the sixteen to twenty Latin businesses—a restaurant and an interpretation service.

At the chamber's annual banquet at Cronk's Cafe in February, the speaker was Barbara Mack, an Iowa State University professor, who gave a demographics lesson. She noted that Iowa's population reached its maximum in 1920 and has since been in decline. Were immigrants a salvation? Perhaps. But were they being welcomed? Mack praised the efforts of Denison's schools. She then asked if the business community had done enough.

"I have a feeling that if you had done the best possible job, I would see different faces here tonight."

The room was filled with whites.

"We have the real opportunity to sow the seeds of unity and hope, or we can sow the earth with the salt of exclusivity, disunity, and factionalism," Mack said. If the latter choice is made, Iowa would be filled with dying communities. She said that Denison was at a critical "tipping point." If it didn't bring the Latinos into the mainstream, the town would not flourish.

In a column on the editorial page of the *Denison Bulletin & Review*, staff writer Gordon Wolf highlighted Mack's comments imploring citizens to reach out by "inviting Latinos to your business and inviting Latino children to your home."

In the next issue of the paper, an anonymous reader's comments were published in Sound Off:

The Latinos are here at the convenience of our packing plants. I would be more than willing to visit their businesses if they would all learn our language. After all, this is our country and they should have more respect for us.

A week after this appeared, I entered Taqueria Los II Hermanos, a two-week-old Uptown restaurant. The family that owned it, watching a Spanish-language movie, was visibly surprised when I walked in. I was the first white customer, I was told by the daughter, who took my order in English.

It was *muy Mexicano.* The room was bare. The only decorations were some Mylar chiles on strings in the window and a lone tiny cactus. They didn't have menus. The daughter ticked off six items I could choose, from tacos to menudo.

"Do you know what a tortilla is?"

On the coasts, such a question would be insulting. Here it was genuine.

"De maize?"

The daughter was surprised by my asking in Spanish if they had corn tortillas.

"Yes. My mom makes them by hand."

I ordered four tacos—pork and beef. As much as I had liked La Estrella, this food was different. These were *campesino* tacos, the "peasant" kind with the thick tortillas common in backwater Mexico. They were stunning. This was the real deal. But the service was also *campesino* Mexico. My Coke came with no glass nor ice. I was given no silverware. I didn't mind, but I couldn't imagine white Denisonites flocking in if they couldn't look at a menu or use a fork.

It seemed simple. If the chamber wanted to pull in new businesses such as this, they would have come in opening day (or sooner). Chamber and city officials told me that they felt they couldn't do such things because they didn't know Spanish. But here, as with many other family businesses, language was not a barrier if the businesses were visited in nonschool hours. The chamber could have advised about making a menu (even photocopies) and what it would take to attract whites, such as two-for-one offers. And the chamber wouldn't have pressed for membership. The family was broke. When I paid, they couldn't change a twenty. The cash drawer had only loose pennies and nickels and dimes.

In time and with luck, the family would thrive and might join the chamber. Or the business would fail. No matter. At the least, word would spread about the helpful chamber advice, and it would be a start at building the bridges Mack talked about.

I was feeling pretty good about this idea as I left Taqueria Los II Hermanos. I slept on these good feelings.

The next day I was at the Hy-Vee purchasing the makings of dinner. A worker I knew helped me. She was a typical Iowan—just plain friendly. The conversation turned to German culture and how Germans were such a huge influence in Denison, and then were bashed in 1918.

"We're all from somewhere else," the woman, of German heritage, said. "It's such a shame we lost the language."

The Hy-Vee management asked if any workers wanted to learn Spanish. Some seventeen employees availed themselves of the program, including her. I mentioned that I was tutoring at Georgia Hollrah's ESL class. The conversation took a sharp turn, like there was an audible snap.

"I saw that article in the paper," she said in reference to Mack's talk. "A lot of people feel like I do. That article makes me so mad! Telling us to take them into our homes. They should be reaching out to us! They don't want to."

The woman railed against Latino youths, whom she felt were rude, others being criminals. I said nothing as she grew increasingly agitated. It was a stunning shift that contradicted what she'd just said about Germans. I'd been hanging around Georgia and others, removed from this dark side of Denison. There was rage in this woman. I suspected she wouldn't go even if Taqueria Los II Hermanos offered her a free meal. I had a sinking feeling. My hope of the previous day vaporized.

"I think I'm going to stop learning," she continued of the Spanish class. "I'm not taking anyone into my home!"

And then she ceased talking about Latinos. She again was so "Iowa"— pleasant and warm, the stereotype of a heartland woman. I too was very Iowa as I smiled and bid a friendly farewell. I hated myself for thinking as I walked away, *The white buffalo is gonna kick your ass.*

* * *

I was in Georgia's class waiting for seven o'clock to strike. It was a Monday, a few days after my encounter with the Hy-Vee woman.

Juan Escobar asked "what have I been to."

I didn't understand. Then it became clear. He asked me to write the correct way to say what he meant. I wrote,

"What have you been up to?"

Or, I wrote, he could say,

"What did you do last weekend?"

Juan copied down both questions. Martha, a very nice middle-aged Salvadoran, also copied them. Juan and William then peppered me with other questions.

"How do you spend your day?"

I again explained that I was writing a book. *"Escribiendo un libro,"* I said. They got that. No, no, they said. What they meant, after some back-and-forth Spanglish, was they could not comprehend how someone paid me to do nothing but live in a town and talk with people.

"I am very lucky," I said.

"What is it about?" asked a man who was listening from a nearby table.

"It's about *todos personas en Denison,*" I said, about all people of Denison. "White, Latino. It's about change, about a town. It's also about cultural change, *cambio de cultura.* Some whites don't like Latinos."

"Oh yes!" Martha said, rolling her eyes. Heads all around bobbed. Georgia began the lesson.

A question in the class workbook asked, "Who does the cooking in your house?" Georgia went around the room seeking volunteers to respond.

"I do the cooking at my house," Martha said.

"I don't do the cooking at my house," a student named Francisco said.

"My wife and I both do the cooking at my house," Juan said.

Martha reached across our table to shake Juan's hand.

"This is good!" Martha said. Everyone laughed.

The class continued. In a lull, when students were writing down an exercise, Juan raised his hand.

"Maestra, what is 'wonderful?'"

"*Es fantástico, comó . . .*"

" . . . Oh, I see!" Juan said. "It's a wonderful life."

"Yes," Georgia said. "It is true."

"It's on the water tower," I said.

"The water tower would not lie," Georgia added.

HOMELAND AND THE HEARTLAND

I was photocopying old records in the Crawford County Courthouse when a worker began talking to her colleagues about a coming tropical vacation to escape the brutal winter. I looked up and said I'd moved here because of the climate. The woman was puzzled. I added, with a serious face, that I'd been told there were palm trees in Denison. Now she looked aghast.

"I was misinformed."

I'd appropriated Humphrey Bogart's line from *Casablanca;* I let on that I was joking. She smiled, a little, and asked why I really had moved to town. Now she even looked more aghast. Why would anyone volunteer to live in Denison when he could have picked anywhere else?

"There's nothing to do here."

"Well, look at the bright side. At least you're not a terrorism target."

"I'm not so sure we aren't. If they were smart, they'd come attack here, hit us in the middle. We don't expect it here."

Her coworkers nodded somberly. Others in town felt the same. It wasn't just Denison paranoia; the mood was similar throughout the rest of the Midwest. Twice while driving through Nebraska on backroads as I came and went from Iowa, police had stopped me for spurious reasons. Once I was told I was going forty-one in the forty zone; I'd seen the cop and knew I was doing thirty-eight. The cop had eyed the bed of my truck, then relaxed; he told me they just had to be careful these days.

At least two Denison companies were doing well because of terrorism. Peterson Manufacturing Company and Bohlmann once made concrete hog watering troughs but now produced antiterrorism concrete barriers. There were eighty-some workers between the companies, and they sold products all over the world.

The U.S. government was beginning to dole out homeland security funds, and Denison, like hundreds of other communities, was eyeing these monies. Fire Chief Mike McKinnon had landed a few of these grants. Perhaps those funds could also help build the golf course conference center. This was the subject of a work session I attended that winter between the project backers, Mayor Ken Livingston, Police Chief Rod Bradley, McKinnon, and others that included a representative of Frontier Communications, the phone company.

"Grants are available through Homeland Security to use for the community center," Ken told the group.

The notion was to put a backup command center for the police and fire services in the basement, as well as communications services for private companies. Ken said the bottom was going to be a foundation over dirt, but if they could get funds, it could be made into a 5,000 square-foot bunker. This "emergency operations center" would cost at least $250,000, perhaps more.

"We just want to get the space occupied and contributing," Ken said.

The Frontier representative said, "Homeland Defense seems to be coming up with a lot of cash."

*　*　*

Sheriff Tom Hogan pulled his unmarked official SUV out of the lot next to the Crawford County Courthouse, taking me to where the eleven railcar dead had been discovered. He is forty-five and for a time worked at the Farmland plant. He is thin, tall, and always wears body armor, but has more the manner of an Eagle Scout than a cop. He approaches his job with passion. One citizen deemed him "Dudley Do-Right."

We hit the Lincoln Highway and drove west to the grain elevators. He turned onto a gravel road and pointed to where the car with the eleven dead had been located. It shook him.

"They weren't coming here. But they ended up here. As I stared into that grain car that day, I thought, there are no borders . . . we are all the same."

Hogan said the national media showed up and got to see "a side of Denison that was very compassionate." But he said the face of town painted by the city's leaders was one of them dealing well with the cultural change, that it was all good.

"People out there are scared. It's not all good."

Tom pulled back onto the Lincoln Highway and asked if I had some time. "Sure," I said. We went north on gravel roads.

"It's real easy to be a racist," he continued. "They're racist out of fear. It's a fear of jobs. They see Hispanics as competing with them. They're not unfounded fears. But they don't look at the real threat. They don't see corporate greed being the reason. They see the Latino taking their job."

Tom seemed atypical of the law officers I'd dealt with, so I brought up an article in the previous day's newspapers about Iowa's just-disbursed $28 million share of antiterrorism homeland security grants. The *Des Moines Register* reported that Des Moines got $250,000 of these monies; the city has a population of 198,700. Sioux County, with 31,600 residents, got $299,000. I asked how much of this money his department ended up with.

"What do you think about Iraq?" Tom asked, not answering my question.

The war was a sensitive subject in town; if it were talked about, I certainly did not hear criticism. Ken Livingston told me any Democrat who publicly questioned President George W. Bush was essentially regarded as committing treason. I pointed out to Ken that even in 1944, Republicans attacked the way Franklin D. Roosevelt was prosecuting the war. This was different, Ken shot back. The Iraq War had to be supported. Period.

"You want to know what I really think?" I asked Tom.

"Yes."

"It's an unmitigated disaster."

"Exactly."

Tom pointed to the Rotary Club where we'd first met when I had given a talk. There were thirty or so Rotarians in the room, and Tom told me each had been in favor of the war except him.

"It bothered me. Rotarians are supposed to be about brotherhood and love. They jumped all over me. I can't talk about this around here. Is it like that everywhere? We don't really know who we're fighting. Now, I believe in war. It has a place. But I believe we should only fight wars in which we are willing to publicly put gas on their children, light a match, and photograph them burning to death. It comes down to that. That's the reality of what war is. You know what? Your cause better be worth it."

He likened the Iraq situation to a domestic disturbance.

"The first thing we learn in law enforcement is we don't give someone a common enemy," Tom said, referring to how an officer doesn't want to give any reason for both spouses to turn on the cop. In other words, don't have two opposing sides unite in hating you. Tom told the story about an Indian reservation near where he grew up in Minnesota. After the Indians were pacified, a trading post opened, owned by a white man. The Indians were starving, and the post would not give them any food.

"The agent told the Indians that they should go out and eat grass. So when there was an uprising, he was the first killed. And they stuffed his mouth with grass."

All this sounded very left wing to a New York and California ear. But I learned Tom is conservative in many ways. He wasn't talking this way as a liberal. Tom is deeply religious, a member of Zion Lutheran Church, and he came to these conclusions based on his abiding Christian beliefs.

"I stopped talking about that," Tom said. People thought he was trying to convert them. "Instead, I talk about Christian ideals. We're all bad at times. We all have bad in us."

He is a man who comfortably quotes Gandhi, Martin Luther King, Eugene Debs. He talked about his jihad, and he used it the correct way—as a personal struggle. He said he didn't like being a cop in the Hollywood sense of the job—pulling a gun, being Rambo. That's not the thrill for him.

"I'm a mediator, a conflict resolution specialist."

He told the story of a local white supremacist who was suspected of growing marijuana. State and federal agents came to Tom and said they heard the man was armed and dangerous, and were going to send officers with guns drawn in a show of force. Tom knew the suspect: he was extremely volatile. The man had children, and Tom warned against pulling guns on his kids.

"I told the head agent, if you do that, he will shoot you. I don't want a Ruby Ridge here. Let me go out there and talk to him. 'You're nuts,' he said to me."

Tom drove up to the man's door. The suspect answered, and Tom asked him to step outside.

"I said, there are twenty state and federal agents waiting down the road.

I'll make a deal with you: no guns on your children and no handcuffs if you come quietly. He said, 'Thank you.'"

The man went without a struggle. He was placed in a cell in Tom's jail. A few days later, Tom was talking to the suspect about the bust and he "told me that, 'yes, I would have shot them if they pulled a gun on my kids.'"

We were now on distant and desolate gravel roads, had been driving about two hours. I got back to my question. How much of the $28 million in homeland security funds did his department apply for?

"None. We didn't request any."

"Why?"

"Because it's a sham. The problem that plagues Crawford County, that money doesn't fix."

The Crawford County Sheriff's Department has nine deputies to patrol the 714-square-mile county, twenty-four hours a day, seven days a week. He needs more officers, not more toys. None of those grants pay for officers.

"Look, we got $15,000 in night vision equipment for free already. It was a grant. All we had to do was attend a training session in Florida. It was Raytheon and those companies. It's all about making money. We didn't have to go to the training session. The equipment has four knobs, and you could figure out how to use it in five minutes. We've used it two times in one and a half years. Could we have gotten away without using it? Yes. We don't really need it."

If terrorists were to do something really big in Crawford County, such as derailing or blowing up a train carrying chlorine gas cars, any equipment Tom's department could get—a few helmets and hazmat suits—would be worthless against a billowing deadly cloud.

"We like being scared. I will not be afraid of terrorism. Some of the bigger cities will get a helicopter to fight terrorism. But do they need it? Before September 11, if it was tied to drug enforcement, you got money. Then came terrorism, and now you get money."

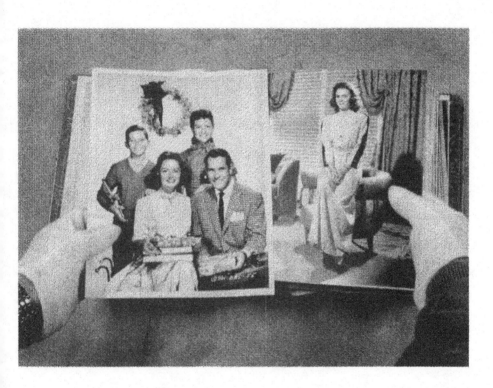

ARTIFACTS, DONNA REED MUSEUM.

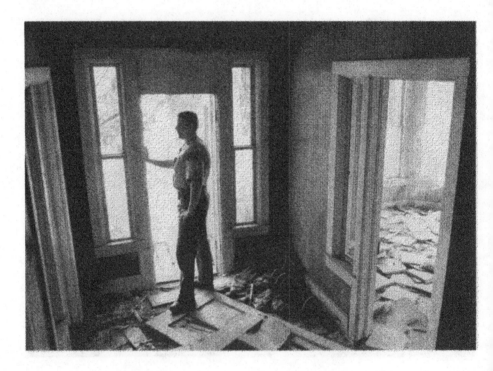

CRAWFORD COUNTY SHERIFF TOM HOGAN.

CRACK DEN IN THE SHAW MANSION.

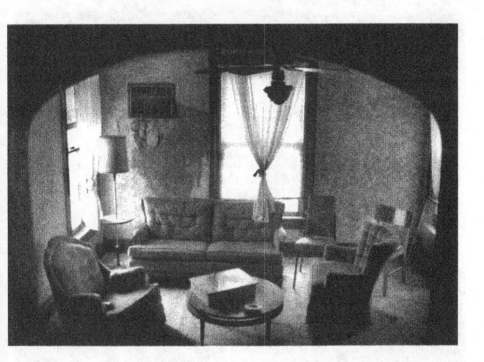

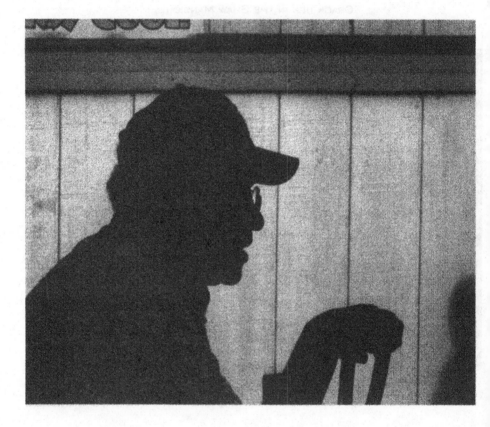

THE OLD MAN.

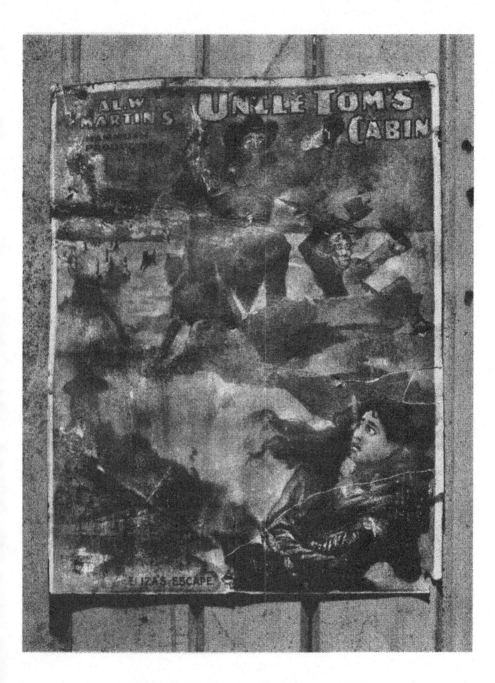

POSTER OF TOURING THEATRICAL PRODUCTION,
CIRCA 1900, DISCOVERED IN 2004 BEHIND A SEALED WALL
OF THE OLD GERMAN OPERA HOUSE.

BROADWAY.

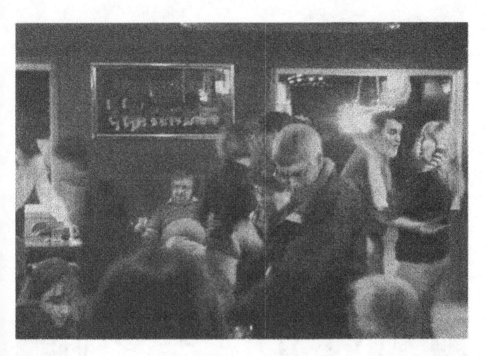

St. Patrick's Day, Prime Times Lounge.

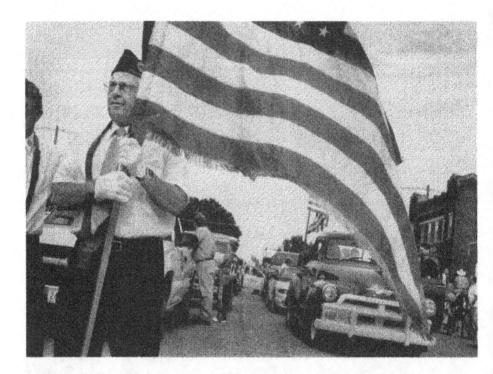

VFW members, Donna Reed Festival parade.

Float, Donna Reed Festival parade.

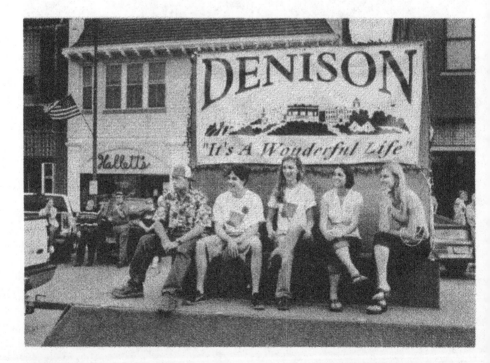

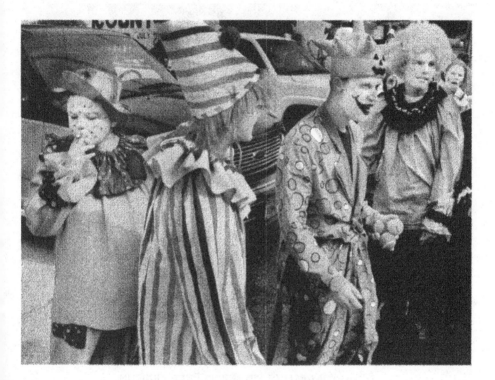

U.S. Job Corps members playing clowns,
Donna Reed Festival parade.

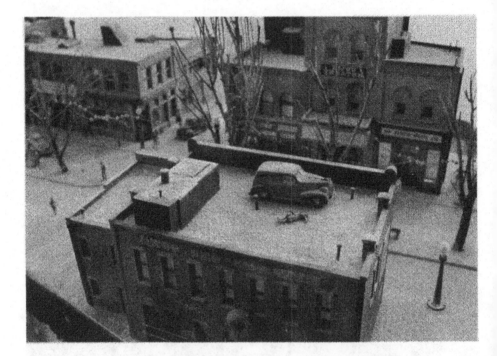

SCALE MODEL OF BEDFORD FALLS FROM
IT'S A WONDERFUL LIFE, DONNA REED MUSEUM.

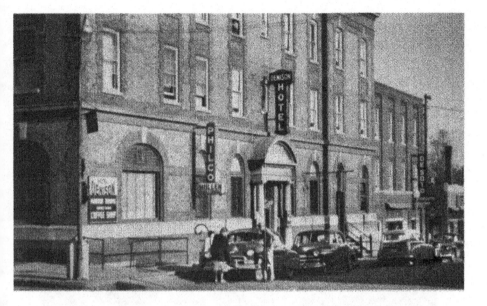

DENISON HOTEL, TOP, REPLACED BY THE TOPKO DRUG STORE.

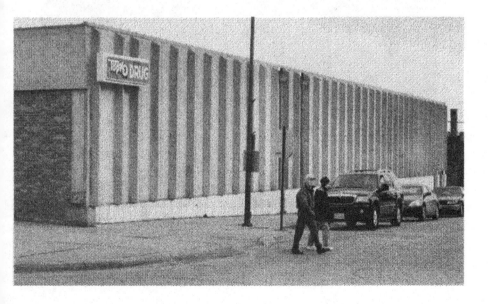

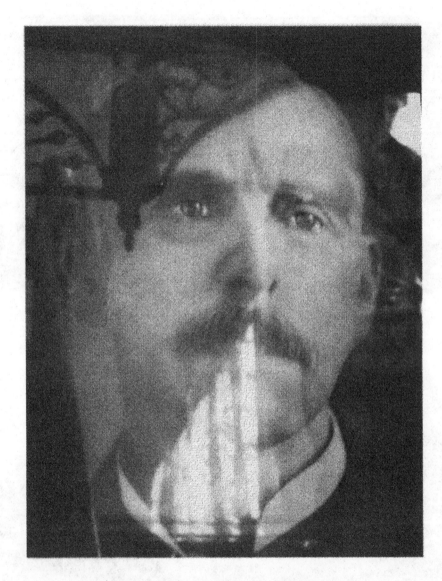

LESLIE SHAW'S PHOTOGRAPH ON THE WALL
OF THE GRAND STAIRCASE, REFLECTING THE
FRETWORK IN HIS MANSION.

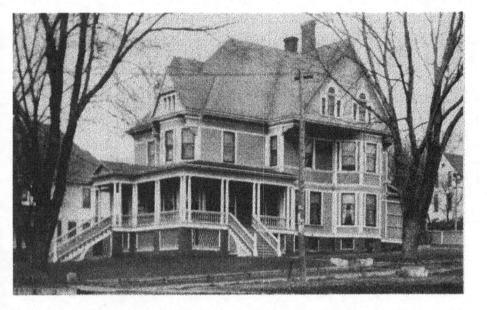

Shaw Mansion, top, in 1905 and in 2004.

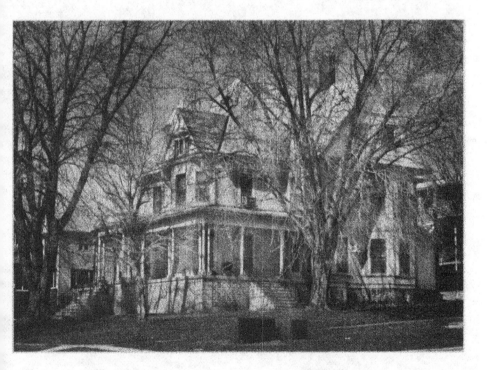

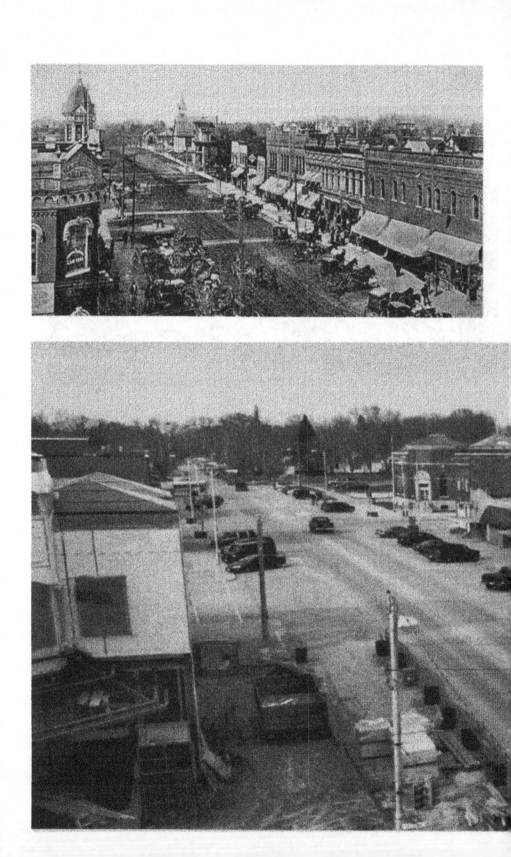

MAIN STREET, LEFT, CIRCA 1900
AND IN 2004.

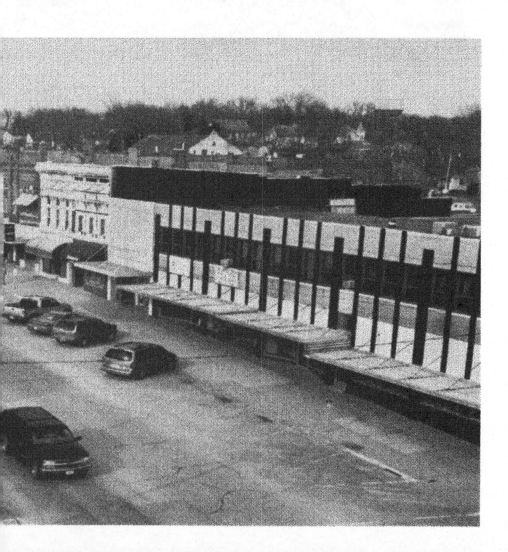

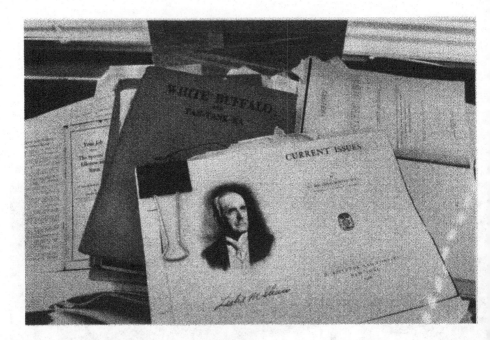

THE WRITER'S DESK.

PART FOUR

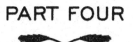

SPRING AND EARLY SUMMER

WILLARD'S DIARY

DEAD DONNA

THE FESTIVAL

The wild marijuana and corn grew robustly that last week of June, in a summer of profuse rainfall. Anyone walking field and creek edges suffered mightily from chiggers, invisible insects that cause an eruption of itchy red welts. The rains had resulted in an abundance of this pest and were also beneficial to the mosquito. The headlines and television news, when not trumpeting the latest Code Red or Code Orange alerts, were energetically sending fears of West Nile virus through the Iowa populace.

It was the time of year for Hollywood to come to corn country, the nineteenth annual Donna Reed Performing Arts Festival and Workshops. It was once again the season for many locals to see the dark side of life.

"Dead Donna Days" was uttered in the cafés, bars, and library, said with an insider's contempt. One elderly woman spoke from experience.

—I went to school with Donna Reed. She wasn't anything special. She was no different than me. So why are they pinning all their hopes on her?

People crossed their arms and said they'd be having nothing to do with the festival. They'd sooner roll naked in prairie grass with chiggers. A smaller number embraced the festival and fretted about its future. The administration was on autopilot at best and seemed inept. In its early years, some 300 aspiring young actors came; this year there were fewer than 100. One leader shared his worries with the writer.

—It's falling apart. We've got to do something. They've blamed 9/11 for the past two years. They say kids are afraid of traveling, but that's not it. It's been going downhill since before 9/11.

The problems had long been known. The 2020 Report said the Donna

Reed Center is potentially an attraction, "yet the community has not determined how to market this resource most effectively." At Mayor Ken Livingston's 2020 Executive Committee, Doug Skarin grumbled that the foundation was not making it more of a street festival with multiple-day outdoor events.

The primary purpose was a series of acting workshops for young people, junior high school age to college, who paid $400 tuition (a few received scholarships) for forty hours of schooling from actors and production people. Another member of the executive committee wondered aloud why the foundation didn't keep this aspect but expand.

—We could stage a week-long stage version of the movie *It's a Wonderful Life* at Christmas. It would draw a different crowd, people from Des Moines and Omaha.

He added it could be one of those plays that moves out of the theater with the audience into the streets of Denison. The writer noted that the town of Monroeville, Alabama, stages Harper Lee's 1960 novel, *To Kill a Mockingbird*, later made into a movie starring Gregory Peck. Each May for three weeks, sellout crowds come to the play put on by the town's citizens, not professional actors, in and out on the lawn of the 1903 courthouse that was replicated exactly in the movie.

Or perhaps they should put on an original play about cultural change in an Iowa town. It would be unique and would attract attention. What was clear to many was that Donna Reed's name was fading. She appealed to an older crowd, did not have an "A" list persona that endured beyond her era, like, say, James Dean.

Another idea was to market other things along with the festival. Denison has another citizen of fame: Clarence Chamberlin. He was trying to be the first aviator to fly nonstop across the Atlantic Ocean, but lost out to Charles Lindbergh. A few weeks after Lindbergh's 1927 flight, Chamberlin and a copilot flew from New York to Berlin in forty-two hours, setting a distance record.

The possibilities were numerous. For now, except for one week in June, the $1 million building sat mostly empty the rest of the year. It allegedly showed films, under the aegis of the company that owned a multiplex theater in a metal warehouse building west of town on the highway, but several times the door was locked when the writer showed up to see a film.

Then came the morning that fire engines from Denison and the communities of Deloit, Kiron, and Ricketts blared sirens as the parade for the Donna Reed Festival started on the corner at the building that once was *Der Denison Herold*. At the head was a Book 'Em Dano float—a cart pulled by a miniature horse. A sign on the cart announced,

BOOK 'EM DANO

COOL BAR

COLD BEER

HOT ENTERTAINMENT

There were floats from Farmland/Smithfield, Tyson, the U.S. Job Corps, the Crawford County Cattlemen's Association. There was an assortment of vintage cars: Joel Franken was in a 1930s vehicle, and the Hollywood types who had come to teach the workshops were in convertibles. Candy was thrown to children from all vehicles as they slowly moved down Main Street and made a left on Broadway past the Donna Reed Performing Arts Center, where a giant black-and-white picture of Donna stared at the street from the window of the newly opened museum.

It was the first time the writer had seen substantial numbers of Latinos and whites together in any public setting outside Wal-Mart. Why did the Latinos come? There were no Latino students taking acting workshops. And they knew very little about this Donna Reed, had trouble pronouncing her name. They were puzzled by most American holidays in which white people just stayed home, did nothing. But they understood a parade. This was a real holiday like they knew, even if they knew nothing about the person it celebrated.

It was a fine day to come out and watch a parade.

And then all the floats had passed, the last white and Latino kids finished picking up candy that remained on the street, and the Donna Reed Performing Arts Festival disappeared for the week behind the doors of the high school and the theater.

FAME

The innkeepers had full houses. One woman showed up with her teenage son at a hotel, only to learn there were no rooms. The clerk called around and found an innkeeper with cancellations.

The mother and son arrived in a real beater of a car at this second inn. The mother asked the price for a room with a single bed. She was nervous about the rate. The innkeeper saw they were poor, talked with the mother, and discovered they had driven up from Missouri. The son had landed some kind of bit speaking part of six or so words in a film, and she was spending her last dollars on her son's dream to become a star based on the training he would get this week. The kid had absolutely no charisma. The innkeeper gave them two rooms for the price of one.

The writer discovered three kinds of students at the festival: untalented locals who were indulging fantasies, those without talent who had come from afar, and those from afar who had real ability and were playing the longest of long shots of any artistic discipline: to make it as actors.

Casting director Eddie Foy III had the latter in his seminar, "Personality and Screen Test," in which he taped the young actors and then played back the test to give them pointers. Foy had thirty years in the business, including working in television on the *Donna Reed Show*, *I Dream of Jeannie*, *That Girl*, and *Barney Miller*, among others. He was straight from central casting as a casting director: a rough voice and a no-bullshit persona, a warped sense of humor, a perpetual lit or unlit cigar stuffed in his smacker or being waved in hand as he made a point.

The writer sat at the back as students filtered in. Foy began the class sitting atop the desk of a beautiful young woman as he lectured. He looked down at the woman.

—Don't touch me.

Foy continued lecturing about how he would film them, showing where they were making mistakes; he interrupted himself.

—At least don't touch me on the thigh.

The lecture resumed. Foy again interrupted himself, pointing to his ankle.

—Well, you can touch me down here. Go ahead. Touch.

The woman touched his ankle.

—Lech!

Foy leaped to his feet, went to the camera, and students began working through scenes. A talented eighteen-year-old woman went through a long scene from a script she'd read and memorized only that day, written by a friend of Foy—a monologue by a snarky waitress that occurred at a restaurant in Malibu. Foy kept interrupting, giving the class pointers about life in acting.

—You'll be surprised what you look like. You'll gain ten pounds. The camera makes you gain weight. It will spread your face out. I have no problem saying it: lose weight. You can't be fat and go into casting. It's death.

He pointed to a college-age woman's face.

—You have to lose weight in here.

She nodded.

—I'm on it.

Foy pointed to another woman's mouth.

—The public likes a woman with a big mouth. Why is Bernadette Peters not a much bigger star? Little, little mouth.

On another day in the classroom of actors Kerry Remsen and Barbara Mallory, it was an entirely different scene in their seminar, "Creative Dramatics." The class had four girls and one overweight boy. Two of the girls, from Chicago, were overeager in a desperate way that one truly understands only after spending time in the Los Angeles film world.

One of the Chicago girls bubbled at one point about Barbara.

—I saw you in *Airplane!* You were great!

The girl, age fourteen, was her parents' DNA when the film was made in 1980. The girl continued starfucking, ignored by the instructors. Barbara told them to role-play. She called the two Chicago girls and another girl to the front of the room.

—What will you talk about?

—Hot guys!

—School!

She sat the three girls in a row. The two on the ends had to talk, and the middle girl had to listen. Then they had to switch roles. The end girls blathered and the middle girl's head shot back and forth. Kerry barked an order.

—Louder! There's a little old lady in the back saying, *What?! What?!*

The girls went back and forth, and when done, Kerry congratulated them.

—Good. You have to do that when you are acting. You have to act like you are listening.

Now it was the fat boy's turn. He overacted to the extreme, both with his motions and emotions. Barbara and Kerry cautioned him to tone down, but it was hopeless. He continued waving his arms, talking about sports as he did an improvisation. Kerry let him go on, then cut him off.

—Why is this a good acting exercise, guys? You have to listen. Spencer Tracy said acting is reacting. Sometimes actors are waiting to say their lines. They aren't listening. And you can see it.

The two women sent the students out into the hall to practice. Barbara looked at the writer and sighed. With the number of students down, their jobs are more difficult, because as a larger number work through routines, the instructors get a break.

—We usually have fifteen to twenty students. It is much harder with so few. And we have them for nine hours!

The kids came back, did the exercise. The two women sent them out again to prepare for another. Kerry shouted.

—Take your time! Take a half-hour!

The students came back in less than a minute. Now they were all overacting. Kerry stopped them again.

—What do we need in acting?

A Chicago girl raised a hand.

—Emotions.

—You want to be as real as possible. You don't want it fake. You don't need to say, "I am real sad."

Kerry went into a scene and overdid being sad. Then she did it correctly, with subtle emotion. Now the students had to run through a gamut of emotions, solo. The girls did the exercise, and they had toned down. The fat boy, however, went into overdrive, droop-eyed and fake-teared.

—I was so sad when Dallas won! How could that happen!? I couldn't believe it . . .

Barbara and Kerry glanced at the clock, counting the seconds until noon struck and they could take a break.

—I was so sad! So sad! I . . .

CONCERNING THE METH FREAK

The writer rapidly exited the classroom at noon, as much fleeing as hurrying to the county jail. For most of the previous year, he'd wondered about the drug scene. The prairie was alive with the sound of meth labs cooking away. A clerk at Kehl Drug said the store had trouble with a cold remedy containing pseudoephedrine, an ingredient in making methamphetamine.

—Kids come in all the time looking to buy Sudafed. It gets stolen. We have the boxes it comes in on the shelf, and they're empty.

In 1995 there were eight meth labs busted in Iowa; in 2002, 1,009 were found. Sheriff Tom Hogan had invited the writer to interview a prisoner—a methamphetamine addict who had robbed a bank to pay off a huge drug bill.

—His dealer was going to kill him if he didn't pay up.

Sheriff Hogan had seen a lot of cranksters in his time, and he saw a pattern—white, black, or Latino. He told the writer,

—You show me the person who is not getting in on the American dream, and I'll show you someone who is chemically dependent.

Denison was rife with people not making it in the dream called America. For every Latino arrival who worked hard and fantasized about stepping up, someone was coming down the ladder.

The writer went to the jail. But as soon as he entered, he wondered if the prisoner would agree to talk, and if he did, what would the writer ask him? The writer suddenly wanted to be somewhere else. At that moment, the woman jailer said the prisoner was ready.

The writer entered the concrete block visiting area, fixated on a one-foot-square glass window in the center of the wall, the intense face that filled that square. The face had a beard, and the skin was bathed in an orange light. But none of that was really noted by the writer: it was the eyes, burning on this man on the free side of the pane. The eyes were terrifying, frightening, timeless, and they asked: Why had he come? The room held nothing but these eyes, and the writer could not leave them, not even to pull out his notebook at first.

The writer picked up the telephone receiver without taking his gaze off the eyes.

—Hi Mr.———

The writer explained why he had come, and he was sure the man would hang up. Why would a writer from the coasts be in this backwater talking to a doomed man? They had him dead cold guilty on the robbery. The writer had to be some kind of a setup. But the addict did not hang up.

—I used meth. Yeah. They have me on suicide watch.

—How old are you?

—Thirty-six.

—You don't look that old.

—Thanks.

A smile, briefly.

—How did you start using, what happened?

—My mom died. Then I wrecked my motorcycle in 2000. I was going 130, hit a deer. I lived through it. Two weeks later, my sister died. I tried to do good. And when I got it together, something always happened. I lost three of my family in a year and a half. It's hard to face life every day. I've just held it all in. Every day when I wake up, I miss my sister. I couldn't talk with my girlfriend about it.

—It's hard when you're a guy, to put it out there . . .

—I got no one. They've all left me. Every day I took my stepson to school, I passed the cemetery where my mom is buried. I'd go to the cemetery . . .

Tears ran from his right eye, then left. They dripped for the rest of the interview.

—I won't lie to you. Don't get me wrong. I've done bad stuff. But I'm not a bad person.

The writer had talked with enough meth addicts to know that nothing was to be trusted. Of all drug users, speed freaks are the most unstable, the scariest. But the raw emotion was real, no matter the man's story. He told the writer he had been working as a welder but had lost that job.

—To be honest, I was numbing myself. I'd do weed. I like weed. Then I started meth. I also did coke. I'll take my punishment like a man. But I don't want to be here. I wish I weren't here. I just want to be with my girl-friend and her kids. I'm tired. So tired.

The writer told him he is young enough that when he gets beyond this rap, he could still fix his life.

His eyes looked down, for a second, came back up.

—I wish I could believe that.

The allotted time was up. The writer had to go.

—Hang in there, man.

It was all the writer could say before he walked from the chamber, backward, looking into the saddest eyes he'd seen in years. The eyes, amid the orange and bearded face, never left the writer. The face now looked like that of Jesus. Or death.

CONCERNING THE BLUE-COLLAR COUPLE

For the older white working-class residents, there were two major peri-ods in their lives. Pre Strike/After Strike. Wages were very good at Farm-land before the strike, and bought a solid middle-class life: good homes, boats, recreational vehicles. Then came after, a long period of struggle.

The Farmland strike began December 1, 1982, and lasted into Febru-ary. The white couple sat in their modest house and recalled the previous two decades. He now saw the larger forces at work.

—When we came back from strike, we realized we never should have gone out. The whole industry had gone backward and we didn't. Farm-land tried. You can't pay $1.50 an hour more than your competitors and stay in business. We were one of the last packers in the country not to cut wages. We came back, and we took a big, big cut. The United States thinks they're entitled to cheap food. If the price of a pork chop goes up, they have a heart attack.

Their income dropped from the mid-thirties to the mid-twenties, not only because of the wage cuts but because orders were down due to the strike. Wages remained frozen. Between 1982 and 2000, there was no real increase, the man said.

What were their options? They had two small boys, and they were a blue-collar family. They hung on. Back then they had a real union, even if it made a mistake. Now they had a union in name only, a whore for the company. It didn't fight for wages, and it did little if anything to help workers unfairly fired or punished. Farmland began hiring Latinos in the 1990s because it couldn't attract the white kids, who were going to college in increasing numbers. But even the wages for Latinos were not enough, he said.

—The wages fell so low it was costing the plant. They had to up the pay, to stop churn [turnover]. It was expensive training new workers. The turnover was atrocious. Management got raises, the bottom didn't get them. But the guy at the top doesn't make money if the janitor doesn't do his job. The USDA could come in and shut us down for being unclean. Or things wouldn't get done and the line would slow or stop. And when you have a few hundred workers on a line waiting, any stoppage is very expensive. I don't blame the Hispanics. If I lived down there, I'd come up here too. They go through a lot just to get here. This is going to sound prejudiced, but they need to be driven. They will do their job, and when they are done, they will just stand there, even though they know what to do next. You have to tell them. There is no motivation. Some aren't that way. But most of them. Yet they'll get up there and do the job the nineteen-year-old white kid won't do. You just cringe when you get a young white guy in there. American kids are spoiled. People in town don't want to believe that the Hispanic person will work harder than the white person. The plant is now over 50 percent Hispanic.

She said many whites in town complain that Latinos have taken the jobs that would have belonged to their children.

—We drilled into our kids that we don't want them to go into the packing plants! Especially after the strike. People say they took the jobs away from their kids. I ask them, "What did you tell your kids to do? The same thing we did. Don't you want them to have a better life?" If it weren't for Hispanics, this town would die.

The town is not just divided between whites and Latinos. There are two classes of whites: the blue-collar workers and the Uptown elites.

He said the elites who run Denison don't understand blue-collar residents.

—They say if you don't like what's going on, get involved. Most of them don't get up at 4:00 A.M. to go to work. The people running the town have jobs that start at 10 o'clock. They don't understand that by the time you get home, mow your yard, make dinner, spend time with your kids, you don't have any time left. I think the 20 percent runs the 80 percent. These 20 percent don't want to admit that the 80 percent might have an idea of how things should be run, too. We're not Carroll. We're a blue-collar meatpacking town. Some people at the top don't want us to be that. We have to cater to the people that we do have. I asked one of the Hispanic interpreters, "What is it that Hispanics want?" I asked him to think about it. They are in the restaurant business and clothing. They frequent those. What do they want that we don't have? He came back and said the Hispanics would like to have current movies in Spanish. They would really go to that.

Neither this husband nor his wife liked Streetscape or the golf course project, but they were for the city helping in other ways to create business. His idea is for the city to give rent subsidies to businesses such as a restaurant, say $300 a month to start, then decreasing, to encourage diverse economic activity.

She said Donna Reed should be exploited more, say by creating a restaurant, a good one, with a Donna Reed theme.

—You tie the restaurant to Dead Donna, so they have the Donna Reed cut. You dress the waitresses like Donna Reed.

CONCERNING KATE SWIFT: SHE REVEALS A TRUTH ABOUT DENISON

As the writer's time in town was winding down, Kate Swift telephoned.

—I have a problem. I thought you might be able to suggest a solution . . . I wouldn't call if it weren't a real serious problem.

They talked for an hour. She insisted he come over that night and solve her problem, which involved visiting her bedroom. Why not, she insisted? *Why not*, he thought. He went.

Later that night the writer talked with Ms. Swift about the Iowa way of dealing with people; that is, most people seldom say what they really mean to anyone's face; that no matter, people will go away hurt and nurture those hurts for days, weeks, or months. Yet they will be pleasant to the offender.

—They'll never let you know they're hurt, but they'll bitterly talk about how you hurt them, however unknowingly, behind your back to others. I don't get it.

—Iowa, it's what I call the "nicey-nice." Everyone is "nice."

The Iowa "nicey-nice" encompassed many things, she said. It was tied in with an enforced modesty. One should not flash money or themselves. They should work hard and not complain about their lives. This is the stereotype of Midwest values and virtue.

She told the story of a man she knew, the father of a friend from high school who was roped into running the family farm at a young age. He read books, and his wife would yell at him: Why was he not out doing the multitude of chores one always has on a farm? There was great tension in the marriage. The man carried index cards in his pocket, and his children often saw him writing on these cards. They thought he was writing notes about farm chores. When he died, one of the kids discovered the index cards were a running diary; they were notes of desperation to himself. He wanted a bigger life than the farm, but was destined to die never having tried for that life.

It was a town filled with people just like this.

—We grew up together, and we think we know each other. But we don't really know each other. It's because of the nicey-nice. It's passive-aggressive.

AN AMERICAN STORY III

Work was slow for Luis Navar as spring advanced. Luis painted his sister's house in Dow City, and he had a minor job removing tar globs from the brick of an Uptown building after the owner had removed the "modernized" facing panels—this was part of Joel Franken's redesign of storefronts to return them to a 1930s motif. None of this was lucrative. He had four children to feed. A big April tax bill loomed.

Phase IV, remodeling of the interior of *Der Denison Herold*, was coming up for bid by the city. (Phase III had been putting on a new roof, which had followed Luis's completion of Phase II, the gutting.) The fourth stage included building a stairwell, replacing joists, rebuilding floors with sixty sheets of plywood, sheetrock work, creating a restroom. Once again Nathan helped Luis cost the job. Nathan admonished Luis for going too low on the previous phase; he now advised him to bid $25,000. Luis absorbed Nathan's counsel as he readied the bid for Bravo Construction.

In this period, the Denison Chamber of Commerce seems to have heeded the censure from the banquet speaker. It found an interpreter and held a ribbon-cutting photo op for the *Bulletin & Review* to mark the grand opening of Tienda Mexicana La Jaliscience II in the old Hardees, owned by Maria Elena Ochoa and her husband, Alfonso. Chamber members showed up, as did Dick Knowles and Mayor Ken Livingston. Maria cut the ribbon, and everyone applauded.

"Welcome," Ken said.

"Thank you, thank you," Maria said through the interpreter. "Thank you to everyone for coming." She then welled with tears of joy.

"How do you say good luck in Spanish?" Ken asked the interpreter.

"*Buena suerte.*"

"Buena suerte."

A few weeks later the Denison City Council scheduled a "work session" for 5:00 P.M. on April 29 for the bids on *Der Denison Herold* and other matters. Dick had long been critical of these sessions. Why didn't the council do like other cities and simply hold one session in which matters were discussed, and then voted on? The meeting was public, but it, like others, was sparsely attended. Mayor Ken Livingston announced there were five bids for the fourth phase of renovation. Four of the bids were:

Ben's Electric & Construction:	$38,600.00
Denison Construction:	$31,054.63
Frazier Construction:	$26,699.00
Bravo Construction:	$22,500.00

The fifth bid was by the golf course fund-raising committee, for $15,694. Ken explained this bid was for materials only and that the labor would be donated, to be handled by Denison Construction. (The company had double-bid in the event the city didn't agree with the plan.) It was being submitted with the understanding that the city would then allow the committee $14,000 worth of in-kind credit toward the $1.5 million it needed to raise for the golf course conference center.

Ken talked about volunteer labor, but left unsaid was how the company could provide a crew of workers for free. Was the company simply being heroic? Or was something else going on? And how would crediting a nonexisting $14,000 pay for materials needed to build the conference center? Would the city have to kick in this money later when the project was signed over from the committee, to be constructed and then owned by the city? It sounded like Enron accounting. In reality, the proposal seemed to be costing the city $29,694, far more than the bids by Luis Navar and Frazier Construction.

Yet the mayor and city manager Al Roder ended the session crowing about the plan. They added the city attorney said it was legal. It would be voted on the coming Monday. It was the latest turn in finding monies for the golf course project: the idea of seeking homeland security funds had fizzled.

I left the meeting puzzled and stunned as I walked to the high school and the last night of Georgia Hollrah's ESL class for that year. For a year and a half, I'd heard Ken talking about bringing Latinos, especially those in business, into the mainstream. Now it was time to walk his talk. Here was a low bid by the first Latino contractor in the city—in desperate need of the job—being cast aside in favor of good-old-boy politics, essentially using city monies to help pay for a clubhouse for the golfing elites.

*　*　*

Two days after the council work session, I was walking down Broadway past the Donna Reed Museum. I spied Nathan working inside. There was just over one month to go before it was to open for the Donna Reed Festival, and time was short. It was Saturday, and he was putting oak trim on the walls. Amber, his wife, didn't know he was here. She was angry that their own house wasn't being finished; the stairwell was missing banisters, and some door frames were bare wood, among many other things. I blurted news about the golf course bid.

"Son of a bitch! It's things like that that make me want to give up!"

Nathan railed against the mayor, the city manager, and the golf course. When he calmed, I pulled out my notebook and read details of what the conference center committee was proposing to do through Denison Construction. I put the notebook back in my pocket.

"Why would they do that?" Nathan asked of the donated labor. "What's in it for them? They lose more than $14,000—they aren't doing another job and making money. This is wrong! You have to tell Luis this!"

As Nathan spouted, he looked out the window and spied a car at the red light.

"There's Luis now!"

Nathan bolted out the door, yelling.

"Luis! Luis!"

Luis was with Lupe. Luis spied Nathan waving; he rolled down the window. The light turned green. There were cars behind him.

"Go through the light, and come back!"

Nathan glanced at his watch, startled. It was 5:15. Amber was expecting him home at 5:00.

"I've got to go. Tell him everything! Tell him to say discrimination lawsuit! They don't like Mexicans!"

Nathan was about to go down the alley next to the Donna Reed Center when Luis came back through the light, beeping and waving for Nathan to wait. Nathan ran to his door as Luis pulled into the spot.

"Tell him what's going on!" Nathan commanded of me. As I pulled out my notebook, Nathan himself blurted the story. Luis's eyes were wide.

"It's wrong! You have to say you're gonna file a discrimination lawsuit! I've got to go!"

Nathan darted off, and the confused Luis looked at me as Nathan vanished; we could hear his running steps in the alley. I filled Luis in on more details. He shook his head and talked about all the discrimination he had experienced.

"I told you about some of the things that happened to me. What happened at the plant, how I lost my job when I went to become a citizen. And now this."

Luis looked dejected.

"You have to go to the meeting on Monday."

"Meeting?"

"The city council. That's when they're voting on the bids."

"You can do that? They do that in public?"

"Hey, this isn't Mexico! It's *Estados Unidos*, man. Yes, they do it in public."

"It's not done in secret?"

"No!"

"I'm tired of some of the things that have happened," Luis said. "You have to stand up."

He didn't have to speak at the meeting, I suggested. Just being present would make a statement. And maybe it would lay some guilt on the mayor and council. Perhaps they'd do the right thing. He was gravely concerned about the bid.

"I really need this job."

"Will you be at the meeting?"

Luis looked unsure. He told me he would think about it.

* * *

That night I had dinner with Joel Franken. I'd long wanted to eat at the German Hausbarn restaurant in the town of Manning to the south to experience some German culinary culture, for none remained in Denison.

We mostly talked about his long-distance relationship and women in general, but halfway through dinner over *schwein schnitzel* and kraut balls, I brought up the bidding process on the old German newspaper building, and how I felt Luis was being wronged. Joel listened but remained silent. I figured he preferred not to discuss city matters on personal time. There was no way he'd take part in voting for such a sham—Joel had been such a champion of Latinos in town. So I turned the conversation back to women.

LA MAESTRA IV

William Galicia drove up to me on Main Street and offered a ride.

"Don't ask if I have a license."

"I will not."

I got into the blue 1986 Honda Accord with over 200,000 miles on the odometer.

"You have to love the engine to make it run," William said, patting the cracked dash. He was good with cars, always working on the motor. He pulled the Accord into traffic, going well under the speed limit of twenty-five miles per hour. I learned he does not drink, either. He does nothing that could get him in trouble. William slipped in a music CD, Los Tigres del Norte, a Mexican group. On the dash was a well-worn Spanish-English dictionary and a toy model of a tractor-trailer truck. Several fortunes from cookies at Little China, a local buffet-style restaurant, were pasted on the dash. One, with some Spanish translation penned in by hand with lines to key words, said

Love is blind.
   (ciego)
Jealousy, however, sees too much.
      (envidia sin embargo)

We went to the British Petroleum station next to Cronk's. There was a row of booths, where we sat after he got a machine espresso and I a coffee. He comes here often.

"I like this place."

From a large envelope, he pulled an eleven-by-seventeen color picture, in a frame stand, of a row of gleaming white condominiums under con-

234

struction in San Salvador. It was a five-thousand-unit project in the sub-
urb of Pinares de Suiza. He was one of 460 workers. He did masonry, laid
tile, and earned about five U.S. dollars for a long day of work. The condos
went for a bit over $100,000 U.S.

"People from America came down to buy them. I am not sure, but I
think they are returning Salvadorans."

The condo picture sat on a dresser near his bed. He'd brought it so he
could show me his other life. He'd worked on four big projects over seven
years, from the time he was sixteen. He began as an apprentice and ended
a self-employed contractor. He loved this work, loved being his own boss.

He held the picture, staring at it for a long time, in the same manner
Nathan had held the 1949 aerial photo of Denison.

"When I look at this picture, I can still smell the paint drying."

It was violence that drove him away, that and the lure of opportunity,
he said as we got back into his car and drove up to Juan Escobar's apartment in a nice complex near Fort Purdy.

Juan, happy to see us, invited us into the spotless and well-furnished
quarters. Everywhere, in dozens of photos, were pictures of his daughter,
age four. The largest was three feet square: the girl was in a white dress,
with imploring eyes. She was in El Salvador with Juan's mother, Juan explained, and his heart was broken. He missed her.

William coming to Denison, as a single man, was one thing. Juan and
his wife, leaving their daughter behind, was another. This constantly
smiling and always nice man contained a depth of anguish. But one never
saw it. This was very Salvadoran. During the war, I was amazed how Salvadorans could so matter-of-factly tell about how they watched mothers
and fathers or siblings killed in front of them by the death squads.

"We are *fuerte* [strong]," William had said to me earlier.

Juan's wife was at work. Juan brought out photo albums. In the pictures the couple walk around the lake in Yellow Smoke Park, are in the
apartment, or are seated in the letters of the giant cement "Denison" sign
on the hillside above Cronk's. In most pictures, Juan is kissing her. "I love
my wife," he said. They had been married for five years.

Juan and William work at Custom Ribs, a specialty meat operation.
Juan is in shipping, William on the line cutting ribs. The pay is about
eight dollars an hour, not as high as Farmland, but they say the bosses are

nicer and conditions better. Both grew up in the Salvadoran state of Ahuachapán, which abuts Guatemala. They didn't know each other there.

"Denison is like Ahuachapán," Juan said of the rural region. "We don't have very many problems in Ahuachapán. But we also don't have any money."

Juan's family ran a statue and tombstone business. His father died when Juan was thirteen. Both men completed high school, and Juan had two years of college, studying to be a civil engineer. Their dreams for America are not huge. I had told them about Luis Navar; they would love to be self-employed contractors like Luis.

Both men picked up English much faster than most other students. Juan had been studying about two years, William only one; his year anniversary of arriving in the United States was just one week away.

I was curious about their journeys. We talked about the eleven railcar dead, and they knew of other stories of those who did not make it. William had experience being locked aboard a freight train: he made it into the Mexican state of Chiapas, where a coyote put him in a sealed container box on a train to Puebla. Then he was driven to Mexico City, where he boarded a bus to the Texas border; he walked into the United States. He came to Denison because his sister was here. Juan had a brother in Denison.

"I heard it was quee—," Juan said, stumbling on the word. "How you say? Oh, quiet. The country was fantastic. And a lot of pay, too!"

The first time Juan came, he was able to get a visa. Then he went home because of his wife and daughter. He couldn't get a visa for a second trip, so he got a visa for Mexico and took a bus from El Salvador to Mexico City. Then he hired a coyote. He flew from Mexico City to Hermosillo, in the north, and walked some 140 miles parallel with the Sierra Madre— roughly the route Michael and I had driven when we smuggled the family in 1984.

"It was very cold walking at that time," Juan said of the April trek, led by the coyote, with eighty others. "Everyone did not make it. No one died, but some people were very tired." They stopped in places on the way, and those who could not continue stayed. "Many people die at other times, when it is hot."

Mexican *migra* had not changed. Juan said he paid *mordida*, bribes.

"They don't like Salvadoran peoples. I like Mexicans. There are good and bad people everywhere. In El Salvador, bad people, good. Mexico, too. United States is the same. But I have to say there are a few more bad peoples in Mexico."

William had immigration problems, and a federal hearing coming up in Council Bluffs. He had papers, given to some Salvadorans after two devastating earthquakes in 2001, but they had expired.

"I don't want to go back," William said. "But if they tell me I have to, I will go back."

"In America, people want to sit and think," Juan said of what he sees Americans in better jobs doing.

"They love computers and cars," William said.

"When we learn English, we get another job, where we sit," Juan said. "I want to sit and think too. And issue orders, no? That is why we study English so very hard."

"We are the *raza*, too, no?" William asked, using the Spanish for race, or people. William doesn't understand why some whites hate them.

"We get this place, will you white people move away?" William asked. "If we got a lot of money in El Salvador, we don't come here. Everyone is looking for the best."

"We are *indio*," Juan says of their native roots. "The English came, but we were here. Everyone is *immigrante*. What is the word for this?"

Juan wrote *razista* in my notebook.

"Racist."

"It is what Georgia is not," Juan said. "How would you say she is?"

I think about it. I write down *multiculturalist*.

"*Multiculturista*," I said.

This Spanglish did not work. Then I wrote down *tolerant*.

"*Tolerencia*."

They understood, nodding.

I added, "She is a saint."

"*Santo?*"

"*Sí!*"

"Yes, she is Saint Georgia," Juan said.

I got up to leave with William. I stared at the large photograph of Juan's daughter hanging in the living room.

"Life goes fast. We must get our daughter here."

He told me they were going to pay to have her smuggled north later in the year. I expressed amazement, muttered about the enormity of doing so.

"Difficult," he said with a smile. "But not impossible."

* * *

The Iowa land finally started greening. And with the growing warmth, fewer students came to Georgia's class, though all the people at my table were diligent. One day Georgia wrote on the overhead, SEASONS.

"There are four seasons."

spring	*primavera*
summer	*verano*
fall	*otoño*
winter	*invierno*

Georgia asked the class to describe two seasons—the one now concluded and the present. Students threw out words.

Spring	*Winter*
Warm, cool, *fresco*	Cold
Green	White, gray
New grass, *pasto*	Snow
New leaves, *hojas*	Bare trees
Rain	Snow
Many birds	Some birds
Flowers, *las flores*	No flowers
Butterflies, lady bugs	No insects, no bugs

"There is the bird with the red breast and big tail feathers," Georgia said of the creature just now being seen in Denison. "What are they?"

"Robins," Juan said.

"They are very intelligent," Georgia said. "They go to Texas and Mexico in the winter."

* * *

April 29 arrived, the last day of the ESL class for the year. Georgia ended it about a month before regular school ceased because of other pressing duties and because even fewer ESL learners would come now as the days turned to summer. Georgia wrote,

1. We are asking and answering questions.
2. We are reading new dialogues.
3. We are creating *(creando)* different dialogues.
4. We are completing exercises.
5. We are saying goodbye.

Georgia wrote important dates on the chalkboard, with ellipses for the answers. One question was, "An important date in May is . . ."

Juan raised his hand.

"An important date in May is May 10. It is Mother's Day."

"No," Georgia said. "It is May 9. May 10 is a Monday."

"In El Salvador, it is always May 10."

"Oh . . . here it is the second Sunday in May."

I was surprised Juan knew Mother's Day so well. Then I remembered his father died when he was young.

The lesson continued, and then whispering erupted. A cry went up from Juan and William, and a second William in the class, for celebration. They suggested the class order pizzas that they would pay for; someone went to the phone and called an order. Georgia taught a bit more, and then the pizzas arrived. As we ate, students gave presents to Georgia. Marilou gave her a music box made of ceramic, in the form of a book. On the pages was written,

God give me the strength to accept those things I cannot change, the courage to change the things I can, and the wisdom to know the difference.

Juan gave Georgia a small globe of the world that was also a clock. And then Juan handed me a wrapped box. I opened it. It was two nice pens, and a note. It read,

I'm proud of have you like a friend, too.

thank you for help us to learn English
I think you are the best writer

"I write that in English, as best I can."

Then he spoke in Spanish about Georgia and me. He was thanking us, but I was so taken with emotion that I didn't catch all of what he said. He too was emotional, and that was the only language required. Georgia addressed the group in Spanish.

"I like this class so much. Thank you—one thousand thank-yous. I am so glad you are in the United States. It is an honor to help you, to work teaching you English. You are our future, the future of Denison, of Iowa."

As we ate pizza, I thought about some things I'd heard. The high school was now 20 percent minority, the middle school 32 percent, the elementary grade school 47 percent, kindergarten 50 percent. A few weeks earlier, Steve Westerberg, the principal of the high school, had told me, "The traditional Denisonians are in my building." He noted that will change in a few years as the younger grades move up. "We're a microcosm in an area that's not used to it. They're used to it on the coasts. We just happen to be an early part of the change here in the Midwest. This is what America is going to be everywhere."

How many lives has Georgia helped? I thought of what Steve said, echoing others: in uncountable hidden ways, Georgia's class softened what otherwise might be harsher attitudes by whites in town. By living her religion by example, perhaps she made some of them feel guilty, muting their anger. Or maybe they'd heard good things first or second hand from those who volunteered with Georgia—that the Latinos were people just like them. At a most basic level, a significant number of Latinos in town had been in her classroom in the previous decade, learning English. She'd taught hundreds.

The four pizzas were consumed. The last of the native Spanish speakers filtered out after lots of hugs. It was just Georgia and me. We sat atop desks, talking. It was now my turn to thank her, but she'd have none of it, saying that I helped her more than she had helped me.

It wasn't true. It had to be one of the more satisfying things I had done, not as a writer but as a human being. As with teaching college students, I discovered that one often gets back more than one gives. But at the universities, I had students who were pretty well assured of making it in American life by the time they entered my classroom. Many had the passports for their lives stamped for success the moment they were born.

Here were people on the front end of the American experience, who were born not with silver spoons but cactus in their mouths, as I was told years earlier by a man, now dead, named Esubio Del Luna who had lived in a hovel in San Antonio, Texas. I thought of how hard the students like William and Juan worked to learn English—humbled by their enthusiasm for life in this country. I again thought of the railcar dead. The U.S. Justice Department in 2003 handed down a twenty-seven-count indictment. In 2004 four smugglers pleaded guilty (including the Union Pacific railworker who assisted); two others remained fugitives. In their desperation to get to a place like Denison, eleven people had placed their trust in someone to open a hatch. Some wanted what was here so badly like Juan, that they left a child behind.

For her part, Georgia was hopeful.

"It's getting better," she said. "I see it in the kids in the halls. They're getting along better."

She told a story from her hairdresser, who has a son in kindergarten.

"She told me he came home one day and said, 'There's a Mexican in the class.'"

This seeming complaint concerned the mom. Her son had been getting along with the Latino kids. The teacher even sent a note home about how her boy had been helping them.

"She said, 'Aaron, you've been helping kids all year. What do you mean?' And he said, 'Oh, he's not a Denison kid. He doesn't speak English. He's not one of ours.' And then she realized he meant the kid was new. It was like a Canadian kid had come in, an outsider. It was not racial."

Georgia said the real change will come when that kindergarten class reaches adulthood. Patience will be required. It will take time. Then, she said, it will be a different Denison.

We hugged, and I went out into the cool spring air. I walked the mile home to the Shaw Mansion, thinking about one Latino adult who didn't have twenty years to wait for cultural inclusion to take hold, the coming Monday and the city council meeting when Luis would learn his fate.

THEY SHOOT BUFFALO, DON'T THEY?

The Denison City Council meeting on Monday was jammed with specta-
tors. The golf course conference center backers were to make a presentation. There was a crucial vote on the Streetscape project. And there was
the vote on the bids for Phase IV of the German newspaper building. I'd
arrived late. There were no seats. Fire Chief Mike McKinnon was bringing in more chairs. I found a place in one of these chairs up front, knock-
kneed against a table holding a computer for a PowerPoint presentation
by Tim Stuart of the conference center committee.

I looked over my shoulder and didn't see Luis. I was bummed. I looked
again as a man two rows back leaned forward. Behind him was Luis,
seated against the wall. He winked. Luis was the sole Latino in the room.
Against the side wall, near the door, was Dick Knowles. Mayor Ken Livingston pounded the gavel. The meeting began.

Stuart rose and went through his presentation on the $2.7 million pro-
ject. An image came up: the committee had $1,172,600 in pledges from
citizens and another $328,000 in "in-kind" monies such as the company
that agreed to pave the parking lot. He announced they had reached their
goal of $1.5 million.

Councilman Earl McCollough asked Stuart if the $1.17 million was in
the bank. No, Stuart said. Now they had to collect on the promises. An architect went through an explanation of the project and showed images of
what it would look like—what I saw was two-story Wal-Mart architecture. It looked cheap.

The architect sat down, and Stuart wheeled away the PowerPoint table.
City manager Al Roder announced with triumph that the committee had
raised its $1.5 million and that the council should now take the next step
"to move the process along." That meant ponying up $1 million in tax-

payer dollars, and then the city would own the project. But no action would be taken tonight.

The next item was the renovation of *Der Denison Herold*. Al said there were five bids ranging from $15,694 to $38,600. He extolled the bid from the golf course/Denison Construction.

"We are not paying for labor under this proposal," Al said. He came up with the $14,000 labor cost that would be credited "in-kind" to the $1.5 million by averaging all the bids.

Councilman Keith Greder, who knew construction, said he costed the job. It would take a team of five workers two weeks. He wondered how the company could afford to pay the workers.

Only then did Ken and Al say that Denison Construction would not do the work—the company would supervise it. The labor would be done by the students of Job Corps, the federal program that trained troubled youths in vocations, including construction.

"I think we are entitled to more than amateurs doing it," Greder said.

As the mayor and city manager spun Greder, I looked back at Luis. He stared intently. It was the stare of a man who needed this work, badly, and who was seeing it vaporize because Greder did not pursue the questioning. Joel was writing notes, not looking up. *Speak up*, I thought. *Say something! Are you selling out? Say it ain't so, Joel!*

Joel spoke. He seconded a motion to give the bid to Job Corps. When he was asked by the city clerk how he was voting, Luis stared hard at him. Joel looked down and through clenched teeth said, "yes." The only councilman to vote "no" was Greder. Tim Stuart looked like a very happy man.

There was more meeting remaining. In the previous council session, it had voted 2–2 in a tie over an aspect of Streetscape: to fill in old coal chutes in front of the buildings beneath the sidewalks. One faction of the council didn't want to pay for this expensive prospect. Because of the tie vote, due to councilman Dan Leinen's being absent, the motion to pay failed. Now Streetscape was threatened because several building owners were talking of suing, and the council agreed to take another vote with all members present. If it didn't pass this time, Streetscape could be dead or tied up for years.

There was debate. In the end Leinen voted in favor of paying to fill in the chutes, and the motion carried 3–2. Streetscape would happen: the downtown would start on the path of Joel's drawings and the feeling of what it was in the 1930s.

And then came the final item on the agenda: comments from the public. Ken asked if anyone wanted to speak. One man did, briefly. Ken asked if there was anyone else. Ken raised the gavel, about to close the meeting. I looked at Dick Knowles, figuring he'd speak as he always did. His lips remained pursed. The gavel was about to drop.

"I have a question."

I looked back to see who belonged to this voice. It was Luis. His eyes were intent on the mayor.

"Yes, Mr. Navarro," Ken said, mangling Luis's last name.

"I would like to ask who's really paying for the $14,000."

Al replied that with this bid, the city didn't have to pay the $14,000 in labor.

"It's a donation. That part is no charge to the city."

"They have to raise one million and a half," Luis responded. "The $14,000 is going to have to come out of somewhere."

Al went into a convoluted explanation about in-kind monies and credits and how it was really free money. Al concluded, saying, "I don't know if that helps, Mr. Navarro."

"Not really."

The audience erupted in laughter. Luis remained stone-faced. But he was not confrontational. He had simply asked questions, and now he conceded the floor.

"Thank you very much," Luis said politely, and he sat down.

I flashed on the diary of Henry C. Finnern all those years after the mob surrounded the German newspaper and how he rued that "in my business career October 6, 1918 will rank as the darkest day." Back then, city officials through inaction allowed the mob to rule. Now here was the city through action on May 3, 2004, devastating the business career of Luis Navar over that same building. For sure, it was not a violent act, and it may not have been illegal. But was it moral? Luis was simply irrelevant. The officials' eyes were on the prize benefiting mostly the white people of the city. It was a stab at Luis nonetheless, his honest bid rendered meaningless. This had nothing to do with "preferences" or affirmative action. Luis's was the lowest bid. Period.

The city had its first major test over doing the right thing by a Latino businessman, and it failed. All the talk I'd heard from Ken and the others about inclusion was only hollow platitudes.

Luis may not have been confrontational, but I was. As soon as the gavel pounded to adjourn, I went up to Al, still seated, and went into big-city reporter mode. Out of the corner of my eye, I saw Joel observing us. He didn't look so good.

"It still will not help build the center," I said of the $14,000 being put toward the $1.5 million.

"Yes, the cash has to come from someplace. The key is the city is not out getting that $14,000. It is simply modifying the amount needed."

"It doesn't pay for any bricks and mortar."

"The $1.5 million is an arbitrary number," Al finally sputtered. "It's the number the council set. The council can change it."

In other words, there were no rules. Gordon Wolf from the *Denison Bulletin & Review* now joined in. It was a rare media feeding frenzy in Denison. I let Gordon have his turn bloodying Al and looked for Luis, but he was gone. I figured he went home.

I hurried on foot up North Main Street. The spring night air was crisp. As I neared Sixth Avenue, I spotted Luis's truck passing me, turning into his drive. I waved; he recognized me in the dark.

"I was looking for you! I need to talk!" Luis said. He was pacing by the truck. "I need to walk!"

Luis was breathless. The enormity of the moment in the council chambers was now hitting him.

"I was so mad!"

"You were great," I said, noting he was like Columbo, the detective played by Peter Falk on the NBC television show that first was on the air from 1971 to 1977—Columbo was bumbling and solved crimes by asking questions, not raging. Luis didn't get the pop culture reference. So I said he could have called them names and said bad things, but it would have gotten him nowhere. Asking questions was the most powerful thing he could have done.

"Yes," he said as we walked along in the dark, back toward city hall four blocks distant. "I'm not smart. But I can see what's going down, clear and simple. Anyone can see it. They are lying. They are giving money away."

"But you are smart," I insisted. Luis didn't want to believe me. I reassured him. All this was new territory for a man who a few days earlier asked if the meetings were held in secret.

We neared Second Avenue North. I could see Ken and Al talking with some folks outside city hall. We were in the shadows. I cautioned Luis in a whisper that it might be best if he weren't seen with me. I went back into small-town mode, fearing repercussions against Luis after my hard line with Al. We walked back. Luis worried about his finances. He had no money. Lupe was working at the Tyson plant, but her salary was not enough. There was a big federal tax bill. And he had $2,000 in bills from an injury at Tyson, from when he said a slab of beef slammed into him. They might lose one of their rental houses. He was considering returning to California to labor at construction, sending money home. He anguished about living away from his family.

We stood near his truck. I expressed worry about his situation, but said I was proud of him. He'd lost a battle, but he gained something in here—I thumped my chest.

"You learned something about America. You lost tonight, but you will win someday."

"I will invite you for *carne asada* when you come back," he said. "If I can afford it. If I am here."

We shook hands, and I watched 'til he climbed his steps. I made the four blocks back to city hall. Al was gone, but Ken was talking with a few people.

"We're going down to Family Table for some pie," Ken said. "Do you want to join us?"

I begged off, said I was tired. I really was. I was too tired to confront Ken. And I was in no mood to play "nicey-nice" over pie. I was soon leaving town on business, and I realized it was a good time to be away, for I'd gone a bit native after the long and cold winter. Not only was Georgia Hollrah's class over; in a lot of ways, my year in Denison was over.

THE BUFFALO TRIUMPHS

Nathan had called minutes after I'd arrived back at the Shaw Mansion following the council session. He hadn't gone to the meeting for the same reason he'd remained publicly quiet for many years—the "nicey-nice." He didn't want to be the nail that stood up, only to get pounded down. But as I related to Nathan what had happened regarding Luis, something snapped. Nathan, sleepless and stewing, called again at 2:00 A.M., yet again at 4:00 A.M. During the final call, he vowed to write a column for the paper condemning what had occurred.

Come morning, I didn't think Nathan would go through with it. He was up for a job at the middle school where there was an opening, and finally, he'd be able to quit the city utilities where he was underemployed. There was solemn risk in going public with his anger in the small-town world where those making the hiring decision could be connected in direct or oblique ways to the golf course project.

Nathan wrote every free moment the next day. At the same time Dick Knowles picked up the phone and made a call—not to the mayor, not to the city manger—but to the director of Job Corps.

"I just said, 'Hey, what is happening here? It's something that doesn't look good for equality and fairness,'" Dick later recounted telling the director. Dick reminded the man that it might be a violation of federal rules for the corps to take work away from local companies, especially a minority-owned business.

"I didn't urge them to make any changes. I just said, 'I'll tell you what, if this happens with the Job Corps being involved, we'll be getting a lot of calls from Washington. They won't like that. That's a fact, not a threat.'"

A two-punch hit that Friday afternoon. The *Denison Bulletin & Review* carried a front-page story about Job Corps pulling out of the renovation of *Der Denison Herold,* commonly known as the North Main Tap. The article didn't mention Dick's phone call. The corps' official statement did not cite a reason that it was withdrawing. Inside, on page two, was the second punch, a column by Nathan, under a headline, "The Public Forum."

> I am not one to voice my opinion publicly. Those [who] know me know that I care about this community a little more than a healthy minded person should. It is in this respect that I am writing this letter.
>
> The city of Denison has sold its soul to the golf course for $14,000. I would have thought that the people of this town were worth more than that.
>
> Recently the city had a bid letting for the North Main Tap renovation. Many contractors responded with qualified bids. The lowest bid was by Luis Navar, a local contractor trying to start a business. It would only stand to reason that his bid was lowest because he needed this job. He would make a name for himself. More important to Luis, he wanted to provide for his family.
>
> The fact that he is Hispanic meshes very well with Mayor Livingston's minority entrepreneurial goals. He encourages Hispanics to start businesses.
>
> The was the first real test to help one of his Hispanic entrepreneurs.
>
> Luis did not get the job. How could this happen?

Nathan went on at length to debate the $14,000 in-kind credit and how it would not help build the center. He continued:

> I do not know of a brick made of in-kind or mortar made of credit. There is a reason the city demanded that there be $1.5 million IN THE BANK before the public would commit the $1 million pledge. Not one dime of city money should be spent until the $1.5 million is in the bank.... There needs to be an audit by a third party accounting firm. The people of Denison deserve this.... The mayor and council should have supported the entrepreneurial efforts of Luis Navar who is only trying to start a business and support his family.

To say there was a firestorm after the letter appeared that Friday afternoon is to understate.

Ken Livingston phoned even before it ran, during lunch hour when Nathan was at home. Ken had heard of the letter, not seen the paper, yet he threatened a lawsuit. Nathan said Ken was shouting.

"He said he consulted the city attorney before they did this and it was all legal," Nathan said. "My reply was if you had to consult an attorney, it was definitely unethical. He hung up on me and then called me right back. He is pissed."

At two o'clock, when the *Bulletin & Review* hit the streets, Ken phoned Nathan at the city utilities, but Nathan refused to take the call. Ken drove there, and Nathan blew him off. On Saturday when Nathan was working finishing the Donna Reed Museum, Ken showed up. Nathan went out on the sidewalk to talk. As Nathan tells it, Ken was poking him in the chest, calling him "stupid," cussing, promising a lawsuit: he told Nathan to expect to be served papers on Monday.

"He said my grandchildren would be paying off my debt," Nathan said.

A backer of the golf course complex ran into Nathan and went ballistic. "If not for it being a prominent public place, he would have punched me out."

This man, who was doing some work gratis for the Donna Reed Museum, told Nathan he would no longer do that work.

Another project backer was in tears.

But a far larger group hailed Nathan as a hero. Nathan's phone rang incessantly as people called to congratulate him.

"Finally someone said it in public!" said one caller.

One blue-collar woman said to me later, "I don't know if he knows how many people support him."

Blue collar or white, there was a broad championing of Nathan. He stopped going out in public that weekend. He couldn't even mow his lawn without cars constantly stopping and drivers exiting to shake his hand. The support had nothing to do with Luis. These townspeople were happy that Nathan had stood up to what they saw as the shenanigans of city hall.

A week after the council vote, it was announced that the golf course group was quitting the German newspaper project. It was stated that the bid was being withdrawn not because of improprieties but due to the "confusion" that had occurred.

What would the city now do? One idea was to call for a new set of bids. Nathan believes the city administration didn't want to give the job to Luis as retribution due to Nathan's letter; officials denied this. But rebidding wouldn't work. Everyone's poker hand was shown. There was only one remaining course of action: give the contract to the next lowest bidder, Luis Navar's Bravo Construction. This would not have happened if not for two white men, Nathan and Dick—one heralded, the other a silent force—who stood up for the Latino who had no political standing to fight back.

Amid this, Nathan was hired as a teacher for the Denison Community School District.

* * *

The pounding of hammers emanated from the shell of *Der Denison Herold*. Inside Luis and his crew were busy. Some men were replacing joists, while Luis was sawing the notches for the stair carriages.

Luis's eyes lit up. He ran over, embraced me. I'd awakened in the Shaw Mansion and had walked up here. I was gone for the immediate fallout from Nathan's letter and was freshly back in town. Luis had started work five days earlier. He was beaming.

"I have to thank Nathan," he says. "What he did, it was something."

Luis was suddenly more involved in the politics of town and was now attending Dick Knowles's Cultural Diversity Committee meetings.

"I like it. And I am going to go to more city council meetings."

I did not want to interrupt Luis's work—we would talk more later. As I turned to leave and Luis picked up a saw, he smiled.

"We are winning the war—with our hearts, and hard work."

* * *

I had heard Mayor Ken Livingston was looking for me from just about everyone I had spoken to on the phone the previous week as I wended my way back to Denison.

"He wants to talk with you—he's worried about how he will come off," one person said.

Minutes after seeing Luis that morning, I was crossing Broadway in front of Reynold's Clothing, and a horn beeped. It was Ken.

"When did you get back in town?"

"Last night."

"We have to have lunch. I want to hear what you think of Denison and what we are doing."

Ken was nervous. I sensed a big spin storm was blowing in. To test the figurative wind with a verbal wetted finger, I told him I'd just come from seeing Luis.

"My good friend!" Ken said.

He said that he'd invited Luis to a meeting to train Denison business-people in entrepreneurial skills; meantime, Luis came up with two needed additions to the contract for which the city had to pony up some extra funds.

"I told him he doesn't need any training as an entrepreneur," Ken said.

I thanked Ken and suggested we could connect later in the week after I settled in. I crossed the street and entered the office of Dick Knowles.

"They do not walk their talk," Dick said. "You don't have anyone championing the rights of Latino people. They make it sound like everything is hunky dory. But it's not."

He said this is true on all levels in the city.

"You tell me where not. What it boils down to is this: let's just not rock the boat. They use code words. When they talk about hiring opportunities, they say it would be good if we had a bilingual doctor. But they have to be 'otherwise qualified.' There's the code words. And that says something to people who know exactly what they mean. We're not going to give them a foot in the door here. These people are good people, making these statements. The reasons that they do it?"

Dick explained that politicians fear the wrath of the voters, who are virtually all white. It's all about resources: monies doled out, sports positions on high school teams, who receives the largesse of churches. Anything given to Latinos means whites miss out.

"See, they don't want any heat. So I push and I needle. It doesn't go over well when I ask questions. Why aren't there any Hispanics who are volunteer firemen? Why aren't there any Hispanics in the Boy Scouts? Teaching in the schools? I ask these questions, and I get the cold shoulder."

The next day, I began what was my morning by taking lunch at the Hy-Vee. As I sat at a table eating a casserole dish, engrossed in the *Des*

Moines Register, a voice greeted me. I looked up to see Ken, in a baseball cap and shorts. I suddenly felt he was stalking me. Or was it a chance meeting? He asked if he was bothering me, and I said no, inviting him to sit. We'd have our talk now. He immediately brought up Nathan.

"Did you see the letter?"

"Yes."

"I would have sued him for slander [libel] if I wasn't mayor."

Ken said Nathan hurt himself.

"He didn't know the whole story. He should have called me before he published that letter."

Ken focused on the part that accused the city of being racist to Latinos. He didn't bring up the weird logic about the funding. The appearance of racism was a much bigger hot button in the prism of hindsight.

"Luis and I are getting closer," Ken said. "I want to see him get more city work."

I thanked Ken, and we parted. I crossed Broadway, entered the Donna Reed Museum where I found Joel Franken in the center of a bustle. It was just days before the museum would open during the Donna Reed Festival. The window exhibits were in, and Joel and the staff were working on niggling details. Joel greeted me with a hug. He looked tired. There was no space to talk; we agreed to go to dinner at The Pub, the best non-Latino food in town.

Joel pulled up to the Shaw Mansion that afternoon. As soon as I climbed into the van, he began explaining his vote—that Nathan didn't have all the facts, that Al Roder did not rig the bid.

"But it looked bad," I said.

"It was not my finest moment, that vote."

Joel agreed to go along with Ken and Al with the understanding that the city would come up with the $14,000. Then they changed things, he said. When Al stumbled and tried to explain the money when I questioned him, Joel thought how horrible it sounded—it had the ring of a backroom deal. But it was one, was it not? Joel insisted it was not. It still sounded very unkosher, I asserted. Joel sighed.

"I told them this was the last time I'd go along with this kind of thing."

We'd arrived at The Pub. I let it go. Joel had repeated his mea culpa several times. I realized that for Joel, the bigger picture that won out was very tiny—the sphere of small-town politics. As head of the Donna Reed Museum, Joel needed to appease the men pushing the golf course project. They were among the wheels of power that could help the museum in numerous ways.

Amid this, the city agreed to submit to an outside audit of the golf course fund-raising to prove the numbers added up. It was later deemed a "review," and Ken Livingston aggressively continued to push the project despite remaining questions over the strength of the financing.

At the end of the week Michael Williamson and I were walking by *Der Denison Herold*. I spied Luis in a second-floor window. He waved.

The stairs were done. We climbed them to the rapidly advancing remodeling of the second story. I sat on the floor, Luis in a glassless window frame, one leg crooked on the ledge, enjoying the mild breeze. Luis looked at city hall about a block away.

"The mayor said that writer guy didn't get you this job, nor did Mr. Mahrt. It was me."

Luis laughed.

"The mayor wants me to play golf with him. Yes, I will play golf with the mayor."

He laughed again. He was philosophical, reciting a Mexican saying about life and work;

> *El sol sale*
> *El sol se mete*
> *y si no te gusta*
> *véte*

"What we say in Mexico. 'The sun comes up, the sun goes down. And if you don't like it, get out.'"

"You should become a city councilman," I said.

Luis laughed yet again. But he stared at city hall for a long time as Michael took his picture.

* * *

That last week in Denison, I walked the streets by day, in the evening, and especially late at night. I was recognized everywhere. A waitress hailed me like an old friend. I was puzzled.

253

"Oh, you came to talk to our high school class."

I'd become a town fixture. I knew the sheriff, the police chief, the mayor, teachers, students, librarians, the men and women slicing at beef and pork in the plants, the woman baking pastries at the Mexican *panadería*, the woman who slopped my lunch onto a foam plate at the Hy-Vee many afternoons, a few farmers, and on. I knew many people, and a lot about them. But I'd been at this kind of work too long to really believe I knew everything. I just knew what I'd seen, what I'd lived. I was humbled by what I did not know.

While a town of 8,000 seems small to someone in a metropolis, there were 8,000 lives being lived, with all the complexities of 8,000 stories. They worked, ate, drank, lusted, were lonely, had hopes and fears, all in their own unique ways. One could not grasp them all, even if one were able to talk with all 8,000—a task that would take one person one year if he or she never slept and talked to each resident for one hour, with a five-minute break between interviews, for twenty-four hours a day, seven days a week.

No truth would come from such an insane undertaking. My head reeled from what I'd learned of the residents I had gotten to know intimately and the truths I'd discovered. I indeed had become a grotesque. These thoughts dominated the night Joel Franken and I entered the lounge at Cronk's Cafe for a final drink days before I left. His relationship was proceeding apace. He was moving east—but not as far as he'd talked months earlier while scraping doors in the Donna Reed Museum. He and the woman would buy a home in Davenport, where she was from. Joel would get out of Denison and to a larger city, albeit not as big as he'd wondered about. He could still confront creativity.

There was a round table in a dark corner where a regular crowd sat, including realtor Doug Skarin and the plant manager who had avoided me for the entire year, Joel, others. The manager slinked to a video game as we neared.

"So you know about our town now," Doug announced as we sat.

Doug smiled. He knew what I had witnessed, and he seemed happy for it. He was one of the smartest people in Denison and did not play "nicey-nice," which made him suspect by many citizens. We drank a round.

Doug was bittersweet about Denison, more bitter at this moment because the work of the 2020 Executive Committee was in a state of fragility. We didn't know it then, but the plan was slowly maturing so that in the coming months, the disparate agencies would put aside turf battles and power-sharing fears, to combine the chamber of commerce and the county development agency into a single entity that would promote the town by hiring a director and marketing person. The Chamber and Development Council of Crawford County became official on January 1, 2005.

"People are scared shapeless around here," Doug said. "They're scared shapeless about failure. Or maybe it's success."

Heads nodded, drinks were tipped. Joel said fear of success is probably the biggest problem.

"Crabs in a pot?" I asked.

Doug especially nodded.

"The person can't be from around here," Doug said of the marketing position they would have to fill. "They have to be willing to take risk. People here aren't willing to take risk."

Eric Skoog, the owner of Cronk's, had said what is needed to fix the business climate is not a one- or two-year proposition—it will require years of focused effort. Something finally would begin to start taking Denison down that road, thanks to Ken Livingston's pushing the 2020 Committee to do something.

Another round was sent over, paid by the plant manager. I looked in his direction to thank him, but his face was in the video machine.

I left and walked the Uptown streets. It was after midnight. A few kids sat atop car hoods in the Safety Zone. The night man wheeled into the Hy-Vee; he had just a few months left to live. More businesses were closing. An interior design store had just put up a going-out-of-business banner. A block away, I peered in the window of the just-closed Brass Shutter, a photography studio. It was being remodeled into an insurance office. It was better than remaining empty, but it marked another Uptown death knell. The loss of retail hurts all businesses, for professional offices have less foot traffic. Talk of the Wal-Mart supercenter was intensifying, though it was still just rumor.

Would the supercenter really come? Wal-Mart never returned my repeated telephone calls for comment.

On the plus side, on Main Street near Book 'Em Dano, a new Mexican restaurant was about to open in a long-empty storefront. And the Streetscape project had now advanced to the Donna Reed building. A mound of dirt was in the center of the intersection, and the curbing and wider sidewalks were about to be poured. Streetscape had been a struggle, but it was happening. It was one good thing, one bit of hope. Would it work? Who knows. The alternative was doing nothing. But it seemed to me that there would be no magic cure to resurrect business, short of the potential marketing person being an absolute genius, both in thinking of the right schtick to attract visitors and in being able to get the distrustful citizenry to support that plan. The odds seemed as long as trying to plant a citrus orchard outside town and hoping that the trees would survive the Iowa winter. And in the months that followed my leaving, bickering over the golf course project continued. The city audit was filled with faults, critics such as Dick Knowles pointed out, and the project seemed to be going nowhere, but in the summer of 2005 its backers succeeded and ground was broken for it.

It was a town of flawed men and women, often well intentioned, trying to do what they saw as the right thing. Sometimes they succeeded. They often stumbled. I wondered how flawed Henry Laub, that original builder of Denison, had been. The available historic record does not reveal this aspect of the man. He certainly was not perfect, as no man or woman ever is. The positives are sometimes negative, and vice versa.

Another night a big storm rolled in out of Nebraska. Thunder shook the Shaw Mansion, followed by a crash. I went down the grand staircase and discovered that a piece of the rotted roof had collapsed to the porch floor. I grabbed a beer, returned to the porch, and sat in a metal rocking chair, watching rain sheet down. I stared at the chunk of roof. The house didn't have much time.

As lightning flashed, illuminating the street below, I thought of what the day must have been like when Leslie Shaw sat here and saw an approaching carriage carrying his enemy, William Jennings Bryan. Bryan was with J. B. Romans, who owned the mansion up the street. Shaw waved and Bryan waved back. The Shaw Mansion had been standing only a bit over twice as long as I had been alive, and the day of the passionate rivals waving had not really been all that long ago; if I went back three times as long in time, there were Indians living here. The arc of history is so very short.

Nathan was still trying to save the house, and my landlord, recovering from a cancer operation, was still saying he was going to clean the ballroom. The good news is that my landlord's procrastination had put off the Des Moines man who had wanted to gut the woodwork; he'd given up. Nathan continued his quest to save history. The restoration of the old opera house remained on hold, but he sold the 1930s garage for a profit and used the money to buy the oldest home in town, a brick dwelling begun in 1860 and finished in 1870. It had caught fire, was now a ruins, and had been within one day of being bulldozed. It was a wreck, but Nathan wanted to rapidly restore it, sell it, and use the profit to finally buy the Shaw house himself.

Then came the last night in the Shaw Mansion. I was packing my vehicle, hauling belongings down the grand staircase. As I carried the last load, I looked at the mansion, aglow and massed against the starry Iowa sky. The crickets were loud. A few late-flying male fireflies plied the airspace beneath the silverleaf maples. I cracked a beer and sat for the last time on the porch. The air blew from the west, and with it came the smell of cooked blood—blood in industrial quantities. I wondered if it had been a perfect kill day at the hog plant.

I had not seen many people I knew well in the previous two days. Some were avoiding me. Perhaps the only people reluctant to see me depart, now that they contemplated the meaning of a Willard in their midst for the previous year, were countable on a few fingers. It truly was time to go. I slept a few hours, awakened to take the September 2001 calendar off the wall, and to place the last items in my truck. I turned the ignition key.

As I drove west on the Lincoln Highway, Denison vanishing in the rearview mirror, I thought of the last person I'd seen—Luis—whom I'd run into the previous afternoon.

Luis spotted me near the phone company where I was headed to disconnect my service. He pulled his truck into the alley and told me about a new job he'd landed, doing a roof for Dick Knowles. Word had filtered back to Al Roder and Ken Livingston.

" 'I thought we were friends,'" one of them said, Luis recalled. In that meeting they teased him about working with their nemesis, under the guise of being good-natured. He detected it was not so benign.

"I told them it was business, that I do business with everyone, that in Mexico it is rougher than here. You don't trust anybody, you are only a friend after you prove it, when it really matters. It is earned. You do business with people, and you shake hands and smile and call each other 'friend,' but you're not really friends. You don't trust them. It is just business. So I am doing business with Mr. Knowles . . ."

With that Luis told me he smiled, extended his right hand to the mayor. They shook.

" . . . and with you, friend."

Dale Maharidge
New York City, April 20, 2005

ACKNOWLEDGMENTS

This book would not have been possible without our agent, James Fitzgerald, whose ideas and guidance were vital. At the Free Press, I want to thank our editor, Dominick Anfuso, and his assistant, Wylie O'Sullivan.

Thanks also to Tom McCarthy for his sharp eye and help. This book was made possible because of the understanding of Dean Nicholas Lemann and Vice Dean David A. Klatell at the Graduate School of Journalism at Columbia University. They generously understood my need to go live in an Iowa town for one year.

In Denison, the list of those to whom I must extend my gratitude are many, and too numerous to list in totality. Among them Nathan Mahrt, for all of his help with the town's history; at the Denison schools, Superintendent Bill Wright, Principal Steve Westerberg, and Georgia Hollrah; at city hall, Mayor Ken Livingston and Councilman Joel Franken; at the the Norelius Community Library, special thanks to Joyce Amdor, Sandy Haynes, and Pam Scanlan and the other librarians; and others: Paul Assman, Sylvia Bachmann, Police Chief Rod Bradley, Joe Chavez, Steve Harris, Sheriff Tom Hogan, Ike Johnson, Dick Knowles, Luis Navar, Doug Skarin, Eric Skoog, Craig Whited.

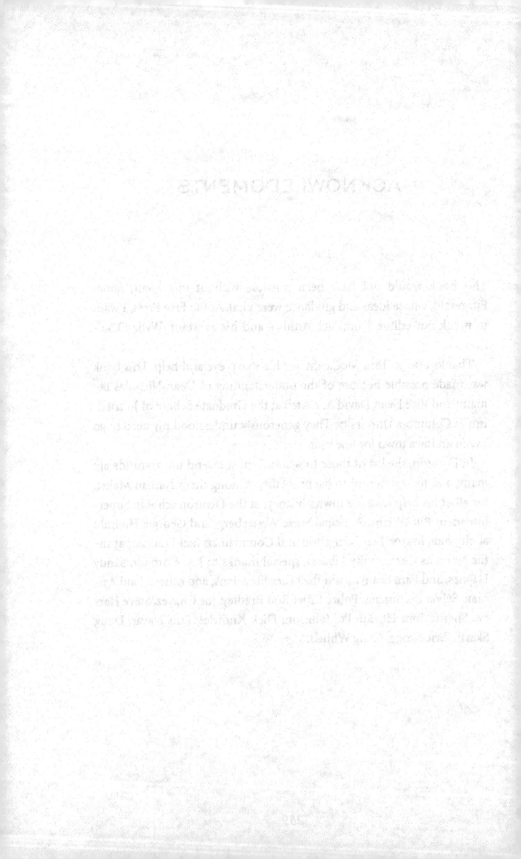

ABOUT THE AUTHORS

Denison, Iowa is the fifth book from the writer/photographer team of Dale Maharidge and Michael Williamson. For over a quarter of a century the duo has documented America, traveling widely to capture the spirit of the nation's workers, the poor, the dispossessed. In 1990 they won the nonfiction Pulitzer Prize for *And Their Children After Them/The legacy of Let Us Now Praise Famous Men: James Agee, Walker Evans, and the rise and fall of cotton in the South.* Their other books are *Journey to Nowhere: The Saga of the New Underclass, The Last Great American Hobo,* and *Homeland.*

Williamson is a staff photographer at the *Washington Post.* He won a second Pulitzer Prize for his work in Kosovo.

Maharidge is a visiting professor at the Graduate School of Journalism at Columbia University in New York City. His other books include *The Coming White Minority: California, Multiculturalism, and America's Future.*